ADDRESSES
UPON
THE AMERICAN ROAD

ADDRESSES

UPON

THE AMERICAN ROAD

BY

Herbert Hoover

1933-1938

———

NEW YORK
CHARLES SCRIBNER'S SONS
1938

COPYRIGHT, 1938, BY
EDGAR RICKARD

Printed in the United States of America

Fourth Printing, October, 1938

Contents

v

ADDRESSES
UPON
THE AMERICAN ROAD

The Consequences of the Proposed New Deal*

THIS campaign is more than a contest between two men. It is more than a contest between two parties. It is a contest between two philosophies of government.

We are told by the opposition that we must have a change, that we must have a new deal. It is not the change that comes from normal development of national life to which I object, but the proposal to alter the whole foundations of our national life which have been builded through generations of testing and struggle, and of the principles upon which we have builded the nation. The expressions our opponents use must refer to important changes in our economic and social system and our system of government, otherwise they are nothing but vacuous words. And I realize that in this time of distress many of our people are asking whether our social and economic system is incapable of that great primary function of providing security and comfort of life to all of the firesides of our 25,000,000 homes in America, whether our social system provides for the fundamental development and progress of our people, whether our form of government is capable of originating and sustaining that security and progress.

*This address is published only in extracts, as it has been hitherto published in book form. The extracts are included here because of their prophetic character. They should be read in conjunction with the address on "The Dangerous Road for Democracy" of May 5, 1938. This address of October 31, 1932, is printed in full in *Campaign Speeches of 1932*, Doubleday, Doran & Co., 1933.

This question is the basis upon which our opponents are appealing to the people in their fears and distress. They are proposing changes and so-called new deals which would destroy the very foundations of our American system.

Our people should consider the primary facts before they come to the judgment—not merely through political agitation, the glitter of promise, and the discouragement of temporary hardships—whether they will support changes which radically affect the whole system which has been builded up by a hundred and fifty years of the toil of our fathers. They should not approach the question in the despair with which our opponents would clothe it.

Our economic system has received abnormal shocks during the last three years, which temporarily dislocated its normal functioning. These shocks have in a large sense come from without our borders, but I say to you that our system of government has enabled us to take such strong action as to prevent the disaster which would otherwise have come to our Nation. It has enabled us further to develop measures and programs which are now demonstrating their ability to bring about restoration and progress.

We must go deeper than platitudes and emotional appeals of the public platform in the campaign, if we will penetrate to the full significance of the changes which our opponents are attempting to float upon the wave of distress and discontent from the difficulties we are passing through. We can find what our opponents would do after searching the record of their appeals to discontent, group and sectional interest. We must search for them in the legislative acts which they sponsored and passed in the Democratic-controlled House of Representatives in the last session of Congress. We must look into measures for which they voted and which were defeated. We must inquire whether or not the Presidential and Vice-Presidential candidates have disavowed these acts. If they have not, we must conclude that they form a portion and are a substantial indication of the profound changes proposed.

And we must look still further than this as to what revolutionary changes have been proposed by the candidates themselves.

We must look into the type of leaders who are campaigning for the Democratic ticket, whose philosophies have been well known all their lives, whose demands for a change in the American system are frank and forceful. I can respect the sincerity of these men in their desire to change our form of government and our social and economic system, though I shall do my best tonight to prove they are wrong. I refer particularly to Senator Norris, Senator LaFollette, Senator Cuttting, Senator Huey Long, Senator Wheeler, William R. Hearst, and other exponents of a social philosophy different from the traditional American one. Unless these men feel assurance of support to their ideas they certainly would not be supporting these candidates and the Democratic Party. The seal of these men indicates that they have sure confidence that they will have voice in the administration of our government.

I may say at once that the changes proposed from all these Democratic principals and allies are of the most profound and penetrating character. If they are brought about this will not be the America which we have known in the past.

Let us pause for a moment and examine the American system of government, of social and economic life, which it is now proposed that we should alter. Our system is the product of our race and of our experience in building a nation to heights unparalleled in the whole history of the world. It is a system peculiar to the American people. It differs essentially from all others in the world. It is an American system.

It is founded on the conception that only through ordered liberty, through freedom to the individual, and equal opportunity to the individual will his initiative and enterprise be summoned to spur the march of progress.

It is by the maintenance of equality of opportunity and therefore of a society absolutely fluid in freedom of the movement of its human particles that our individualism departs from the individualism of Europe. We resent class distinction because there can be no rise for the individual through the frozen strata of classes and no stratification of classes can take place in a mass livened by the free rise of its particles. Thus in our ideals the able and ambitious are able to rise constantly from the bottom to leadership in the community.

This freedom of the individual creates of itself the necessity and the cheerful willingness of men to act co-operatively in a thousand ways and for every purpose as occasion arises; and it permits such voluntary co-operations to be dissolved as soon as they have served their purpose, to be replaced by new voluntary associations for new purposes.

There has thus grown within us, to gigantic importance, a new conception. That is, this voluntary co-operation within the community. Co-operation to perfect the social organizations; co-operation for the care of those in distress; co-operation for the advancement of knowledge, of scientific research, of education; for co-operative action in the advancement of many phases of economic life. This is self-government by the people outside of Government; it is the most powerful development of individual freedom and equal opportunity that has taken place in the century and a half since our fundamental institutions were founded.

It is in the further development of this co-operation and a sense of its responsibility that we should find solution for many of our complex problems, and not by the extension of government into our economic and social life. The greatest function of government is to build up that co-operation, and its most resolute action should be to deny the extension of bureaucracy. We have developed great agencies of co-operation by the assistance of the Government which promote and protect the interests of individuals and the smaller units of business. The Federal Reserve System, in its strengthening and support of the smaller banks; the Farm Board, in its strengthening and support of the farm co-operatives; the Home Loan banks, in the mobilizing of building and loan associations and savings banks; the Federal land banks, in giving independence and strength to land mortgage associations; the great mobilization of relief to distress, the mobilization of business and industry in measures of recovery, and a score of other activities are not socialism—they are the essence of protection to the development of free men.

The primary conception of this whole American system is not the regimentation of men but the co-operation of free men. It is founded upon the conception of responsibility of the individual to the community, of the responsibility of local government to the State, of the State to the national Government.

It is founded on a peculiar conception of self-government designed to maintain this equal opportunity to the individual, and through decentralization it brings about and maintains these responsibilities. The centralization of government will undermine responsibilities and will destroy the system.

Our Government differs from all previous conceptions, not only in this decentralization, but also in the separation of functions between the legislative, executive, and judicial arms of government, in which the independence of the judicial arm is the keystone of the whole structure.

It is founded on a conception that in times of emergency, when forces are running beyond control of individuals or other co-operative action, beyond the control of local communities and of States, then the great reserve powers of the Federal Government shall be brought into action to protect the community. But when these forces have ceased there must be a return of State, local, and individual responsibility.

The implacable march of scientific discovery with its train of new inventions presents every year new problems to government and new problems to the social order. Questions often arise whether, in the face of the growth of these new and gigantic tools, democracy can remain master in its own house, can preserve the fundamentals of our American system. I contend that it can; and I contend that this American system of ours has demonstrated its validity and superiority over any system yet invented by human mind.

It has demonstrated it in the face of the greatest test of our history—that is the emergency which we have faced in the last three years.

When the political and economic weakness of many nations of Europe, the result of the World War and its aftermath, finally culminated in collapse of their institutions, the delicate adjustments of our economic and social life received a shock unparalleled in our history. No one knows that better than you of New York. No one knows its causes better than you. That the crisis was so great that many of the leading banks sought directly or indirectly to convert their assets into gold or its equivalent with the result that they practically ceased to function as credit institutions; that many of our citizens sought flight for their capital to other countries; that many of them attempted to hoard gold in large amounts. These were but indications of the flight of confidence and of the belief that our Government could not overcome these forces.

Yet these forces were overcome—perhaps by narrow margins —and this action demonstrates what the courage of a nation can accomplish under the resolute leadership in the Republican Party. And I say the Republican Party because our opponents, before and during the crisis, proposed no constructive program; though some of their members patriotically supported ours. Later on the Democratic House of Representatives did develop the real thought and ideas of the Democratic Party, but it was so destructive that it had to be defeated, for it would have destroyed, not healed.

In spite of all these obstructions we did succeed. Our form of government did prove itself equal to the task. We saved this Nation from a quarter of a century of chaos and degeneration, and we preserved the savings, the insurance policies, gave a fighting chance to men to hold their homes. We saved the integrity of our Government and the honesty of the American dollar. And we installed measures which today are bringing back recovery. Employment, agriculture, business—all of these show the steady, if slow, healing of our enormous wound.

I therefore contend that the problem of today is to continue these measures and policies to restore this American system to its normal functioning, to repair the wounds it has received, to correct the weaknesses and evils which would defeat that system. To enter upon a series of deep changes to embark upon this inchoate new deal which has been propounded in this campaign would be to undermine and destroy our American system.

Before we enter upon such courses, I would like you to consider what the results of this American system have been during the last thirty years—that is, one single generation. For if it can be demonstrated that by means of this, our unequalled political, social, and economic system, we have secured a lift in the standards of living and a diffusion of comfort and hope to men and women, the growth of equal opportunity, the widening of all opportunity, such as had never been seen in the history of the world, then we should not tamper with it or destroy it; but on the contrary we should restore it and, by its gradual improvement and perfection, foster it into new performance for our country and for our children.

Now, if we look back over the last generation we find that the number of our families and, therefore, our homes, has increased from sixteen to twenty-five million, or 62 per cent. In that time we have builded for them 15,000,000 new and better homes. We have equipped 20,000,000 homes with electricity; thereby we have lifted infinite drudgery from women and men. The barriers of time and space have been swept away. Life has been made freer, the intellectual vision of every individual has been expanded by the installation of 20,000,000 telephones, 12,000,000 radios, and the service of 20,000,000 automobiles. Our cities have been made magnificent with beautiful buildings, parks, and playgrounds. Our countryside has been knit together with splendid roads. We have increased by twelve times the use of electrical power and thereby taken sweat from the backs of men. In this broad sweep real wages and purchasing power of men and women have steadily increased. New comforts have steadily come to them. The hours of labor have decreased, the 12-hour day has disappeared, even the 9-hour day has almost gone. We are now advancing the 5-day week. The portals of opportunity to our children have ever widened. While our population grew by but 62 per cent, we have increased the number of children in high schools by 700 per cent, those in institutions of higher learning by 300 per cent. With all our spending, we multiplied by six times the savings in our banks and in our building and loan associations. We multiplied by 1,200 per cent the amount of our life insurance. With the enlargement of our leisure we have come to a fuller life; we gained new visions of hope, we more nearly realize our national aspirations and give increasing scope to the creative power of every individual and expansion of every man's mind.

Our people in these thirty years grew in the sense of social responsibility. There is profound progress in the relation of the employer and employed. We have more nearly met with a full hand the most sacred obligation of man, that is, the responsibility of a man to his neighbor. Support to our schools, hospitals, and institutions for the care of the afflicted surpassed in totals of billions the proportionate service in any period of history in any nation in the world.

Three years ago there came a break in this progress. A break of the same type we have met fifteen times in a century and yet we have overcome them. But eighteen months later came a further blow by shocks transmitted to us by the earthquakes of the collapse in nations throughout the world as the aftermath of the World War. The workings of our system were dislocated. Millions of men and women are out of jobs. Business men and farmers suffer. Their distress is bitter. I do not seek to minimize the depth of it. We may thank God that in view of this storm 30,000,000 still have their jobs; yet this must not distract our thoughts from the suffering of the other 10,000,000.

But I ask you what has happened. This thirty years of incomparable improvement in the scale of living, the advance of comfort and intellectual life, inspiration and ideals did not arise without right principles animating the American system which produced them. Shall that system be discarded because vote-seeking men appeal to distress and say that the machinery is all wrong and that it must be abandoned or tampered with? Is it not more sensible to realize the simple fact that some extraordinary force has been thrown into the mechanism, temporarily deranging its operation? Is it not wiser to believe that the difficulty is not with the principles upon which our American system is founded and designed through all these generations of inheritance? Should not our purpose be to restore the normal working of that system which has brought to us such immeasurable benefits, and not destroy it?

And in order to indicate to you that the proposals of our opponents will endanger or destroy our system, I propose to analyze a few of the proposals of our opponents in their relation to these fundamentals.

First: A proposal of our opponents which would break down the American system is the expansion of Government expenditure by yielding to sectional and group raids on the Public Treasury. The extension of Government expenditures beyond the minimum limit necessary to conduct the proper functions of the Government enslaves men to work for the Government. If we combine the whole governmental expenditures—national, State, and municipal—we will find that before the World War each citizen worked, theoretically, twenty-five days out of each year for the Government. In 1924 he worked forty-six days a year for the Government. Today he works for the support of all forms of Government sixty-one days out of the year.

No nation can conscript its citizens for this proportion of men's time without national impoverishment and destruction of their liberties. Our Nation cannot do it without destruction to our whole conception of the American system. The Federal Government has been forced in this emergency to unusual expenditure, but in partial alleviation of these extraordinary and unusual expenditures the Republican Administration has made a successful effort to reduce the ordinary running expenses of the Government. Our opponents have persistently interfered with such policies. I only need recall to you that the Democratic House of Representatives passed bills in the last session that would have increased our expenditures by $3,500,000,000, or 87 per cent. Expressed in days' labor, this would have meant the conscription of sixteen days' additional work from every citizen for the Government. This I stopped. Furthermore, they refused to accept recommendations from the Administration in respect to $150,000,000 to $200,000,000 of reductions in ordinary expenditures, and finally they forced upon us increasing expenditure of $322,000,000. In spite of this, the ordinary expenses of the Government have been reduced upwards of $200,000,000 during this present administration. They will be decidedly further reduced. But the major point I wish to make —the disheartening part of these proposals of our opponents— is that they represent successful pressures of minorities. They would appeal to sectional and group political support and thereby impose terrific burdens upon every home in the country. These things can and must be resisted. But they can only be resisted if there shall be live and virile public support to the Administration, in opposition to political log-rolling and the sectional and group raids on the Treasury for distribution of public money, which is cardinal in the congeries of elements which make up the Democratic Party.

These expenditures proposed by the Democratic House of Representatives for the benefit of special groups and special sections of our country directly undermine the American system. Those who pay are, in the last analysis, the man who works at the bench, the desk, and on the farm. They take away his comfort, stifle his leisure, and destroy his equal opportunity.

Second: Another proposal of our opponents which would destroy the American system is that of inflation of the currency. The bill which passed the last session of the Democratic House called upon the Treasury of the United States to issue $2,300,-000,000 in paper currency that would be unconvertible into solid values. Call it what you will, greenbacks or fiat money. It was that nightmare which overhung our own country for years after the Civil War. . . .

Third: In the last session the Congress, under the personal leadership of the Democratic Vice-Presidential candidate, and their allies in the Senate, enacted a law to extend the Government into personal banking business. This I was compelled to veto, out of fidelity to the whole American system of life and government. . . .

Fourth: Another proposal of our opponents which would wholly alter our American system of life is to reduce the protective tariff to a competitive tariff for revenue. The protective tariff and its results upon our economic structure has become gradually embedded into our economic life since the first protective tariff act passed by the American Congress under the Administration of George Washington. There have been gaps at times of Democratic control when this protection has been taken away. But it has been so embedded that its removal has never failed to bring disaster. . . .

Fifth: Another proposal is that the Government go into the power business. Three years ago, in view of the extension of the use of transmission of power over State borders and the difficulties of State regulatory bodies in the face of this interstate action, I recommended to the Congress that such interstate power should be placed under regulation by the Federal Government in co-operation with the State authorities.

That recommendation was in accord with the principles of the Republican Party over the last fifty years, to provide regulation where public interest had developed in tools of industry which was beyond control and regulation of the States.

I succeeded in creating an independent Power Commission to handle such matters, but the Democratic House declined to approve the further powers to this commission necessary for such regulation.

I have stated unceasingly that I am opposed to the Federal Government going into the power business. I have insisted upon rigid regulation. The Democratic candidate has declared that under the same conditions which may make local action of this character desirable, he is prepared to put the Federal Government into the power business. He is being actively supported by a score of Senators in this campaign, many of whose expenses are being paid by the Democratic National Committee, who are pledged to Federal Government development and operation of electrical power.

I find in the instructions to campaign speakers issued by the Democratic National Committee that they are instructed to criticize my action in the veto of the bill which would have put the Government permanently into the operation of power at Muscle Shoals with a capital from the Federal Treasury of over

$100,000,000. In fact thirty-one Democratic Senators, being all except three, voted to override that veto. In that bill was the flat issue of the Federal Government permanently in competitive business. I vetoed it because of principle and not because it was especially the power business. In that veto I stated that I was firmly opposed to the Federal Government entering into any business, the major purpose of which is competition with our citizens. I said:

There are national emergencies which require that the Government should temporarily enter the field of business but that they must be emergency actions and in matters where the cost of the project is secondary to much higher consideration. There are many localities where the Federal Government is justified in the construction of great dams and reservoirs, where navigation, flood control, reclamation, or stream regulation are of dominant importance, and where they are beyond the capacity or purpose of private or local government capital to construct. In these cases, power is often a by-product and should be disposed of by contract or lease. But for the Federal Government to deliberately go out to build up and expand such an occasion to the major purpose of a power and manufacturing business is to break down the initiative and enterprise of the American people; it is destruction of equality of opportunity among our people; it is the negation of the ideals upon which our civilization has been based.

This bill raises one of the important issues confronting our people. That is squarely the issue of Federal Government ownership and operation of power and manufacturing business not as a minor by-product but as a major purpose. Involved in this question is the agitation against the conduct of the power industry. The power problem is not to be solved by the Federal Government going into the power business, nor is it to be solved by the project in this bill. The remedy for abuses in the conduct of that industry lies in regulation and not by the Federal Government entering upon the business itself. I have recommended to the Congress on various occasions that action should be taken to establish Federal regulation of interstate power in co-operation with State authorities. This bill would launch the Federal Government upon a policy of ownership of power utilities upon a basis of competition instead of by the proper Government function of regulation for the protection of all the people. I hesitate to contemplate the future of our institutions, of our Government, and of our country, if the preoccupation of its officials is to be no longer the promotion of justice and equal opportunity but is to be devoted to barter in the markets. That is not liberalism; it is degeneration.

From their utterances in this campaign and elsewhere we are justified in the conclusion that our opponents propose to put the Federal Government in the power business with all its additions to Federal bureaucracy, its tyranny over State and local governments, its undermining of State and local responsibilities and initiative.

Sixth: I may cite another instance of absolutely destructive proposals to our American system by our opponents.

Recently there was circulated through the unemployed in this country a letter from the Democratic candidate in which he stated that he

. . . would support measures for the inauguration of self-liquidating public works such as the utilization of water resources, flood control, land reclamation, to provide employment for all surplus labor at all times.

I especially emphasize that promise to promote "employment for all surplus labor at all times." At first I could not believe that any one would be so cruel as to hold out a hope so absolutely impossible of realization to those 10,000,000 who are unemployed. But the authenticity of this promise has been verified. And I protest against such frivolous promises being held out to a suffering people. It is easily demonstrable that no such employment can be found. But the point I wish to make here and now is the mental attitude and spirit of the Democratic Party to attempt it. It is another mark of the character of the new deal and the destructive changes which mean the total abandonment of every principle upon which this Government and the American system are founded. If it were possible to give this employment to 10,000,000 people by the Government, it would cost upwards of $9,000,000,000 a year. . . .

I have said before, and I want to repeat on this occasion, that the only method by which we can stop the suffering and unemployment is by returning our people to their normal jobs in their normal homes, carrying on their normal functions of living. This can be done only by sound processes of protecting and stimulating recovery of the existing economic system upon which we have builded our progress thus far—preventing distress and giving such sound employment as we can find in the meantime.

Seventh: Recently, at Indianapolis, I called attention to the statement made by Governor Roosevelt in his address on October 25th with respect to the Supreme Court of the United States. He said:

After March 4, 1929, the Republican Party was in complete control of all branches of the Government—Executive, Senate, and House, and I may add, for good measure, in order to make it complete, the Supreme Court as well.

I am not called upon to defend the Supreme Court of the United States from this slurring reflection. Fortunately that court has jealously maintained over the years its high standard of integrity, impartiality, and freedom from influence of either the Executive or Congress, so that the confidence of the people is sound and unshaken.

But is the Democratic candidate really proposing his conception of the relation of the Executive and the Supreme Court? If that is his idea, he is proposing the most revolutionary new deal, the most stupendous breaking of precedent, the most destructive undermining of the very safeguard of our form of government yet proposed by a Presidential candidate.

Eighth: In order that we may get at the philosophical background of the mind which pronounces the necessity for profound change in our American system and a new deal, I would call your attention to an address delivered by the Democratic candidate in San Francisco, early in October.

He said:

Our industrial plant is built. The problem just now is whether under existing conditions it is not overbuilt. Our last frontier has long since been reached. There is practically no more free land. There is no safety

valve in the Western prairies where we can go for a new start. . . .
The mere building of more industrial plants, the organization of more
corporations is as likely to be as much a danger as a help. . . . Our task
now is not the discovery of natural resources or necessarily the production of more goods, it is the sober, less dramatic business of administering the resources and plants already in hand . . . establishing markets
for surplus production, of meeting the problem of under-consumption,
distributing the wealth and products more equitably and adapting the
economic organization to the service of the people. . . .

There are many of these expressions with which no one would
quarrel. But I do challenge the whole idea that we have ended
the advance of America, that this country has reached the zenith
of its power, the height of its development. That is the counsel
of despair for the future of America. That is not the spirit by
which we shall emerge from this depression. That is not the
spirit that made this country. If it is true, every American must
abandon the road of countless progress and unlimited opportunity. I deny that the promise of American life has been fulfilled, for that means we have begun the decline and fall.
No nation can cease to move forward without degeneration of
spirit. . . .

If these measures, these promises, which I have discussed; or
these failures to disavow these projects; this attitude of mind,
mean anything, they mean the enormous expansion of the Federal Government; they mean the growth of bureaucracy such
as we have never seen in our history. No man who has not oc-
cupied my position in Washington can fully realize the constant
battle which must be carried on against incompetence, corruption, tyranny of government expanded into business activities.
If we first examine the effect on our form of government of
such a program, we come at once to the effect of the most gigantic increase in expenditure ever known in history. That alone
would break down the savings, the wages, the equality of opportunity among our people. These measures would transfer
vast responsibilities to the Federal Government from the States,
the local governments, and the individuals. But that is not all;
they would break down our form of government. Our legisla-

tive bodies cannot delegate their authority to any dictator, but without such delegation every member of these bodies is impelled in representation of the interest of his constituents constantly to seek privilege and demand service in the use of such agencies. Every time the Federal Government extends its arm, 531 Senators and Congressmen become actual boards of directors of that business.

Capable men cannot be chosen by politics for all the various talents required. Even if they were supermen, if there were no politics in the selection of the Congress, if there were no constant pressure for this and for that, so large a number would be incapable as a board of directors of any institution. At once when these extensions take place by the Federal Government, the authority and responsibility of State governments and institutions are undermined. Every enterprise of private business is at once halted to know what Federal action is going to be. It destroys initiative and courage. We can do no better than quote that great statesman of labor, the late Samuel Gompers, in speaking of a similar situation:

It is a question of whether it shall be government ownership or private ownership under control. If I were a minority of one in this convention, I would want to cast my vote so that the men of labor shall not willingly enslave themselves to government in their industrial effort.

We have heard a great deal in this campaign about reactionaries, conservatives, progressives, liberals, and radicals. I have not yet heard an attempt by any one of the orators who mouth these phrases to define the principles upon which they base these classifications. There is one thing I can say without any question of doubt—that is, that the spirit of liberalism is to create free men; it is not the regimentation of men. It is not the extension of bureaucracy. I have said in this city before now that you cannot extend the mastery of government over the daily life of a people without somewhere making it master of people's souls and thoughts. Expansion of government in business means that the government, in order to protect itself from the political consequences of its errors, is driven irresistibly without peace to greater and greater control of the Nation's press and platform. Free speech does not live many hours after free industry and free commerce die. It is a false liberalism that interprets itself into Government operation of business. Every step in that direction poisons the very roots of liberalism. It poisons political equality, free speech, free press, and equality of opportunity. It is the road not to liberty but to less liberty. True liberalism is found not in striving to spread bureaucracy, but in striving to set bounds to it. True liberalism seeks all legitimate freedom first in the confident belief that without such freedom the pursuit of other blessings is in vain. Liberalism is a force truly of the spirit proceeding from the deep realization that economic freedom cannot be sacrificed if political freedom is to be preserved.

Even if the Government conduct of business could give us the maximum of efficiency instead of least efficiency, it would be purchased at the cost of freedom. It would increase rather than decrease abuse and corruption, stifle initiative and invention, undermine development of leadership, cripple mental and spiritual energies of our people, extinguish equality of opportunity, and dry up the spirit of liberty and progress. Men who are going about this country announcing that they are liberals because of their promises to extend the Government in business are not liberals, they are reactionaries of the United States.

And I do not wish to be misquoted or misunderstood. I do not mean that our Government is to part with one iota of its national resources without complete protection to the public interest. I have already stated that democracy must remain master in its own house. I have stated that abuse and wrongdoing must be punished and controlled. Nor do I wish to be misinterpreted as stating that the United States is a free-for-all and devil-take-the-hindermost society.

The very essence of equality of opportunity of our American system is that there shall be no monopoly or domination by any group or section in this country, whether it be business, sectional, or a group interest. On the contrary, our American system demands economic justice as well as political and social justice; it is not a system of *laissez faire.*

I am not setting up the contention that our American system is perfect. No human ideal has ever been perfectly attained, since humanity itself is not perfect. But the wisdom of our fore-fathers and the wisdom of the thirty men who have preceded me in this office hold to the conception that progress can be attained only as the sum of accomplishments of free individuals, and they have held unalterably to these principles.

In the ebb and flow of economic life our people in times of prosperity and ease naturally tend to neglect the vigilance over their rights. Moreover, wrongdoing is obscured by apparent success in enterprise. Then insidious diseases and wrongdoings grow apace. But we have in the past seen in times of distress and difficulty that wrongdoing and weakness come to the surface, and our people, in their endeavors to correct these wrongs, are tempted to extremes which may destroy rather than build.

It is men who do wrong, not our institutions. It is men who violate the laws and public rights. It is men, not institutions, who must be punished.

In my acceptance speech four years ago at Palo Alto I stated that—

One of the oldest aspirations of the human race was the abolition of poverty. By poverty I mean the grinding by under-nourishment, cold, ignorance, fear of old age to those who have the will to work.

I stated that—

In America today we are nearer a final triumph over poverty than in any land. The poorhouse has vanished from among us; we have not reached that goal, but given a chance to go forward, we shall, with the help of God, be in sight of the day when poverty will be banished from this Nation.

. . . .

My countrymen, the proposals of our opponents represent a profound change in American life—less in concrete proposal, bad as that may be, than by implication and by evasion. Dominantly in their spirit they represent a radical departure from the foundations of 150 years which have made this the greatest nation in the world. This election is not a mere shift from the ins to the outs. It means deciding the direction our Nation will take over a century to come.

My conception of America is a land where men and women may walk in ordered liberty, where they may enjoy the advantages of wealth not concentrated in the hands of a few but diffused through the lives of all, where they build and safeguard their homes, give to their children full opportunities of American life, where every man shall be respected in the faith that his conscience and his heart direct him to follow, where people secure in their liberty shall have leisure and impulse to seek a fuller life. That leads to the release of the energies of men and women, to the wider vision and higher hope; it leads to opportunity for greater and greater service not alone of man to man in our country but from our country to the world. It leads to health in body and a spirit unfettered, youthful, eager with a vision stretching beyond the farthest horizons with an open mind, sympathetic and generous. But that must be builded upon our experience with the past, upon the foundations which have made our country great. It must be the product of our truly American system.

Reform in Our Financial System

LETTER TO ARCH W. SHAW, CHICAGO

[February 17, 1933]

DEAR Mr. Shaw:

I have your request that I should state in writing what I said to you a few days ago* as to the broad conclusions I have formed from experience of the last four years as to the functioning of our economic system. It is, of course, impossible in the time I have left at my disposal or within the reach of a short statement, to cover all phases of the problem.

Our whole economic system naturally divides itself into production, distribution, and finance. By finance I mean every phase of investment, banking and credit. And at once I may say that the major fault in the system as it stands is in the financial system.

As to production, our system of stimulated individual effort, by its creation of enterprise, development of skill and discoveries in science and invention, has resulted in production of the greatest quantity of commodities and services of the most infinite variety that were ever known in the history of man. Our production in 1924–28, for instance, in the flow of commodities, service and leisure, resulted in the highest standard of living of any group of humanity in the history of the world. Even in these years, with our machinery and equipment and labor and business organizations, we could have produced more and could have enjoyed an even higher standard of living if all the adjustments of economic mechanism had been more perfect. We can say,

*February 10, 1933.

however, without qualification, that the motivation of production based on private initiative has proved the very mother of plenty. It has faults, for humanity is not without faults. Difficulties arise from overexpansion and adjustment to the march of labor-saving devices, but in broad result it stands in sharp contrast with the failure of the system of production as in its greater exemplar—Russia—where after fifteen years of trial in a land of as great natural resources as ours, that system has never produced in a single year an adequate supply of even the barest necessities in food and clothing for its people.

In the larger sense our system of distribution in normal times is sufficient and effective. Our transportation and communication is rapid and universal. The trades distribute the necessities of life at profits which represent a remarkably small percentage of their value.

The system moves supplies of everything into remotest villages and crossroads; it feeds and clothes great cities each day with the regularity and assurance which causes never a thought or anxiety. The diffusion of commodities and services in a social sense has faults. In normal times out of our 120,000,000 people there are a few millions who conscientiously work and strive, yet do not receive that minimum of commodities and services to which they have a just right as earnest members of the community. The system does not give to them that assurance of security and living which frees them from fear for the future.

There is another fringe of a few hundred thousand who receive more than they deserve for the effort they make. But taxes are furnishing rapid correction in this quarter. The great mass of people enjoy in normal times a broader diffusion of our wealth, commodities and services than ever before in history. The enlarging social sense of our people is furnishing the impulse to correction of faults. That correction is to be brought about by diffusion of property through constructive development within the system itself, with social vision as well as economic vision. It is not to be brought about by destruction of the system.

The last four years have shown unquestionably that it is

mainly the third element of our system—that is, finance—which has failed and produced by far the largest part of the demoralization of our systems of production and distribution with its thousand tragedies which wring the heart of the nation. I am not insensible to the disturbing war inheritances, of our expansion of production in certain branches, nor to the effect of increased labor-saving devices on employment, but these are minor notes of discord compared to that arising from failure of the financial system. This failure has been evidenced in two directions: That is, the lack of organization for domestic purposes and the weakness presented by a disintegrated front to the world through which we have been infinitely more demoralized by repeated shocks from abroad.

The credit system in all its phases should be merely a lubricant to the systems of production and distribution. It is not its function to control these systems. That it should be so badly organized, that the volume of currency and credit, whether long or short term, should expand and shrink irrespective of the needs of production and distribution; that its stability should be the particular creature of emotional fear or optimism; that it should be insecure; that it should dominate and not be subordinate to production and distribution—all this is intolerable if we are to maintain our civilization. Yet these things have happened on a gigantic scale. We could have weathered through these failures with some losses and could have secured reorganization as we went along, planing out failures in the fundamental organization of the financial system. The rain of blows from abroad, however, on the system of such weakness has wholly prostrated us by a second phase of this depression which came from a collapse of the financial systems in Europe.

In this system I am not referring to individual banks or financial institutions. Many of them have shown distinguished courage and ability. On the contrary I am referring to the system itself, which is so organized, or so lacking in organization, that it fails in its primary function of stable and steady service to the production and distribution system. In an emergency its very mechanism increases the jeopardy and paralyzes action of the community.

Clearly we must secure sound organization of our financial system as a prerequisite of the functioning of the whole economic system. The first steps in that system are sound currency, economy in government, balanced governmental budgets, whether national or local. The second step is an adequate separation of commerical banking from investment banking, whether in mortgages, bonds or other forms of long-term securities. The next step is to secure effective co-ordination between national and state systems. We cannot endure 49 separate regulatory systems which are both conflicting and weakening. We must accept the large view that the mismanagement, instability and bad functioning of any single institution affects the stability of some part of production and distribution and a multitude of other financial institutions. Therefore there must be co-operation within the financial system enforced by control and regulation by the Government, that will assure that this segment of our economic system does not, through faulty organization and action, bring our people again to these tragedies of unemployment and loss of homes which are today a stigma upon national life. We cannot endure that enormous sums of the people's savings shall be poured out either at home or abroad without making the promoter responsible for his every statement. We cannot endure that men will either manipulate the savings of the people so abundantly evidenced in recent exposures.

That it has been necessary for the Government, through emergency action, to protect us while holding a wealth of gold from being taken off the gold standard, to erect gigantic credit institutions with the full pledge of Government credit to save the nation from chaos through this failure of the financial system, that it is necessary for us to devise schemes of clearing-house protections and to install such temporary devices throughout the nation, is full proof of all I have said. That is the big question. If we can solve this, then we must take in hand the faults of the production and distribution systems—and many problems in the social and political system. But this financial system simply must be made to function first.

There is a phase of all this that must cause anxiety to every American. Democracy cannot survive unless it is master in its own house. The economic system cannot survive unless there are real restraints upon unbridled greed or dishonest reach for power. Greed and dishonesty are not attributes solely of our system—they are human and will infect Socialism or any ism. But if our production and distribution systems are to function we must have effective restraints on manipulation, greed and dishonesty. Our Democracy has proved its ability to put its unruly occupants under control but never until their conduct has been a public scandal and a stench. For instance, you will recollect my own opposition to Government operation of electric power, for that is a violation of the very fundamentals of our system; but parallel with it I asked and preached for regulation of it to protect the public from its financial manipulation. We gained the Power Commission but Congress refused it the regulatory authority we asked. I have time and again warned, asked and urged the reorganization of the banking system. The inertia of the Democracy is never more marked than in promotion of what seem abstract or indirect ideas. The recent scandals are the result. Democracy, always lagging, will no doubt now act and may act destructively to the system, for it is mad. It is this lag, the failure to act in time for prevention which I fear most in the sane advancement of economic life. For an outraged people may destroy the whole economic system rather than reconstruct and control the segment which has failed in its function. I trust the new Administration will recognize the difference between crime and economic functioning; between constructive prevention and organization as contrasted with destruction.

During these four years I have been fighting to preserve this fundamental system of production and distribution from destruction through collapse and bad functioning of the financial system. Time can only tell if we have succeeded. Success means higher and higher standards of living, greater comfort, more opportunity for intellectual, moral and spiritual development. Failure means a new form of the Middle Ages.

If we succeed in the job of preservation, certainly the next effort before the country is to reorganize the financial system so that all this will not happen again. We must organize for advance in the other directions, but that is another subject.

Yours faithfully,
HERBERT HOOVER.

The Gold Standard and Recovery

THE people determined the election. Those of us who believe in the most basic principle insisted upon by Abraham Lincoln—the transcendent importance of popular government—have no complaint. We accept and, as Americans, will continue wholeheartedly to do our part in promoting the well-being of the country. Our party can truly feel that we have held the faith; that we shall do so in the future is our solemn responsibility.

It has ever been the party of constructive action. The Republican Party will support the new administration in every measure which will promote public welfare. It must and will be vigilant in opposing those which are harmful.

My purpose is not to speak upon divided issues on this occasion, rather it is to discuss matters concerning which there should be no partisanship.

Further steps toward economic recovery is the urgent problem before the entire world. Ceaseless effort must be directed to restoration of confidence, the vanquishing of fear and apprehension, and thus the release of the recuperative spirit of the world.

It is, therefore, my purpose to discuss some of the broad measures which confront us in reaching further to the roots of this tragic disturbance, particularly in the field of foreign relations. While we have many concerns in the domestic field we must realize that so long as we engage in the export and import of goods and in financial activities abroad our price levels and credit system, our employment, and above all our fears will be greatly affected by foreign influences. During the past two years the crash of one foreign nation after another under direct and indirect war inheritances has dominated our whole economic life. The time has now come when nations must accept, in self-interest no less than in altruism, the obligations to co-operate in achieving world stability so mankind may again resume the march of progress. Daily it becomes more certain that the next great constructive step in remedy of the illimitable human suffering from this depression lies in the international field. It is in that field where the tide of prices can be most surely and quickly turned and the tragic despair of unemployment, agriculture and business transformed to hope and confidence.

Economic degeneration is always a series of vicious cycles of cause and effect. Whatever the causes may be, we must grasp these cycles at some segment and deal with them. Perhaps it would add clarity to the position I wish to make later if I should shortly follow through the cycle of financial failure which has at least in part taken place in countries abroad. Many countries in addition to the other pressures of the depression were over-burdened with debt and obligations from the World War or from excessive borrowing from abroad for rehabilitation or expansion. Many created or added to their difficulties through unbalanced budgets due to vast social programs or armament, finally reaching the point where collapse in governmental credit was inevitable. Foreigners in fear withdrew their deposits in such countries. Citizens in fright exported their capital. The result was a large movement of gold from such a country followed by the immediate undermining of confidence in its currency and its credit system. Runs on its banks ensued. Restrictions were imposed upon exchange to stop the flight of capital. Barriers were erected against the imports of commodities in endeavor to reduce the spending of the citizens for foreign goods and in an effort to establish equilibrium in exchange and retention of their gold reserves. Failure in such efforts resulted in abandonment of the gold standard. Currency depreciation, stagnation of their industries, increase in their unemployment and further shrinkage in consumption of world goods, again and again affecting all other nations. Depreciated currencies gave some nations the hope to manufacture goods more cheaply than their neighbors and thus to rehabilitate their financial position by invasion of the markets of other nations. Those nations in turn have sought to protect themselves by erecting barriers, until today as the result of such financial breakdown we are in the presence of an incipient outbreak of economic war in the world with the weapons of depreciated currencies, artificial barriers to trade by quotas, reciprocal trade agreements, discriminations, nationalistic campaigns to consume home-made goods, and a score of tactics each of which can be justified for the moment, but each of which adds to world confusion and dangers.

Out of the storm center of Europe this devastation has spread until, if we survey the world situation at the present moment, we find some 44 countries which have placed restrictions upon the movement of gold and exchange or are otherwise definitely off the gold standard. In practically all of them these actions have within the past twelve months been accompanied by new restrictions upon imports in an endeavor to hold or attract gold or to give some stability to currencies.

These depreciations of currency and regulations of exchange and restrictions of imports originated as defense measures by nations to meet their domestic financial difficulties. But a new phase is now developing among these nations—that is the rapid degeneration into economic war which threatens to engulf the world. The imperative call to the world today is to prevent this war.

Ever since the storm began in Europe the United States has held stanchly to the gold standard. In the present setting of depreciated currencies and in the light of differences in costs of production our tariffs are below those of most countries; we have held free from quotas, preferences, discriminations among nations. We have thereby maintained one Gibraltar of stability in the world and contributed to check the movement to chaos.

We are ourselves now confronted with an unnatural movement of goods from the lowered costs and standards of countries of depreciated currencies, which daily increase our unemployment and our difficulties. We are confronted with discriminatory actions and barriers stifling our agricultural and other markets. We will be ourselves forced to defensive action to protect ourselves unless this mad race is stopped. We must not be the major victim of it all.

In all this competition of degeneration, these beginnings of economic war between scores of nations, we see a gradual shrinkage in demand for international commodities throughout the world, and continuing fall in prices in terms of gold. From falling prices and unemployment we have at once the inability of debtors to meet obligations to their creditors, the dispossession of people from their farms and homes and businesses.

If the world is to secure economic peace, if it is to turn in the tide of degeneration, if it is to restore the functioning of the production and distribution systems of the world, it must start somewhere to break these vicious fiscal and financial circles. I am convinced that the first point of attack is to secure assured greater stability in the currencies of the important commercial nations. Without such stability the continued results of uncertainty, the destruction of confidence by currency fluctuations, exchange controls, and artificial import restrictions cannot be overcome but will continue to increase. With effective stability of currencies these dangers can be at once relaxed. I am not unaware that currency instability is both a cause and an effect in the vicious cycle—but we must start somewhere.

This brings me to a phase which has gradually developed during the past months, and that is the reactions and relation of gold itself upon this situation. For, independent of other causes of degeneration, I am convinced that the circumstances which surround this commodity are contributing to drive nations to these interferences with free commerce and to other destructive artificialities.

Outside minor use in the arts there are two dominant uses of gold. First, the important commercial nations have builded their domestic currency and credit systems upon a foundation of convertibility into gold. Second, gold is the most acceptable of all commodities in international payments. Even the nations that have abandoned the gold standard must still depend upon gold for this purpose. It is true that nations must in the long run balance their international trade by goods, services, or investments, but in the intermediate ebb and flow, balances must still be settled by the use of gold.

In all the welter of discussion over these problems we find some who are maintaining that the world has outgrown the use of gold as a basis of currency and exchange. We can all agree that gold as a commodity of universal exchange has not worked perfectly in the face of this great economic eruption. But we have to remember that it is a commodity the value of which is enshrined in human instincts for over 10,000 years. The time may come when the world can safely abandon its use altogether for these purposes, but it has not yet reached that point. It may be that by theoretically managed currencies some form of stability may be found a score or two years hence, but we have no time to wait. They are subject to great human fallibilities. Sooner or later political pressure of special groups and interests will direct their use. But in any event it would take many years' demonstration to convince men that a non-gold currency would certainly a year hence be worth what he paid for it today.

It is noticeable that most of the nations off the gold standard are even today seeking to increase their gold reserves. In the view of many economists these measures and the restrictions which have been placed on the movement of gold or exchange by two score of nations have created the same practical effect as if there were a scarcity of gold in the world. That while there has in the last few years been a very large increase in the quantity of visible gold in the possession of institutions and governments, the effect of all these regulatory actions by governments attempting to protect their gold reserves from runs and flights of capital and their attempts to increase their supply has been to divide the gold of the world into two score of pockets and in many of them to freeze it from full freedom of action. In other words, this view holds that we are today not dealing with a shortage of the commodity; we are dealing with its being partly immobilized in its functioning.

To add to the confusion, another phenomenon of the gold situation has increased disturbance and wrought havoc. That is the effect of waves of fear and apprehension. We have a parallel in nations to an unreasoning panic run on a bank. The fears and apprehensions directed in turn to the stability of first one nation and then another have caused the withdrawal of foreign balances from a particular nation, followed by flights of capital, through purchases of exchange by its own citizens seeking refuge and security for their property. These movements are followed by large flows of gold to meet exchange demands, thus undermining the domestic currency and credit system of the victim nation and leading to an unnatural piling up of gold in some nation temporarily considered safe. These movements, themselves in large degree unwarranted, have forced some nations off the gold standard that could otherwise have maintained their position. We ourselves a year ago suffered from the effect of such a movement. Thus a mass of the gold dashing hither and yon from one nation to another, seeking maximum safety, has acted like a cannon loose on the deck of the world in a storm.

In the meantime the currencies of the world are fluctuating spasmodically. Countries off the gold standard are in reality suffering from their managed paper currencies by reason of the fact that men are unable to make contracts for the future with security, and that insecurity itself again dries up enterprise, business, employment, consumption of goods, and further causes reductions of prices. Other nations to hold their own are attempting to compete in destruction.

Broadly the solution lies in the reestablishment of confidence. That confidence cannot be reestablished by the abandonment of gold as a standard in the world. So far as the human race has yet developed and established its methods and systems of stable exchange that solution can only be found now and found quickly through the reestablishment of gold standards among important nations. The huge gold reserves of the world can be made to function in relation to currencies, standards of value and exchange. And I say with emphasis that I am not proposing this as a favor to the United States. It is the need of the whole world. The United States is so situated that it can protect itself better than almost any country on earth.

Nor is it necessary from an international point of view that those nations who have been forced off the gold standard shall be again restored to former gold values. It will suffice if it only is fixed. From this source are the principal hopes for restoring world confidence and reversing the growing barriers to the movement of goods and making possible the security in trade which will again revive a demand for such goods. To do this it is necessary to have strong and courageous action on the part of the leading commercial nations. If some sort of international financial action is necessary to enable central banks to co-operate for the purpose of stabilizing currencies, nations should have no hesitation in joining in such an operation under proper safeguards. If some part of the debt payments to us could be set aside for temporary use for this purpose we should not hesitate to do so. At the same time the world should endeavor to find a place for silver at least in enlarged subsidiary coinage.

If the major nations will enter the road leading to the early reestablishment of the gold standard, then and then only can the abnormal barriers to trade, the quotas, preferences, discriminatory agreements, and tariffs which exceed the differences in costs of production between nations be removed, uniform trade privileges among all nations be reestablished and the threat of economic war averted. A reasonable period of comparative stability in the world's currencies would repay the cost of such effort a hundred times over in the increase of consumption, the increase of employment, the lessening of the difficulties of debtors throughout the land, with the avoidance of millions of tragedies. The world would quickly see a renewed movement of goods and would have an immediate rise in prices everywhere, thereby bringing immediate relief to the whole economic system.

I do not underestimate the difficulties nor the vast fiscal and financial problems which lie behind the restoration of stability and economic peace. Bold action alone can succeed. The alternative to such constructive action is a condition too grave to be contemplated in passive acceptance.

The American people will soon be at the fork of three roads. The first is the highway of co-operation among nations, thereby to remove the obstructions to world consumption and rising prices. This road leads to real stability, to expanding standards of living, to a resumption of the march of progress by all peoples. It is today the immediate road to relief of agriculture and unemployment, not alone for us but the entire world.

The second road is to rely upon our high degree of national self-containment, to increase our tariffs, to create quotas and discriminations, and to engage in definite methods of curtailment of production of agricultural and other products and thus to secure a larger measure of economic isolation from world influences. It would be a long road of readjustments into unknown and uncertain fields. But it may be necessary if the first way out is closed to us. Some measures may be necessary pending co-operative conclusions with other nations.

The third road is that we inflate our currency, consequently abandon the gold standard, and with our depreciated currency attempt to enter a world economic war, with the certainty that it leads to complete destruction, both at home and abroad.

The first road can only be undertaken by the co-operation among all important nations. Last April, in conjunction with the leaders of Europe, our government developed the idea of a World Economic Conference to deal with these questions. It is unfortunate that the delay of events in Europe and the election in the United States necessarily postponed the convening of that conference. It has been further delayed by the change of our administration.

The question naturally arises whether other nations will co-operate to restore world confidence, stability, and economic peace. In this connection, I trust the American people will not be misled or influenced by the ceaseless stream of foreign propaganda that cancellation of war debts would give this international relief and remedy. That is not true. These debts are but a segment of the problem. Their world trade importance is being exaggerated. In this respect I stated some months ago, the American people can well contend that most of the debtor countries have the capacity to raise these annual amounts from their taxpayers, as witness the fact that in most cases the payments to us amount to less than one-third of the military expenditures of each country. But at the same time we can well realize that in some instances the transfer of these sums may gravely disturb their currency or international exchanges. But if we are asked for sacrifices because of such injury we should have assurances of co-operation that will positively result in monetary stability and the restoration of world prosperity. If we are asked for sacrifices because of incapacity to pay we should have tangible cultural and other imports. The world should have relief from the sore burden of armaments. If they are unwilling to meet us in these fields, this Nation, whether you or I like it or not, will be driven by our own internal forces more and more to its own self-containment and isolation, as harmful to the world and as little satisfactory to us as this course may be.

But this is the counsel of despair. The full meed of prosperity among nations cannot be builded upon mutual impoverishment. It is to the interest of the world to join in bold and courageous action which will bring about economic peace—in which the benefits to the rest of the world are as great as to us—and we should co-operate to the full. Any other course in the world today endangers civilization itself. Unless the world takes heed it will find that it has lost its standards of living and culture, not for a few years of depression but for generations.

Despite many discouragements, the world has shown an increasing ability in establishment of effective agencies in the solution of many controversies which might have led to war. When we compare the attitude of nations toward each other which existed 20 years ago with that of today, we can say that there have been developed both the spirit and the method of co-operation in the prevention of war which gives profound hope of the future.

In its broad light the problem before the world today is to

work together to prevent the dangers of developing economic conflict—to secure economic peace. That is a field in which the world can co-operate even more easily than in the field of prevention of war, because there is involved in it no background of century-old controversies, injustices, or hates. The problems in that economic field contain less of the imponderables and more of the concrete. There is involved in it the most important and appealing self-interest of every nation. Through such co-operation the world can mitigate the forces which are destroying the systems of production and distribution upon the maintenance of which its gigantic population is dependent. There is a driving force before the eyes of every statesman in the misery and suffering which have infected every nation. Throughout the world the people are distraught with unemployment; the decline of prices which has plunged farmers into despair; the loss of homes, of savings and provisions for old age. Therefore, just as there is an obligation amongst nations to engage in every possible step for the prevention of war itself, there is before us today the necessity for world co-operation to prevent economic warfare. And who can say but the greatest act in prevention of war is to allay economic friction?

On our side this problem is not to be solved by partisan action but by national unity. Whatever our differences of view may be on domestic policies, the welfare of the American people rests upon solidarity before the world, not merely in resisting proposals which would weaken the United States and the world but solidarity in co-operation with other nations in strengthening the whole economic fabric of the world. These problems are not insoluble. There is a latent, earnest, and underlying purpose on the part of all nations to find their solution. Of our own determination there should be no question.

The problem before the world is to restore confidence and hope by the release of the strong, natural forces of recovery which are inherent in this civilization. Civilization is the history of surmounted difficulties. We of this world today are of the same strain as our fathers who builded this civilization.

They passed through most terrible conflicts. They met many great depressions. They created a state of human well-being in normal times such as the world has never seen. The next forward step is as great as any in history. It is that we perpetuate the welfare of mankind through the immense objectives of world recovery and world peace.

The Role of the Republican
Party in Opposition

WASHINGTON, D. C.

[*February 27, 1933*]

HON. EVERETT SANDERS, CHAIRMAN
REPUBLICAN NATIONAL COMMITTEE,
WASHINGTON, D. C.

MY DEAR Mr. Chairman:
You have asked that I should address a few words upon questions of party organization to the Executive Committee which meets today. I first wish to take this opportunity to express my appreciation of the loyal and effective work of your Committee and the thousands of party workers.

This work of party organization is a public duty often thankless to a degree, yet in the highest sense a public service, for organized political parties have become an absolute necessity for the functioning of popular government in so large a population as ours. Only through such organization can the people express their will. The nation would be a bedlam of wholly discordant voices without such organization, without loyalty to it. Party organization must assure cohesion in public action and upon their pledges, their principles and their ideals. A party deserves to exist only as it embodies the thought and conviction of earnest men and women who have the welfare of the nation at heart. It must be a party of ideals since only exalted purpose can bring great numbers of people together in united action. But the consummation of ideals must be organized.

You have also asked for some word on the policies to be pursued by the party.

Political parties have great obligations of service whether the party be in power or not. In these times co-operation and not partisanship is the need of the country but it is no less an obligation of the party to subject all proposals to the scrutiny of constructive debate and to oppose those which will hurt the progress and the welfare of the country.

The proposals, the principles and the ideals of the party were set out in the last campaign. They require no repetition here. They will justify themselves. Rather than to review them even in the setting of present events, I prefer to say a word as to a platform upon which all Americans can stand without partisanship.

There are certain fundamentals and safeguards of our government which are not the property of any political party. They are the common necessity to the entire people. They embrace rigid adherence to the Constitution; enforcement of the laws without respect to persons; assurance of the credit of the government through restraint of spending and provision of adequate revenue; preservation of the honor, and integrity of the government in respect to its obligations, its securities and its sound currency; insistence upon the responsibilities of local government; advancement of world peace; adequate preparedness for defense; the cure of abuses which have crept into our economic and political systems; development of security to homes and living; persistence in the initiative, equal opportunity and responsibilities of individuals and institutions; and finally every encouragement to the development of our intellectual, moral and spiritual life. In great emergencies humanity in government requires the utilization of the reserve strength of all branches of the government, whether local or national, to protect our institutions and our people from forces beyond their control. This must and can be accomplished without violation of these fundamentals and safeguards.

Upon these foundations lies the freedom, the welfare and the future of every citizen in the country. By them we will march forward. We do not claim them as the exclusive property of the Republican Party. They are the inheritance of all parties. This is a program which can command the respect and support of all who would maintain the United States in the high position amongst nations it now holds, and one from which we should not deviate fidelity.

Yours faithfully,
HERBERT HOOVER

Responsibility of the Republican Party to the Nation

SACRAMENTO, CALIFORNIA

[March 22, 1935]

THE Republican Party today has the greatest responsibility that has come to it since the days of Abraham Lincoln. That responsibility is to raise the standard in defense of fundamental American principles. It must furnish the rallying point for all those who believe in these principles and are determined to defeat those who are responsible for their daily jeopardy.

1. The American people have directly before them the issue of maintaining and perfecting our system of orderly individual liberty under constitutionally conducted government, or of rejecting it in favor of the newly created system of regimentation and bureaucratic domination in which men and women are not masters of government but are the pawns or dependents of a centralized and potentially self-perpetuating government. That is, shall we as a nation stand on the foundations of Americanism, gaining the great powers of progress inherent in it, correcting abuses which arise within it, widening the security and opportunities that can alone be builded upon it?

Before us is the sink into which first one great nation after another abroad is falling. America must look today, as in the past, to the creative impulses of free men and women, born of the most enterprising and self-reliant stock in the world, for productive genius, for expansion of enterprise, for economic recovery, for restoration of normal jobs, for increased standards of living, for reform of abuse of governmental or economic powers, and for advance from outworn modes of thought. The freedom of men to think, to act, to achieve, is now being hampered.

2. The American people have a right to determine for themselves this fundamental issue, and it is solely through the Republican Party that it can be presented for determination at the ballot box. To accomplish this the country is in need of a rejuvenated and vigorous Republican organization. That rebirth of the Republican Party transcends any personal interest or the selfish interest of any group. That organization will be the stronger if, like your own sessions, it springs from the people who believe in these principles.

3. It is well that the young men and women of the Republican Party should meet and give attention to this drift from national moorings. Some of the concrete results of these policies are already apparent. The most solemn government obligations have been repudiated. The nation is faced with the greatest debt ever known to our country. The currency has been rendered uncertain. The government has been centralized under an enormous bureaucracy in Washington which has dictated and limited the production of our industries, increasing the costs and prices of their products with inevitable decreased consumption. Monopolistic practices have been organized on a gigantic scale. Small business men have been disabled and crushed. Class conflicts have been created and embittered. The government has gone into business in competition with its citizens. Citizens have been coerced, threatened and penalized for offenses unknown to all our concepts of liberty. The courts are proclaiming repeated violations of the Constitution.

Because of food destruction and restraint on farm production, foreign food is pouring into our ports, purchase of which should have been made from our farmers. The cost of living is steadily advancing. More people are dependent upon the government for relief than ever before. Recovery is still delayed. The productive genius of our people, which is the sole road to recovery and to increased standards of living, is being stifled, the nation impoverished instead of enriched. The theories of this Administration do not work. They are no longer a propagandized millennium; they are self-exposed.

4. The people have a right to an opportunity to change these policies. It is the duty of the Republican Party to offer that opportunity. And beyond insistence upon American foundations of government, it is the duty of the Party to insist upon realistic methods of recovery, real jobs for labor and real markets for the farmer. Those methods lie in removing the shackles and uncertainties from enterprise. After nearly six years of depression, liquidation, restriction of all manner of purchases and improvements, we stand on the threshold of a great forward, economic movement, if only the paralyzing effects of mistaken governmental policies and activities may be removed.

The present conception of a national economy based upon scarcity must in all common sense be reversed to an economy based upon production, or workman, farmer, and business man alike are defeated. Surely economic life advances only through increasing production by use of every instrument science gave to us, through lowering of costs and prices with consequent increase in consumption, and through higher real wages to the worker and real return to the farmer. Effective reform of abuses in business and finance must be undertaken through regulation and not through bureaucratic dictation or government operation. Protection to individual enterprise from monopolies must be re-established whereby the smaller businesses may live. Stifling uncertainties of currency manipulation must be removed. Government expenditures which, if continued on the present scale, can create only bankruptcy or calamitous inflation, must be curtailed. The effective participation of the States and local governments in relief under non-partisan administrators must be re-established so that waste, extravagance, and politics may be eliminated and the people better served. Great social problems of better safeguards to the individual against the dislocations of advancing industry, national calamity and old age must be discovered. But these problems of business, agriculture, and labor become much easier with a restoration of economic common sense. Indeed, a score of economic and social questions must be solved, and in their answers are locked the real advancement of life and the attainment of security and contentment in the American home—for that is the ultimate expression of American life. But their solution will not be found in violation of the foundations of human liberty.

5. It is well that we pause a moment to examine what objectives we wish to secure from the vast complex of invisible governmental, economic and social forces which dominate our civilization. The objective of American life must be to upbuild and protect the family and the home, whether farmer, worker, or business man. That is the unit of American life. It is the moral and spiritual as well as the economic unit. With its independence and security come the spiritual blessings of the nation. The fundamental protection of these homes is the spirit as well as the letter of the Bill of Rights, with the supports from the framework of the Constitution. They must be given peace with the world. There must be confidence in the security of the job, of the business, of the savings which sustain these homes. Increased standards of living, leisure, and security can come to that home through unshackling the productive genius of our people. The advancement of knowledge must be translated into increasing health and education for the children. There must be constantly improved safeguards to the family from the dislocations of economic life and of old age. With the growth of great industrial forces we must continue to add unceasing protections from abuse and exploitation. We must be liberal in reward to those who add service, material or spiritual wealth to these homes. Those deserve no reward who do not contribute or who gain from exploitation of them. The windows of these homes must be bright with hope. Their doors must be open outward to initiative, enterprise, opportunity, unbounded by regimentation and socialism. Today there must be restoration of faith, the removal of fear and uncertainty that these ideals and these hopes will be open to those who strive.

To the young men and women it is vital that their opportunity in life shall be preserved; that the frontiers of initiative and enterprise shall not be closed; that their future shall not be burdened by unbearable debt for our follies; that their lives and opportunities shall not be circumscribed and limited; that they shall have the right to make their homes and careers and achieve their own position in the world. There are a host of problems to solve if we attain these ideals; but again I repeat, that the first condition in their solution is orderly individual liberty and responsible constitutional government as opposed to un-American regimentation and bureaucratic domination.

The NRA

IN REPLY to your question, the one right answer by the House of Representatives to the Senate's action extending the life of the NRA is to abolish it entirely.

Present NRA proposals are as bad, in many ways, as the original. With its continuation until the next Congress and with Federal agents putting pressure on State legislatures to get them to enact State laws in support of NRA, it is evident that there has been no real retreat.

This whole idea of ruling business through code authorities with delegated powers of law is un-American in principle and a proved failure in practice. The codes are retarding recovery. They are a cloak for conspiracy against the public interest. They are and will continue to be a weapon of bureaucracy, a device for intimidation of decent citizens.

To the customary answer of "destructive criticism" or the other question "what substitute is offered?" I suggest that the only substitute for an action that rests on definite and proved economic error is to abandon it. We do not construct new buildings on false foundations, and we cannot build a Nation's economy on a fundamental error.

The beneficent objectives of a greater social justice and the prevention of sweating, child labor and abuse in business practices should be and can be better attained by specific statutory law.

There are already sufficient agencies of government for enforcement of the laws of the land. Where necessary those laws

45

should be strengthened, but not replaced with personal government.

The prevention of waste in mineral resources should be carried out by the States operating under Federally encouraged interstate compacts. That is an American method of eradicating economic abuses and wastes, as distinguished from Fascist regimentation.

The multitude of code administrators, agents or committees has spread into every hamlet, and, whether authorized or not, they have engaged in the coercion and intimidation of presumably free citizens. People have been sent to jail, but far more have been threatened with jail. Direct and indirect boycotts have been organized by the bureaucracy itself. Many are being used today. Claiming to cure immoral business practices, the codes have increased them a thousandfold through "chiseling." They have not protected legitimate business from unfair competition but they have deprived the public of the benefits of fair competition.

This whole NRA scheme has saddled the American people with the worst era of monopolies we have ever experienced. However monopoly is defined, its objective is to fix prices or to limit production or to stifle competition. Any one of those evils produces the other two, and it is no remedy to take part of them out. These have been the very aim of certain business elements ever since Queen Elizabeth. Most of the 700 NRA codes effect those very purposes.

Exactly such schemes to avoid competition in business were rejected by my Administration because they are born from a desire to escape the anti-trust laws. If the anti-trust laws had not been effective in a major way, there would have been no such desire to escape them. If they do not meet modern conditions, they should be openly amended or circumvented.

My investigations over the country show that the codes have increased costs of production and distribution, and therefore prices. Thus they have driven toward decreased consumption and increased unemployment. They have increased the cost of living, and placed a heavier burden on the American farmer.

NRA codes have been crushing the life out of small business, and they are crushing the life out of the very heart of the local community body. There are 1,500,000 small businesses in this country, and our purpose should be to protect them.

The codes are preventing new enterprises. In this they deprive America's youth of the opportunity and the liberty to start and build their independence, and thus stop the men and women of tomorrow from building soundly toward a true social security.

Publishers have had to resist arduously the encroachment of these NRA codes upon such fundamental, constitutionally guaranteed American liberties as free speech.

The whole concept of NRA is rooted in a regimented "economy of scarcity"—an idea that increased costs, restricted production and hampered enterprise will enrich a Nation. That notion may enrich a few individuals and help a few businesses, but it will impoverish the nation and undermine the principles of real social justice upon which this Nation was founded.

If the NRA has increased employment, it is not apparent. If we subtract the persons temporarily employed by the coded industries as the direct result of the enormous Government expenditures, we find that the numbers being employed are not materially greater than when it was enacted. NRA's pretended promises to labor were intentionally vague and have never been clarified. They have only promoted conflict without establishing real rights.

That original ballyhoo used to hypnotize and coerce the people into acquiescence is now gone. Most of the originally grandiose schemes now are conceded to be a violation of the spirit and the letter of the American Constitution.

Some business interests already have established advantages out of the codes, and therefore seek the perpetuation of NRA. Even these interests should recognize that in the end they themselves will become either the pawns of a bureaucracy that they do not want or the instruments of a bureaucracy the American people do not want.

Commencement Address

STANFORD UNIVERSITY

[June 16, 1935]

THE ESSENTIALS OF SOCIAL GROWTH IN AMERICA

SOME years ago I marched up, as you do, to receive the diploma of this University. Like some of you here present, my occasion was somewhat distracted by the sinking realization of a shortage of cash working capital and the necessity to find an immediate job. Put into economic terms, I was earnestly wishing some person with a profit motive would allow me to try to earn him a profit. At the risk of seeming counter-revolutionary or as a defender of evil, I am going to suggest that basis of test for a job has some advantages. As Will Payne has aptly mentioned, it does not require qualifications as to either ancestry, religion, good looks, or ability to get votes.

I did not immediately succeed in impressing any of the profit or loss takers with the high profit potentialities of my diploma. The white-collar possibilities having been eliminated, my first serious entrance into the economic world was by manual labor. But somehow, both in the stages of manual labor and professional work, I missed the discovery that I was a wage slave. I at least had the feeling that it was my option that if I did not like that particular profit taker I could find another one somewhere. But what mainly interests you is the fact that I found them a cheery and helpful lot of folk who took an enormous interest in helping young people to get a start and get along in life. And you will find that is the case today. Indeed human helpfulness has improved rather than deteriorated in this generation. You will find many friendly hands. Moreover, as our world has become more intricate, special training has become more respected. They will give more credence to your diploma.

There has indeed been great change in our American world since that time. Our huge surge forward in the conquests of science and of mechanical power has brought new visions and a new vista of further advance in social justice and the general welfare among our people. As we have nearly doubled in numbers, we jostle our elbows more. We must have more rules of the road. In the midst of this changing scene there has been injected the inflation and destruction of the greatest war of history. Its shivering instabilities still remain with us. Surplus production is pitted against mass poverty. Under these pressures every weakness of the system has come to the surface. The wounds of war are made to appear as the result of organic disease of the system. New systems of life are urged as a cure for all human ills. Our economic and governmental system is slow to adjust itself to these changes and aspirations. There is great confusion of thought and ideals.

Such periods of confused thought are not new in the world. You will find an uncanny parallel in England during the period following the Napoleonic Wars. They had also seen a great stride in productivity from the early installation of the factory system, the steam engine, the expansion of world trade. The Napoleonic Wars added to this all the false prosperities of inflation. Then with the inevitable depression they too faced the most acute agricultural distress and unemployment. Agriculture and industry remained out of balance for a score of years. Hectic periods of partial recovery in the cities were followed by outbursts of mad speculation and greed. Economic wounds were painful then as now. They too tried some of the sedatives which we have recently embraced. It was a period seething with contention. Their very expressions have a modern ring. But to the discerning student of that period there emerged one outstanding result of lasting importance. Out of that seething of misery and that violent movement of social and economic forces there came gradually a great clarification of thought and stronger foundations of social growth.

Our standards of life have immensely increased since Napoleonic times. Then the Englishman had less than 100 mechanical horsepower at his command for each thousand adults. Today we command 6,000 mechanical horsepower for each thousand adults. And this does not include the private automobiles. At that period a skilled mechanic with his whole week's wages could purchase less than 200 pounds of the fixings from which bread and butter are made. Today he can purchase 500 pounds, if he were disposed to take all his week's wages in that form. At that time I doubt that 5 per cent of the population enjoyed what we would today call a reasonable standard of living.

In our times over eighty per cent of our people have enjoyed such standards. That was when our economic machine was working on all eight cylinders. Faith in its wider spread was universal. When prosperity was suddenly dimmed, faith was turned to fear. Men today naturally feel all the impulses of distress. Confusion of thought is inevitable.

But we should be of greater faith. The new surge forward in our productivity of this last generation has for the first time in history given us the possibility and the vision that we can raise our whole people to higher standards of living. Capacity to produce a plenty is one of the triumphs of American civilization. It creates the real basis of hope of economic security for all the people who will work. We want to be secure against unemployment, old age, and misfortune, so that fear of poverty will be driven from among us. And social security demands more than economic security. It would have health, education, and strengthening of character, the time and opportunity for recreation and the cultivation of the most desirable things of life.

This aspiration is not new in this part of the world. It has been an American ideal from the beginning. We have brought a larger part of our people within the walls of social security than any nation hitherto. But we have yet in ordinary times somewhat less than a quarter of them for which we must find these protections. The new possibilities of productive capacity

and the poignant miseries of the day are pressing for immediate action. It is not upon this ideal or this aspiration that the
babel of tongues arises today. It is upon the method by which
it is to be accomplished. If our thought is clear and our methods are rightly directed, we should see another era of advancement as great as the hundred years which followed the Napoleonic Wars. If our course is wrongly directed, civilization can
go as deeply into eclipse as it did in the Middle Ages, despite
all our gas and electricity and our knowledge of atoms and
micro-organisms.

You are entering into life at a time when these problems,
vivid from distress, are tense in public mind. Your own future
will depend upon the manner of their solution. I would be
glad indeed if I could contribute only a mite of direction to
your thinking on them.

I shall not take your time to even summarize the facts and
forces which underlie the problem. You will find that task
ably accomplished for the first time in the report of the Committee on Recent Social Trends which I appointed some five
years ago. Nor is it my purpose to discuss all of the principles
or methods of social growth—or even to discuss them at length.
What I wish to do is to enumerate certain essentials for the accomplishment of these ideals which I am convinced stand out
so far from our racial experience and from these bitter years
since the Great War. And do not forget that while our objectives lie in the realm of idealism, these essentials and methods
must be stripped to sheer realism if we are to succeed.

1. The first of social securities is freedom—freedom of men
to worship, to think, to speak, to direct their energies, to develop their own talents and to be rewarded for their effort.
Too often plans of social security ignore these the primary
forces which make for human progress, without which America as we know it could not exist. Freedom is a spiritual need
and a spiritual right of man. We can get security in food,
shelter, education, leisure, music, books, and what not, in some
jails. But we don't get freedom. Those who scoff that individual liberty is of no consequence to the under-privileged and

the unemployed are grossly ignorant of the primary fact that it is through the creative impulses of liberty that the redemption of these sufferings and that social security must come.

2. The second of social securities is the capacity to produce a plenty of goods and services with which to give economic security to the whole of us. Scientific discovery, this vast technology and mechanical power, are the achievement of personal and intellectual freedom. Creativeness, intellectual accomplishment, initiative, and enterprise are the dynamic forces of civilization. They thrive alone among free men and women. It is these impulses which have built this capacity to produce a plenty that society must now learn to employ more effectively. This freedom and this plenty came into western civilization hand in hand—they are inseparable. This vastly complicated mechanism is not alone a mass of machines. These engines and machines are inert materials which require every hour of the day new human initiative, new enterprise, and new creative action, or they will not work. No other group of impulses would have produced this productivity. No other method but that of orderly personal liberty can operate or improve it. Economic security is lost the moment that freedom is sacrificed.

Any system which curtails these freedoms or stimulants to men destroys the possibility of the production which we know we must have to attain economic security. Social security will never be attained by an economy of scarcity. That is the economy of fear. Not out of scarcity or restriction but out of abundance can society make provision for all its members and support the unemployed, the sick, the aged, and the orphan. That is the economy of hope.

3. The safeguards of freedom lie in self-government. There never has been nor ever will be freedom when powers of government are lodged in a man or a group of men. Moreover, all history teaches us that even majorities cannot be trusted with the ark of freedom without checks. Constitutional government, the division of powers, are the only successful protections the human race has devised. To transgress or to override them will weaken and finally destroy freedom itself.

4. The hope of social security can be destroyed both from the right and the left. From the right come the abuses of monopoly, economic tyranny, exploitation of labor, or of consumers or investors. From the left come power-seeking, job-holding bureaucracies, which bleed our productive strength with taxes and destroy confidence and enterprise with their tyrannies and their interferences. The concentration of economic power and the concentration of political power are equally destructive. The weeds of abuse will always grow among the fine blossoms of free initiative and free enterprise. Evil as these weeds are, we can better spend the unceasing labor to dig them out than to have the blossoms killed by the blights of little and big governmental tyrannies.

5. If we are to attain social security we must find remedy or mitigation of interruptions and dislocations in the economic system. Its stable functioning must be our first objective. War and its long dreadful aftermaths of instability is the first and worst of these interruptions. War in defense of our country and our rights is justified. But we should not blame the social and economic system for injuries produced by war. We should sacrifice until they are healed and cease passing the infection to the next generation.

The next worst interruption is the business cycle with all its waste in booms and the vast miseries of slumps. We can never get wholly free from them because sometimes they sweep our borders from abroad. But depressions other than from war origins are capable of great mitigation by wiser conduct of our credit machinery.

6. In any process of returning the machine to stable operation we must consider the problems arising from the dislocation of individuals as well as the dislocation of the system. It is the individual who suffers from these instabilities. We must conclude that it will be a slow and difficult job to bring stability to the system as a whole, and we must realize that every interruption brings misfortune to individuals. Moreover, the rapid advance of labor-saving devices imposes upon us individual dislocations pending re-employment. Therefore, the founda-

tions of individual security must in the end be strengthened beyond relief work. Over the century we have seen the vast development of insurance against the effect of fire, flood, sickness, accident, and death. The expansion of these principles to the remaining fields of human accident, that is, security against poverty in old age, to unemployment, must now be brought into action. While the aid of the government is necessary to overcome the initial risks, yet the world has not yet developed a satisfactory system of doing it.

7. Even if we attained as much economic and social security in these areas as could be expected of human endeavor, we still have the problem of distribution of our productivity so as to find security for the remaining ten or twenty-five per cent, whatever it may be, who are not yet upon the ladder of social security.

Having the vast majority economically secure when the system is stable, our job is not to pull down this great majority but to build up those who lag. And herein lies a great area of unclarified national thought. Here America has, however, developed one new idea—that wages are linked to ability to consume goods; that the highest possible real wage is the necessary accompaniment of mass production. No one denies today that the road to higher consumption of goods and services is lower costs, lower prices, and thus higher real wages and incomes.

Theoretically, the end of that road would be complete economic security. But there is and will be a segment of the dislocated, the less fortunate, the misused and the less wise. Herein we have vast problems of eliminating sweated labor, child labor, marginal farmers, slums, industrial conflicts, and a score of others. That is indeed a far-flung battle front in human welfare.

8. Economic security and in fact social security can be greatly strengthened by wider-spread property ownership. The home, farm, business, savings insurance, and investment are not only a reserve of economic security but by their wide distribution they become of vast social importance far beyond their mone-

tary value. Here lies a sense of freedom from fear, a sense of independence, the accomplishment of personal endeavor and choice.

9. Sometimes we can find our feet if we examine what sort of civilization we seek to secure from all this vast complex of visible and invisible forces which dominate our civilization. Surely our social objective must be to upbuild and protect the family and the home. The family is the unit of American life; it is the moral and spiritual unit as well as the economic unit. With the independence and the security of the family have come the spiritual blessings of the nation. In that home must be men and women of individuality and character. There must be security in education and health, safety from invasion and crime. There must be increasing protections from exploitation, whether from private economic tyranny or governmental tyranny. We must build security in the individual job, for the individual business, for the thrift and savings which sustain it. Fear of ruin, fear of poverty, fear of old age and dislocation must be removed from the individual and thus from the heart of the family. The doors of freedom must be kept open wide to initiative, to honest enterprise, to effort. The windows must be kept bright with hope and confidence in the future. These are the standards and tests which may be applied to every social proposal made to you.

10. Upon all these three categories of objectives for greater stability in the economic system, protections to the individual victims of dislocation, and the distribution of the national product—I should like to make four observations.

(*a*) Universal social security cannot be had by sudden inspiration of panaceas. There are no short cuts. Permanent social growth cannot be had by hothouse methods. The soil of human nature requires infinite patience in search for useful plants and equally in search for methods of elimination of weeds and pests. It requires experiment to develop the plants and to poison the pests. And the essence of experiment is not to transform the whole field but to try with a small part. It implies willingness to abandon failure; for in the field of society futile experimental growth of today becomes the pests of the future. It requires that we do not repeat experiments long since proved futile. Just as we must be bold in experiment also it is doubly necessary that we use caution in experimenting with the welfare of human beings or we can produce infinite misery—not social security.

(b) The functioning of any economic system is peculiarly based upon faith in the future and confidence in certain constants in life. Without that faith all effort slackens. They are not only liberty in the broad sense but these constants include the detail of sanctity of contracts which are not unconscionable, the stability of the currency and credit, the maintenance of legitimate competition, government by specific laws, not by the uncertainties of administrative fiat. Without security in those constants, confidence and faith are impossible. Indeed, today our daily life and the whole world are seized with fears. There are within our ranks defeatists who in despair abandon all confidence in the race, in our accomplishment hitherto, and all hope that upon this rich experience we can further advance. Our sympathetic thought properly drives to consideration of the twenty-five per cent of the less fortunate. It is right that it should be so. But let us not forget that the seventy-five per cent need consideration also. They alone can carry the burden of the twenty-five per cent in these times until that minority per cent can begin their own upward climb. Through them is the sole hope of the twenty-five per cent. If they be harassed, coerced, intimidated, discouraged, unduly taxed, the whole fabric will fall. The times demand a determined spirit whose faith is not dulled by the mere aftermaths of a great war, a vicious business cycle, or the sudden triumphs of science.

(c) Democracy will not function without free debate. Every experiment, every proposal or method is a compromise in judgment as to the weight which must be attached to the different factors, or forces, involved in it. Their relative importance cannot be shaped except upon the anvil of debate. There is no genuine debate unless there is tolerance and intellectual honesty. The whole social order must be critically and constantly examined. But criticism is of no value which either ignores the good of the old or the value of the new. Propaganda which partially presents facts is not debate. Its use under government authority is a pollution of free press and free thought. It is a violation of the spirit of the Bill of Rights. Calling names is not debate. It is a confession of defeat by logic and fact. It is more—it is the infallible sign of intellectual dishonesty.

(*d*) Social security must be builded upon a cult of work, not a cult of leisure. The judgment on Adam has not yet been reversed. That proscription was for his better health and life. Work fails without thrift. It also fails without leadership; leadership fails without character, education, special training, the stimulation of intelligence and genius, the advance of knowledge. All these seem platitudes, but they are worth mentioning because some systems which pretend to social security forget them all or in part. It is to provide leadership that this University labors. This is the service for which you are selected. Just as surely as all the directors and leaders of today must die, just that surely will their responsibilities be taken by you.

None of these attainments is beyond America's capacity to realize. They can be realized in the pure air of orderly liberty. They can be nurtured only through sacrifice in our generation, through faith, courage, and a steady will. Herein is to be found the new spirit of American life and a new triumph in your generation.

Constitution Day Address

THE BILL OF RIGHTS

IN THE twelve minutes which I occupy in this discussion I shall refer to but one phase of the Constitution in its many bearings upon national life—that is the Bill of Rights.

Today the Constitution is indeed under more vivid discussion than at any time since the years before the Civil War. The background of that issue was Negro slavery, but in the foreground was the Constitutional question of States' rights and in the final determination was the fate of the Union. The aroused interest of today is again the rights of men. Today the issue is the rights of the individual in relation to the government; this too involves the fate of the nation. If for no other reason, this discussion has been forced upon us because new philosophies and new theories of government have arisen in the world which militantly deny the validity of our principles.

Our Constitution is not alone the working plan of a great Federation of States under representative government. There is embedded in it also the vital principles of the American system of liberty. That system is based upon certain inalienable freedoms and protections which not even the government may infringe and which we call the Bill of Rights. It does not require a lawyer to interpret those provisions. They are as clear as the Ten Commandments. Among others the freedom of worship, freedom of speech and of the press, the right of peaceable assembly, equality before the law, just trial for crime, freedom from unreasonable search, and security from being deprived of life, liberty, or property without due process of law, are the principles which distinguish our civilization. Herein are the invisible sentinels which guard the door of every home from invasion of coercion, of intimidation and fear. Herein is the expression of the spirit of men who would be forever free.

These rights were no sudden discovery, no over-night inspiration. They were established by centuries of struggle in which men died fighting bitterly for their recognition. Their beginnings lie in the Magna Charta at Runnymede five hundred and seventy years before the Constitution was written. Down through the centuries the Habeas Corpus, the "Petition of Rights," the "Declaration of Rights," the growth of the fundamental maxims of the Common Law, marked their expansion and security. Our forefathers migrated to America that they might attain them more fully. When they wrote the Declaration of Independence they boldly extended these rights. Before the Constitution could be ratified patriotic men who feared a return to tyranny, whose chains had been thrown off only after years of toil and bloody war, insisted that these hard-won rights should be incorporated in black and white within the Constitution—and so came the American Bill of Rights.

In the hurricane of revolutions which have swept the world since the Great War, men, struggling with the wreckage and poverty of that great catastrophe and the complications of the machine age, are in despair surrendering their freedom for false promises of economic security. Whether it be Fascist Italy, Nazi Germany, Communist Russia, or their lesser followers, the result is the same. Every day they repudiate every principle of the Bill of Rights. Freedom of worship is denied. Freedom of speech is suppressed. The press is censored and distorted with propaganda. The right of criticism is denied. Men go to jail or the gallows for honest opinion. They may not assemble for discussion. They speak of public affairs only in whispers. They are subject to search and seizure by spies and inquisitors who haunt the land. The safeguards of justice in trial or imprisonment are set aside. There is no right in one's savings or one's own home which the government need respect.

Here is a form of servitude, of slavery—a slipping back toward the Middle Ages. Whatever these governments are, they have one common denominator—the citizen has no assured rights. He is submerged into the State. Here is the most fundamental clash known to mankind—that is, free men and women, co-operating under orderly liberty, as contrasted with human beings made pawns of dictatorial government; men who are slaves of despotism, as against free men who are the masters of the State.

Even in America, where liberty blazed brightest and by its glow shed light on all the others, it is besieged from without and challenged from within. Many, in honest belief, hold that we cannot longer accommodate the growth of science, technology and mechanical power to the Bill of Rights and our form of government. With that I do not agree. Men's inventions cannot be of more value than men themselves. But it would be better that we sacrifice something of economic efficiency than to surrender these primary liberties. In them lies a spiritual right of men. Behind them is the conception which is the highest development of the Christian faith—the conception of individual freedom with brotherhood. From them is the fullest flowering of individual human personality.

Those who proclaim that by the Machine Age there is created an irreconcilable conflict in which Liberty must be sacrificed should not forget the battles for these rights over the centuries, for let it be remembered that in the end these are undying principles which spring from the souls of men. We imagine conflict not because the principles of Liberty are unworkable in a machine age, but because we have not worked them conscientiously or have forgotten their true meaning.

Nor do I admit that sacrifice of these rights would add to economic efficiency or would gain in economic security, or would find a single job or would give a single assurance in old age. The dynamic forces which sustain economic security and progress in human comfort lie deep below the surface. They reach to those human impulses which are watered alone by freedom. The initiative of men, their enterprise, the inspiration of thought, flower in full only in the security of these rights.

And by practical experience under the American system we have tested this truth. And here I may repeat what I have said elsewhere. Down through a century and a half this American concept of human freedom has enriched the whole world. From the release of the spirit, the initiative, the co-operation, and the courage of men, which alone comes of these freedoms, has been builded this very machine age with all its additions of comfort, its reductions of sweat. Wherever in the world the system of individual liberty has been sustained, mankind has been better clothed, better fed, better housed, has had more leisure. Above all, men and women have had more self-respect. They have been more generous and of finer spirit. Those who scoff that liberty is of no consequence to the underprivileged and the unemployed are grossly ignorant of the primary fact that it is through the creative and the productive impulses of free men that the redemption of those sufferers and their economic security must come. Any system which curtails these freedoms and stimulants to men destroys the possibility of the full production from which economic security can alone come.

These rights and protections of the Bill of Rights are safeguarded in the Constitution through a delicate balance and separation of powers in the framework of our government. That has been founded on the experience over centuries including our own day.

Liberty is safe only by a division of powers and upon local self-government. We know full well that power feeds upon itself—partly from the greed of power and partly from the innocent belief that utopia can be attained by dictation or coercion.

Nor is respect for the Bill of Rights a fetter upon progress.

It has been no dead hand that has carried the living principles of liberty over these centuries. Without violation of these principles and their safeguards we have amended the Constitution many times in the past century to meet the problems of growing civilization. We will no doubt do so many times again. Always groups of audacious men in government or out will attempt to consolidate privilege against their fellows. New invention and new ideas require the constant remolding of our civilization. The functions of government must be readjusted from time to time to restrain the strong and protect the weak. That is the preservation of liberty itself. We ofttimes interpret some provisions of the Bill of Rights so that they override others. They indeed jostle each other in course of changing national life—but their respective domains can be defined by virtue, by reason, and by law. And the freedom of men is not possible without virtue, reason, and law.

Liberty comes alone and lives alone where the hard-won rights of men are held inalienable, where governments themselves may not infringe, where governments are indeed but the mechanisms to protect and sustain these principles. It was this concept for which America's sons have died on a hundred battlefields.

The nation seeks for solution of many difficulties. These solutions can come alone through the constructive forces which arise from the spirit of free men and women. The purification of Liberty from abuses, the restoration of confidence in the rights of men, from which come the release of the dynamic forces of initiative and enterprise, are alone the methods through which these solutions can be found and the purpose of American life assured.

Spending, Deficits, Debts, and Their Consequences

YOU represent the young men and women in American life. Before you is the responsibility of determining the fate of your generation. Three years ago we were warning America against the consequences of the adoption of the ideas and the system which have since been forced upon us. You have now had nearly three years in which these ideas and policies have dominated the nation. They are no longer glowing promises of the more abundant life. They are no longer emotional expressions of high objectives or good intentions. They are practices in government. You now deal with somber realities. Now they can be examined and appraised in the cold light of daily experience.

And we have need to awake from the spell of hypnotic slogans. Phrases can be made to scintillate like the aurora borealis, but such phrases are of as much practical utility in government of a great people as the aurora itself. But the issue of America is not a battle of phrases, but a battle between straight and crooked thinking. We need a return from muddling to sanity and realism. We need to test ideas and actions with the plain hard common sense which the American people possess more greatly than any other nation. We must bring that common sense into use if we are to resume the march of real progress.

The few minutes of this occasion do not afford time for examination or discussion of the enormous range of actions and confusions of public mind in these last three years. I therefore shall confine myself to one hard practical subject—the fiscal policies of this administration. In plain words I will discuss this policy of deliberate spending of public money.

I am taking up this issue because in this gigantic spending and this unbalanced budget is the most subtle and one of the most powerful dangers which has been set in motion by this administration. If it be continued, its result to you, the young men and women of America, is as inexorable as an avalanche.

We must first examine the record as to what is being done and then diagnose the consequences.

As to the records, if you will examine the Reports of the Bureau of the Budget, you will find that the Roosevelt administration has changed the form of publishing governmental accounts. That raises a barrier against easy comparisons with previous administrations. All administrations since Washington were old-fashioned and simply put expenses down on one side of the ledger and receipts on the other. They did not try to fool the taxpayer or make the taxpayer feel better than he really was. Under the New Deal the expenditures have been divided into "Regular" expenditures and "Emergency" or "Recovery" expenditures. These are new words for an old South American and European device of dividing the budget into "ordinary" and "extraordinary" budgets.

That device is most helpful in abundant spending. By liberalism in what you designate as the "emergency" and "regular" expenditures you can blandly pronounce the ordinary budget as balanced. Then all your deficit is concentrated in the "extraordinary" or "emergency" part of the budget, and having made the deficit a plausible necessity you justify borrowing, and make the spending happier for everybody. The theory is that the next generation should pay for the emergencies of this generation.

The report of the Federal Budget Bureau shows that large items which have been an essential part of the government expenditures for years have now been styled "emergency." The vast area of spending through loans guaranteed by the government is not represented in the budget with any taxpayer's liability. Under this arrangement the losses on that will come to the next generation. And there are large items now excluded from the statements of expenditures which improve the looks of the accounts. These jugglings will no doubt ease the taxpayer's mind, but they will not relieve his pocket.

However, we can with diligence dig the facts out from under these methods, and despite all these obstacles can compute with fair certainty from the present commitments where the nation will be in another fifteen months.

The first conclusion is that all losses counted in the expenditures are now running over $8,000,000,000 a year. The annual deficit is running nearly three and a half billions, and each dollar of deficit is of course added to the national debt.

The second conclusion is that the unpaid government obligations which will fall upon the taxpayer at the end of the Roosevelt administration will exceed $35,000,000,000.

The third conclusion is that this peace-time debt will at the end of 1936 exceed our World War debt by ten billions, and the cost of the New Deal threatens to exceed that of the Great War.

Incidentally, outside of recoverable loans, the Roosevelt administration spending will exceed the Hoover administration by from $14,000,000,000 to $15,000,000,000. I always have difficulty trying to comprehend what $14,000,000,000 or even $3,-500,000,000 really is. But I know that even the mere $3,500,-000,000 would buy me 90,000,000 suits of clothes. At least that is about one suit for every mile between the earth and the sun.

It is of course true that during the last years of the last Republican administration deficits were incurred. Just as advance information on misrepresentation, I may state that the deficits of those years were not as large as are being made to appear by the New Deal publications. They include expenditures which the New Deal now excludes in publishing its own accounts. They also include over two billions of loans to industry, agriculture, and banks, which have since been mostly collected and spent by the New Deal administration. But the important thing is that the Republican administration genuinely endeavored to balance the whole government budget. That was not a pious subterfuge. It was a definite program. The record shows that in the year 1931 the Democratic Congress was urged by the Republican administration to enact additional revenues of $1,200,000,000 and to co-operate in a cut of $600,000,000 of less pressing expenditures. Only a part of this revenue was wrung from the Democratic Congress after nearly six months of fighting, delay, and obstruction, punctuated by vetoes of pork-barrel appropriations. Even then over half of the recommended decreases in expenditures were rejected. Again in 1932, $700,000,000 of additional revenues and $300,000,000 of additional reductions in expenditures were urged, and again, after months of delay, were refused altogether.

It is not overstatement to say that had the Republican principles of balancing the budget been accepted in 1931 and 1932, the final stone in the foundation of permanent recovery would have been laid three years ago instead of deferred for years hence.

I do not need recall the promises so vigorously put forward by the Democratic platform, the Democratic candidate, and the Democratic orators in the campaign of 1932—the promises that they would balance the budget and reduce expenditures by one billion a year. I may suggest that our opponents in 1932 would have received far less votes had they disclosed to the country their intention to increase the expenditures by $14,000,000,000 in four years; or had they disclosed that they would maintain a deficit of three and a half billions per annum; that they would increase the number of the government bureaucracy by 160,000 persons and create five thousand paid committees and commissions. They would have lost still more votes had they informed us that they would abandon the gold standard; that they would devalue the dollar by 41 per cent; that they would repudiate government obligations; that they would seek to circumvent the Constitution; that they would attempt to socialize and regiment Americans. It is perhaps not an overstatement that on the now demonstrated principles of this administration they could not have won the election of 1932.

But the wreckage of representative governments is strewn with broken promises.

I do not need to tell any one within the sound of my voice of that huge waste in government expenditures that is going on. Every one of you knows instance after instance of waste and folly in your own city and village. It appears day by day in the headlines of your papers. Think it over and multiply it by all the thousands of other towns and communities in the United States and get the appalling total.

I would call your attention to the numbers and potency of the army of spenders which has been created. According to the reports of the Civil Service Commission, there were about 573,-000 civilian employees in the Federal Government at the end of the Coolidge administration. There were about 565,000 at the end of the Hoover administration. There are 730,000 today. And this does not include some 100,000 part-time paid members of some 5,000 committees and agencies of one sort or another who all spend money. Nor does it include the people on relief. The whole system of non-political appointments under the Civil Service which had been steadily built up by every administration for years has now been practically ignored. Almost this whole addition of 260,000 new people on the Federal payroll constitutes the most gigantic spoils raid in our history. Even Andrew Jackson appointed less than ten thousand.

Whenever you increase the numbers of political bureaucracy you not only have to pay them but they are veritable research laboratories for new inventions in spending money. Bureaucracy rushes headlong into visions of the millennium and sends the bill to the Treasury. And there are three implacable spirits in bureaucracy—self-perpetuation, expansion, and demand for more power. Moreover, they also serve to help win elections.

The Roosevelt administration is now clutched in the meshes of the gigantic spending bureaucracy which it has created. Even with expenditures of some eight billions annually, with deficits of about $3,500,000,000, there is to be no "breathing spell" in spending, as witness the ten billions of new appropriations just passed by Congress. One administration writer kindly assures us that the budget will be balanced four years hence in 1939. That happy ending no doubt marks the end of anything to spend.

Incidentally the Congress supinely surrendered one of the hardest-won battles of human liberty—the control of the nation's purse.

When we protest at those expenditures we are met with the sneer, "Would you let the people starve?" No, never! It was, in fact, a Republican administration that in 1930 announced that no American should go hungry or cold through no fault of his own. It organized the relief so effectively by co-operation of the Federal Government with the state and local authorities that the public health actually improved during that whole period. And here let me pay tribute to the thousands of devoted men and women who gave of their time and energies to conduct that relief over three long years. Theirs was no political objective. Nor was it their object to spend the people's money to prime economic pumps, nor to make social experiments which delayed real jobs. Theirs was a solicitude that those in distress from no fault of their own should be tided over until productive jobs returned.

Real relief is imperative, but its necessary and generous cost unmixed with other objectives would be but a minor part of this eight billions per annum. The presumed purpose of this spending has been to secure recovery. And we may well inquire what has been accomplished toward finding real jobs in productive industry and commerce by this roaring torrent of Federal spending and deficit. The best measure of the depression is the number of unemployed. Justly, I take the date of the election of November, 1932, for this test. For months prior to that election unemployment had been steadily decreasing, but with the election, industrial orders were canceled; the nation at once slowed down its engine. As the fiscal and currency policies of the New Deal were gradually disclosed, the nation skidded into a bank panic. From the day of that election, the New Deal policies dominated economic and business life. In October, 1932, prior to the election, there were 11,585,000 people out of work, according to the American Federation of Labor. Sixty days ago, two years and eight months after the election, after all this gigantic spending, there were still 10,900,000 unemployed, according to the same authority, or a decrease of only 700,000. And if it were not for artificial support of industry by this hugely increased flood of government money, the unemployment would be greater than in 1932.

In any event, all this spending of deficits has not consequently restored genuine jobs in industry and commerce. The reduction of the unemployed was its only conceivable justification. As a matter of fact, until the Supreme Court decisions of last spring, the industrial world had been so scared as to stifle employment. By destroying confidence the administration has retarded recovery.

Since those Supreme Court decisions, the nation is showing some hopeful signs of progress. Every American prays that it may be genuine and come quickly—not alone because it would end infinite misery but because with recovery would come an atmosphere in which the vast problems of the nation can be solved more rationally and more fully. They could be solved in a spirit of Americanism rather than be dominated by the spirit of Europeanism. But whatever recovery we have is constantly endangered by this riotous spending and this unbalanced budget. We cannot spend ourselves into real prosperity. Certainly an artificial prosperity can be created by borrowing to spend, whether by individuals or governments. That is joy-riding to bankruptcy.

These gigantic budget deficits must inevitably be paid for somehow, sometime. There are only three ways to meet the unpaid bills of a government. The first is taxation. The second is repudiation. The third is inflation.

Already our country is highly taxed. Our total taxes today —Federal, state and local—are the highest of any great country in the world except the British, even in proportion to our national income. But the British have a balanced budget and are yearly reducing taxes. We, even with our burden of taxes today, must take on the further load from a budget about fifty per cent balanced. We are on the way deeper into the morass of more and more taxes. The British are on their way out of the stifling swamp of taxation.

Who will pay these taxes? We have just seen a tax bill estimated to produce $300,000,000 per annum. That apparently could not have been designed to meet the regular annual deficit of three and a half billions. It was put forward with the slogan "Soak the Rich." But with the passage of that bill the rich are now "soaked." We may therefore conclude that some one else will have to meet the $3,250,000,000 remaining annual deficit if the bill is paid. If it is paid by taxes those taxes must fall on the so-called economic middle class and the poor. There is no one else left. The poor will pay out of indirect taxes, hidden in the rent and everything they buy. And when the price of the necessaries of life to those who have but a living wage is advanced by hidden taxes, those people are not sharing a surplus with the government. They have no surplus. The poor must go without something in order to pay the taxes wrapped up in the package they take from the store. Every butcher knows that today the poor are depriving themselves of bacon and meat. The economic middle class—whether they be farmers or workers at the bench or the desk, professional or business men—produce eighty per cent of the national income. They, like the poor, will pay by indirect taxes in the cost of living, and in addition, they will pay again and again in direct taxes. No matter where you place taxes, the bulk of them must come from those who work and produce.

The subtle process of issuing government bonds to pay that deficit not only leaves it to be paid from your lifelong earnings, but it daily creates new dangers. No doubt these unpaid bills can be canceled by repudiation. The New Deal form of repudiation is devaluation. We can further devalue the dollar—which is, of course, repudiation on the installment plan. Devaluation is a modern and polite term for clipping the coin. Rome relied upon this method during its decline. If devaluation has the inflationary effect that the New Deal claims, then in the long run it raises the prices of everything we buy and the cost of living goes up to everybody, farmer and worker alike. The loss comes out of the people. But more than that, the returns from your insurance policy, your savings account for old age and for your children, your veteran's allowance, and your old-age pension, are also depleted in purchasing power. Who then pays? It is the same economic middle class and the poor. That would still be true if the rich were taxed to the whole amount of their fortunes.

It is not my purpose to discuss the credit or currency policies of this administration, but you may put it down both economically and historically that every continued government deficit has led to inflation in some form. That is the implacable avenger of profligate spending in government. Our government today is in large degree financing its deficit by credits from banks and financial institutions upon the government promise to pay. By this action a large part of that credit is being manufactured. I will not take your time to describe the process. It is a sort of dervish dance, whirling from budget deficits to government bonds, from bonds to bank credit, from bank credit to more government spending. That is one of the oldest and most dangerous expedients used by spendthrift governments. The new banking laws make it all easy. Governments must, in some emergencies, finance through the banks. But it must be only for the short interval necessary to raise increased revenues and reduce expenses.

The general public mind has been focused on the notion that inflation consists merely of printing-press money. There is also printing-press credit. That is a subtle daily increasing danger. Already it has contributed to increase the price of the things you buy and the cost of living. The present rise in the stock market is ample proof that some people know it. There is a place on that road where there lurks an appalling national peril. We have not reached these extremes, but that is the road we are traveling. The administration may not know where they are going, but they are taking us with them.

Let us not forget that deficits and their resulting debts can be subtly accumulated to a volume where in agony democracy cannot be led to shoulder the taxes to lift them. The tragedy is that the people at large are lulled into the belief that these borrowed deficits cost them nothing; that they do not have to pay; that the money comes out of some indefinite source without obligation or burden to them.

Deficits and debts can be paid by other forms of inflation, such as printing-press money—and then you go down the road that led Germany to ruin. Who paid in Germany? The economic middle class and the poor. The farmer, the worker, the business and professional people—none escaped ruin. They paid by the loss of all their savings; they paid until they were reduced to a universal and unparalleled poverty. They paid more than this; they paid with liberty in the gutter, for universal poverty created a gigantic tyranny.

These indirect or direct schemes of inflation have been the curse of the earth since the World War. They were one of the causes of our mad speculation in 1927 to 1929. They were the immediate cause of the European collapse in 1931 and the world-wide depression. And let me say that if the history of the last hundred years teaches anything, it is that inflation is more dangerous to a people than war. It has been the abyss into which democracy has fallen in these recent years. It has been the cradle of tyranny in a dozen countries. And they all started by inflating bank credit.

It is easy to overstate the dangers. We yet have time to save any such peril. But you will find that my view is a mild remonstrance compared to that of President Roosevelt's own Director of the Budget, who resigned because of these policies.

Even if these greater dangers of inflation be avoided, who will pay the bill in the end? These billions of wasteful deficits will be paid by putting our hands into the pockets of you who are young and keeping them there all your lifetime. It is not only a reduction of your standard of living but of your freedom and your hopes.

There can be no device by which the people may escape paying for this spending.

Here is where common sense cries out to be heard. The folly

and waste must be cut out of this expenditure and the Federal Budget balanced, or we shall see one of these three horsemen ravage the land—Taxation, or Repudiation, or Inflation.

We are asked for a constructive program. The first step is a sound fiscal policy.

This flood of spending is but one of the many realities of the New Deal. It is your duty to examine them all with the torch of common sense and appraise them in the sole light of the future of America. And you should examine them with open mind. You will find some that you should commend. You will find some of right objective and wrong method, such as the acts regulating securities, the old-age pensions, and unemployment insurance. You will find many that are destructive of every ideal and aspiration of American life and will destroy the value of all the acts that are good—and more.

And there is but one test you should apply—will these measures restore the prosperity of America? Will they restore agriculture? Will they give real jobs instead of the dole? Will they maintain personal liberty? Will they make America a happier, a better place in which to live?

In dealing with these great problems you need to remember that the shocks we have received from the War and the depression have created great despair and great discontent with representative government and individual freedom. Our system has faults but these faults are but marginal. They must be constantly corrected. Special privilege, exploitation of labor, the consumer, or the investor have no right or part in it. But the soil of the American heritage of liberty is still fertile with vast harvest of human security and human betterment.

Alert opposition and incisive criticism and debate are the safeguards of a Republic. But that is not enough. The vast revolution in the powers of science and technology has placed within our grasp a future and a security never hitherto glimpsed by mankind. The people hunger for the comfort, the security, and the freedom of spirit which we know they may bring. But we would have but an empty husk should they come at the sacrifice of liberty. Those securities will come if we do not stifle and handcuff the productive genius which alone thrives in freedom. In the large, our problem is to stimulate and utilize the great productive capacity of our people. Herein is the great constructive program—to find the road by which we may attain the vast enrichments of science and technology within the province of private enterprise and personal liberty. Therein we must add the new upon the structure of the old—for therein lie the foundations of centuries of human effort. It will succeed not through vast generalizations but through human sympathy, detailed policies, hard common sense, and political realism. That is the greatest opportunity of statesmanship in two generations.

In the coming months the Republican Party will meet in convention with the responsibility of determining its policies. It will be the most vital convention since 1860. That convention should comprise the thousand best men of the Republican Party. Theirs is the duty to enunciate great principles. They should be inspired to determine a program of policies to solve great issues. Minor issues, petty opposition, sectional interest, group ideas, and every shred of personal ambition must be dumped, that this great responsibility, this great spiritual purpose may be accomplished. None of these things must count in the fate of the nation. Upon the wisdom and courage of these men will depend the future of America.

The Consequences of "Economic Planning" and Some Remedies for It

NEW YORK CITY

[November 16, 1935]

YOUR committee extended to me a cordial invitation to address you on public questions. I urged that they should find somebody else. I explained that even if I were simply to read the Ten Commandments it would be interpreted as critical by the Administration at Washington. Even that hint failed to dampen their insistence. I then stated that the situation of our country was in too great danger for me or any one to waste time in an academic discussion. That what I had to say would be in opposition to certain policies. They insisted that the Ohio Society had invited me because it was a serious body anxious for the stark, rugged truth.

Indeed, discussion of public questions is the first necessity in a republic. Free government cannot exist without free debate. By honest and bold debate alone may we prevent disaster to the security and happiness of this nation. On that anvil alone we may shape the intellectual instruments of human betterment.

I recently made an address upon the New Deal Spending, Debts, and their Consequences. I purpose on this occasion to discuss what the New Deal calls "National Planning," the expenditures it imposes on the people, its consequences, and some remedies that it requires. This old and respected phrase "National Planning" has been disclosed to have powerful meanings. You

75

might think that meant blueprints. But this sort of "National Planning" includes political management of money, credit, farming, industry, morals, and the more abundant life. Two years ago the phrase more frequently used was "Planned Economy." But as that has become so obviously "Planned Extravagance," it has been less used in these last few months. Even "National Planning" is threatened with ejection by a still newer glittering phrase, the "Third Economy." I trust it is not so expensive as the others.

Let me say at once that I am not here criticizing all the measures taken in Washington. Whatever is good should be continued. Republics must go forward, not backward, but if they would go forward they must promptly discard the bad. I am here discussing those measures which threaten to impoverish the nation.

There are two different groups of opponents of the New Deal sort of "National Planning" or "Planned Economy." One group holds that it is a deliberate plan for centralizing authority to a point where we the people can be made to do what starry-eyed young men in Washington think is good for us—whether it is good for us or not. This group believes "Planned Economy" is the American name for the European diseases which have infected us for the past three years. They feel these catch-words cloak that incarnate passion for power, the insidious end of which is the destruction of liberty and the rise of the regimented state.

The other group of opponents hold that the new "National Planning" is an attempt of a collegiate oligarchy to sanctify by a phrase a muddle of unco-ordinated reckless adventures in government—flavored with unctuous claims to monopoly in devotion to their fellow men. These opponents believe "National Planning" has neither philosophy nor consistency of action.

My own conclusion is that the new "National Planning" contains any or all these elements, depending upon which New Dealer is doing the Planning for the day.

Any of these views could be confirmed by the writings of a dozen charter members of the New Deal who have now turned against the order. They could be substantiated by the writings of many who remain in it.

I do not intend on this occasion to elaborate the philosophy of "Planned Economy." It is neither conservative, liberal, nor common sense. Nor do I propose on this occasion to discuss its Constitutional aspects. There are nests of Constitutional termites at work.

I shall simply inquire whether we ought to want this sort of "Economic Planning" and its invisible costs. It has unfolded itself through some scores of new bureaus of the Federal Government. I will not take your time to enumerate all the alphabetical agencies. I may say, however, there are only four letters of the alphabet not now in use by the Administration in Washington. When we establish the Quick Loans Corporation for Xylophones, Yachts, and Zithers, the alphabet of our fathers will be exhausted. But of course the New Russian alphabet has thirty-four letters.

We have now had three years in which to appraise the work of these agencies. They are no longer in the aurora borealis stage, with all its excitement and false promises of light. We emerge from illusion into the daylight of practical experience.

There is one consistency in all this new "National Planning," or "Planned Economy," or "Third Economy." Every branch of these plans has the habit of carefree scattering of public money. They are haunted by no old ghost of a balanced budget. But "National Planning" thinks in phrases and slogans rather than the exactitude of the cash register. We now know that in addition to increased taxes after four years of it the bill of increased taxpayers' liabilities will be about $14,000,000,000. If they have a cash register it certainly has an astronomical keyboard.

The obvious hope of this new "National Plan" is that by creating bank credit they can avoid adding more burdens on the poor and the economic middle class—until after the election.

These are, however, only the visible expenditures imposed on the people. The taxes of today and their sure increase in the future if these policies are not stopped are but a small part of even the money cost of "National Planning." And let no one be deluded. It is the farmer, the worker, as well as the business man, who pay the invisible costs, just as they pay the bulk of the tax assessments.

I may give you a few examples.

Judged by works and not by words, another consistency in this sort of "Economic Planning" is to limit competition and restrict production—the essence of monopoly. They have given us planned scarcity—upon which civilization always degenerates —in the place of economic plenty, upon which America has grown great. It is the more abundant life—without bacon.

One of the wheel-horses of the "National Planning"—that is the NRA—was thought to have been killed by the Supreme Court. That decision has not yet been claimed as part of the new "National Planning," although every day men are getting jobs because of it. But we are now promised a resurrection of this dead. The price of it was and will be in every household budget.

The new "National Planning" is building vast projects—perhaps useful to our grandchildren. We have to pay the cost of interest and maintenance until they come of age. This is also the New Deal door by which the government rushes into business in competition with its own citizens. The citizen loses because he cannot compete with government bookkeeping and the pipe line into the treasury. Few of these projects were even mentioned until after blank checks were drawn by Congress. This method of planning avoids exhaustion from Congressional debate—and takes the limit off spending.

The new "National Planning" of relief shifted its administration from local and state authorities to a political bureaucracy centralized at Washington. That has resulted not only in stupendous waste but in the creation of a great group of permanent dependents. It has added nothing to the security and care of those deserving in distress except—expense. And we are destroying the self respect and the responsibility of self government by turning the treasury into a national grab bag. Our national ideals get little of a lift from the general attitude, "If we don't get ours some one else will."

The new "National Planning" of taxes, currency, credit, and business has raised and will continue to raise the cost of living to the farm housewife, the worker's housewife, and all other housewives. It is a deduction from economic and social security of the poor—it is not a more abundant life. It erodes the purchasing power of wages. It gives birth to strikes and inflames class conflict. During the depression years of the last Administration the loss of man days from strikes and lockouts averaged about 5,-000,000 per year. During this Administration it has averaged a loss of about 18,000,000 man days per year. These gigantic losses appear in the worker's budget, not in the treasury.

The new "Economic Planning" has included repudiation of government covenants, which raises somber questions of government morals and honor. In any event it devalued the dollar by 41 per cent. It gave us the gift of "Managed Currency." As potent devices for destroying confidence these have merit. Through politically managed credit it has brought us to the threshold of devastating inflation. The stock market is already peeking into that Bluebeard's cave.

In the few moments of this address I shall explore a little further into the price and consequences of these monetary and credit policies.

There is the folly of buying foreign silver. I could at least see some reason for spending ten to fifteen million a year to subsidize employment in our Western silver mines by buying their product at a profitable price. But what earthly reason we have for buying vast amounts of foreign silver will take generations of politicians to explain. If we are to have managed currency, we do not require any metallic base. There is in fact no metallic base today. If there were, you could exchange currency for gold. If we want a metallic base, the government already has $9,700,000,000 of gold and only $5,600,000,000 of currency in circulation. Thus it would seem that we have plenty of metallic base for the currency when we have nearly one dollar and eighty cents in gold metal for every dollar of currency. That leaves plenty over to pay international balances. Yet we deliberately bid up the price of foreign silver by 50 per cent. Then we proceed to buy vast quantities of that commodity, for which we have no earthly use, at enormous profits to foreigners. Upon that folly we have already spent about $250,000,000 and under the new "Economic Planning" we are to spend about $1,000,000,000 more. The siphon runs either through the taxpayer's pocket or inflation. You can be sure no foreigner would buy this silver back from us at what we pay for it.

It is no doubt a part of our good-neighbor policies that we have joyfully subsidized every foreign speculator in silver. We have also subsidized every silver mine in Australia, India, Mexico, and Peru. But we have pursued these good-neighbor policies further. We have stirred up currency troubles in China and other silver currency countries. We have stimulated their good feelings by flooding them with brankruptcies, labor troubles, and jiggling their cost of living.

Another result of "Economic Planning" has been the attraction of billions of gold—over two billions in two years—that we do not need for any conceivable purpose. We ought to have had goods instead. Apparently "Planned Economy" aims to become a bi-metallic Midas.

Although we cannot recall the 100 per cent dollars we can well consider the results of devaluation. We devalued the dollar 41 per cent under the hypnosis that if we reduced the length of a yard to 21.2 inches we would have more cloth in the bolt. One result is that the foreigner is shipping us more gold every day to buy our good domestic assets for the price of 21.2 inches to the yard. That is a complicated problem of New Deal economics, but if you will search around in it you will find much of interest. It is likely to represent more loss to the American people than a whole year's treasury deficit.

While on this romantic subject of currencies I may mention that when we entered new "National Planning" in currency we were promised a "managed currency" that would be adjusted to American life and conditions. Of course if it worked it would increase the cost of living by 41 per cent. Thus it would reduce the living to be obtained from all life insurance policies, college endowments, pensions, wages and salaries, and would increase the housewife's cost of living. By it we forgave 41 per cent of most of our foreign debts. That is, they can pay them today with 41 per cent less gold than they expected to pay. You will remember those private foreign loans. They were denounced as the cause of all evil, so we now reduce the evil by reducing them 41 per cent. But offsetting all these pains, it was supposed to reduce the burden of mortgages. And equally if it works it lessens the burdens of all bonds, government and otherwise. Here we again enter higher economics, but if you explore it thoroughly you will find that the 10,000,000 stockholders of corporations, including the wicked power companies, profit at the expense of the 65,000,000 insurance policy holders. The sum of all these shifts does not make the poor any richer.

But above all this managed currency was to be thoroughly American and would make us independent of world influences. Two billions of dollars were appropriated to stabilize secretly foreign exchange and no accounting of the losses appears in the national deficit—that is, not yet. But behold! Our mystery fund has been most successful in stabilizing our currency to within a few per cent of the pound sterling for over a year. We have attained that stability which comes from leaning up against the British. We are the thirty-first member of the "Sterling Bloc" of nations. Let us remember that the British also have a managed currency, and in the "Sterling Bloc" we are only one of the thirty-one planets which revolve around the British sun. We have thus trustingly reposed in London a large influence in American values and freedom of American trade. I do not pretend to know where all this will take us, but I do know that I prefer a currency that no "National Planning" can manage for us, not even the British.

In any event so long as "managed currency" lasts the purchasing value of the dollar lies at the whim of political government. Politics are bound to be in every government-managed currency. You can never make the American dollar ring true on the counters of the world nor on the counters of our savings banks so long as there is the alloy of politics in it. So long as it has that alloy in it people cannot invest $100 today with full confidence as to what it will be worth in old age. One result has been delayed recovery in the construction industries and continued unemployment in millions of unhappy homes. That goes into the realm of higher economics, but I assure you it is a huge burden in money and misery on the country not included in the budget.

There is another of these huge penalties of this "Economic Planning" which may be illustrated by a bit of American history. It concerns a great mistake of the Federal Reserve System in 1927. That was before my Administration, and in any event at that time the system was independent of the Administration. It also concerns a gigantic price in human suffering.

In an effort to support the shaky financial structure of Europe, our Reserve System in 1927 joined with foreign government banks in expansion or inflation of bank credits. Some of us laymen had bitterly protested that we had no need of expanded credits, that in view of the then situation it would be dangerous. We were told it could and would be easily controlled. There were other impulses, but this inflation of bank credit contributed to set off the greatest madness of speculation and greed since the Mississippi Bubble. Men then also dreamed they were in a New Era. They resisted every warning. The controls proved ineffective. The movement collapsed of its own weight in 1929.

No human being could have believed that such griefs and tragedies ever lay in so obscure a thing as bank credit inflation. It brought hunger to the door of millions of homes. It destroyed the savings of millions of families. It created a scene of financial misdoings which have furnished the material for ceaseless attacks upon honest business. This inflation perhaps staved off for a year or two the inevitable collapse in Europe. That struck us in 1931 an already weakened nation. But such strength as we had left saved both ourselves and the world from chaos.

There are morals in that story. But there is something of far more present importance in that story than postmortem moralizing. Despite that bitter experience the new National Planners, to finance their huge spending and other purposes, have desperately resorted to the same inflation of bank credits. They, however, apparently do not believe in homeopathic doses. The dose of that same poison now injected into our national bloodstream by the New Deal is already three or four times as great as that of 1927.

They say also it can be controlled. But will the politically controlled Reserve system prove any more successful? Stated in its mildest form, this is gambling with the fate of a nation. Should these controls fail, this democracy will not survive the shock.

And "National Planning" was supposed to shake us free from vicious speculation and money changers. Of this you can be sure. Instability of currencies and inflation of credit are the green pastures upon which the speculator grows fat. He is the sole beneficiary from instability. The costs of that instability do not appear in the government budget, yet they appear in every honest business. They add to the price of every commodity.

And here the "National Planning" collides with itself. Of what value are old age pensions, or unemployment insurance, savings for old age, or any other beneficent effort under the scourge of devaluation and inflation?

I will not tire you with further examples of these invisible costs which far exceed even the torrent of government spending. There are scores more.

We can express government expenses in figures. But no mortal man can compute the costs, the burdens, and dangers imposed upon 120,000,000 people by these actions. Its cost in national impoverishment far exceeds even taxes. Its losses will be larger than the national debt.

It is a time for plain speaking and blunt statement of some fundamental principles upon these monetary and fiscal questions. And let me speak to you in old-fashioned language. When I was a boy in Iowa I learned some very simple truths about finance. I learned that money does not grow on trees; it must be earned. I learned that the first rule of a successful career is to keep expenditures within the means of paying them. I learned that the keeping of financial promises is the first obligation of an honorable man. And I learned that the man who borrows without intent to repay is headed for bankruptcy or disgrace or crime. These may be platitudes, but they are still truths.

As I have increased in years and in opportunity to study the affairs of governments, I have made a very simple but vital observation. That is that a government should have in financial matters the same standards that an honorable man has. A government must realize that money must be earned before it is spent, that a nation's word in finance must be sacredly kept, that a nation is immoral if it repudiates its obligations or inflates its mediums of exchange or borrows without regard to posterity; and, finally, that a nation which violates these simple principles will, like a man, end in dishonor and disaster. A government cannot expect financial honor in its people unless it maintains honor itself. A large part of the world's misery in all ages has come from the acts of government that ignored these principles and entered upon policies of reckless spending and debasement and repudiation.

Our country shows hopeful signs of recovery despite great hindrances. That convalescence should be speeded and made secure. We should no longer tolerate financial policies that prolong unemployment, that create fear and distrust and uncertainty, that slowly but surely undermine the industrial structure on which the living of the whole nation depends. We should no longer tolerate a money system that is not a money system, but a hodge-podge of promiscuous ingredients that not even the Administration will attempt to name, define, or defend. We should no longer tolerate gambling in the future of a nation with the dice of inflation. We should no longer tolerate a financial policy that does not balance the budget.

The American citizen wants to know whether his savings are to be confiscated. The plain man wants to know whether his little life insurance policy is going to be worth anything at his death. The housewife wants to know whether her husband's wages are going to buy food for his family.

There is a way to settle all these questions. That way is through abandonment of present financial and fiscal policies and return to sound policies. Do you wish a constructive fiscal program?

The waste of taxpayers' money on unnecessary public works should end.

The administration of relief should be turned over to local authorities. Federal expenditures for relief should be confined to cash allowances to these authorities to the extent that they are unable to provide their own funds.

The spending for visionary and un-American experiments should be stopped.

This horde of political bureaucracy should be rooted out.

The provision of the Constitution requiring that expenditures shall only be in accordance with appropriations actually made by law should be obeyed. And they should be made for specific purposes.

The budget should be balanced, not by more taxes, but by reduction of follies.

The futile purchases of foreign silver should be stopped.

The gold standard should be re-established, even on the new basis.

The act authorizing the President to inflate the currency should be repealed.

The Administration should give and keep a pledge to the country that there will be no further juggling of the currency and no further experiments with credit inflation.

Confidence in the validity of promises of the government should be restored.

The nation seeks for solution of its many difficulties. It is groping for security from economic storms and from individual poverty. But economic security, social security, or any other security cannot be found without first restoring these primary policies of government.

These matters are no abstractions. They are not theoretical

questions of academic debate. They are the invisible forces which surround every American fireside. They determine the happiness of every American home. In their rightful direction lies the safety of these homes and the fruition of their hopes. They determine the welfare of our children and the progress of our nation.

The Bank Panic and Relief
Administration Reform

ST. LOUIS, MO.

[December 16, 1935]

I T WAS a pleasure to accept your invitation to debate national policies. There has been no time in two generations
when it is more needed that men stand up and discuss public questions. The welfare of our people can make progress only
upon the sunlit road of frank debate. The witchery of half truth
fades only under the exposure of discussion. And there is only
disaster in the dark alleys of inspired propaganda. There ideals
and men are assassinated with poisonous whisperings.

I have recently discussed the New Deal at Oakland and again
at New York. Since then President Roosevelt at Atlanta has
entered the debate in defense of the New Deal—particularly its
spending, deficits, and debts. I propose to debate so much of
that statement as time permits.

You will not be astonished if we do not agree.

There recently have been some premonitions of change. In
that aspect I find a newspaper dispatch dated November 28 from
Los Angeles. After announcing the naming of a new street as
New Deal Avenue it says: "The new street is located near the
Tugwell resettlement colony. . . . Because New Deal Avenue
comes to a dead end the county supervisors will arrange ample
room . . . to turn around."

Perhaps more than any other living person I can sympathize
with the President in his burdens. We could agree upon some
acts of this Administration, but we disagree upon profound principles of human liberty. In its larger dimensions this irrepres-

sible conflict is between the American system of liberty and New Deal collectivism. May I again say that true American Liberalism is not the possession of any political party. Belief in it does not constitute men either Republicans or Democrats.

Three years ago, speaking in New York City, I said, "This . . . is a contest between two philosophies of government. The expressions our opponents use must refer to important changes in our . . . system . . . otherwise they are nothing but vacuous words. . . . They are proposing changes which would destroy the very foundations. . . ." That warning was denied by our opponents.

We have now had three years of it. We have seen the weakening of self-government by Federal centralization. We have seen the color of personal government in the abandonment of Congressional responsibilty under Executive pressure. We have seen executive orders, propaganda, and threats substituted for specific laws. We have seen the color of despotism in the creation of a huge bureaucracy. We have seen the color of Fascism in the attempt to impose government-directed monopolies. We have seen the color of Socialism by government in business competition with citizens. We have followed the old Roman pattern in the repudiation of government obligations by the clipping of the coin. We are now speeding down the road of wasteful spending and debt, and unless we can escape we will be smashed in inflation. This is not forward-looking American Liberalism. These are the suicide roads along which so many liberal governments in Europe have plunged over the precipice to despotism. It is no kaleidoscope of glittering forms for the amusement of children.

The practical questions we have to debate separate themselves into two great battle fronts.

The first is the insidious expansion of government over the lives of the people. Unless it is arrested it means the strangling of the liberties that were born with this nation.

The second is the spending, debt, currency, and credit policies of the government. Even if they stood alone they would by continuation bring poverty and despair.

In speaking at Atlanta two weeks ago the President's first basis of defense for his gigantic spending, deficits, and debts was the assertion that "The mechanics of civilization came to a dead stop on March 3, 1933."

What happened on March 3, 1933, was an induced hysteria of bank depositors. The banking structure at large subsequently proved to be sound. That is scarcely a dead stop to civilization.

I have always believed that the newspapers are one of the mechanisms of civilization. They did not quit. At that time I saw no headlines that the farmers had ceased to till the fields. Most of you did not detect that the delivery of food to your doors had stopped. Railway managers apparently did not know that their trains had stalled. Somebody failed to inform us that the hum of our factories was silent. We still had to jump out of the way of the twenty-three million automobiles. Our churches, schools, and courts are a part of the mechanics of civilization. They did not close. And the Supreme Court seems to be functioning yet. If civilization came to a dead stop the press missed a great piece of news that day.

If this notion is to be the excuse for this spending and other vagaries of the New Deal, we had better examine into it further.

The truth is that the world-wide depression was turned in June–July, 1932, all over the world. That was before the election of the New Deal. That is supported by scores of leading American economists, business men, and public leaders. It is supported by the economic publications throughout the world.

That turning was aided by the measures of our Republican government. These measures were within the Constitution of the United States. They were not that futile financial juggling which has violated economic law, morals, the Constitution, and the structure of American liberty. The turning was aided by the efforts of foreign governments. Every commercial country, including the United States, surged forward. Prices rose, employment increased, the whole agricultural, financial, and business structure grew in strength. After the election of the New Deal we began a retreat. Only in the United States was there an interruption. We were the strongest and should have led the van. And we lagged behind for two years. The other countries of the world went forward without interruption. They adopted no New Deal. Apparently those nations did not hear that the mechanics of civilization came to a dead stop on March 3, 1933.

It did not come to a stop even in the United States. It was meddled with. We have not got over it yet. But why did we have a panic of bank depositors in 1933? Because they were scared. We had no bank panic from the crash of the boom in 1929. We had no panic at the financial collapse in Europe in 1931. We had no panic at the most dangerous point in the depression when our banks were weakest in the spring of 1932. There was no panic before the election of November, 1932. When did they become frightened? They became scared a few weeks before the inauguration of the New Deal on March 4, 1933.

What were they frightened of? They could not have been scared by the outgoing administration which had only a few days to run. They were frightened at the incoming New Deal. Why were they scared at the New Deal? Because soon after the election large numbers of people awoke to the fact that promises given in the campaign would be violated. Among other things it gradually spread that the gold standard would be abandoned or that the currency would be tinkered with. It was evident that a wholesale orgy of spending of public money would be undertaken. Business slackened its energies. Shrewd speculators shipped their money abroad at fabulous profits. Bankers tried to protect themselves. The public in blind fear demanded gold and the "covenants" of the United States which called for gold. Some of them were scared at the banks by the destructive publication of RFC loans. The banking structure was not insolvent. After the banks were closed it was found that the solvent banks, measured by deposits, comprised 92 per cent of the banking strength of the country. The President himself stated they were sound. Subsequently more banks were found sound and reopened. And beyond this, important banks wrongfully closed by the New Deal, such as in the Detroit area, are now paying out 100 per cent to the depositors. It was the most political and the most unnecessary bank panic in all our history. It could have been prevented. It could have been cured by simple co-operation.

The President in further elucidation of the stop of civilization says: "At that time our national balance sheet, the wealth versus the debts of the American public, showed we were in the 'red'." The value of America is not the quotations in the market place —either the highs of inflation booms or the lows made in anticipation of the New Deal. He informs us, however, that some great bankers told him that the country could safely stand an increase in the national debt to between 55 and 75 billions. He adds "remember this was in the spring of 1933." Thus we are to believe that when our wealth was less than our debts we were so strong we could still borrow 55 billions. It certainly is a confusing thought. It indicates some little excess of assets and at the same time great restraint on the part of the New Deal.

The breakdown in confidence which sounded the advent of the New Deal is of course a helpful statistical point when they want to show how good they have been to us.

I have no desire to waste time over historical discussion. But correction of distortion which is used to justify destructive national policies and this high piling up of debt and taxes is imperative. It is even more imperative, as the documented facts upon that subject were published by Myers and Newton six months ago and have not been refuted.

A second defense of this spending is a grand example of New Deal bookkeeping. The President justifies the 8½ billion rise in debt by the New Deal by suggesting it is offset by "nearly 4½ billions of recoverable assets." He states also that the debt increased a little less than four billions in my Administration. The little less was $400,000,000 less. But of more importance, he received more than $2,200,000,000 of these recoverable assets from my Administration; or alternatively, they have realized those assets and spent the money. The President seems to have forgotten the very powerful agencies set up which were making loans for relief of agriculture and unemployment long before his Administration.

With these corrections the increase in burdens of the depression on the taxpayers in the Hoover Administration was under 1½ billion. Also in addition to his 2½ billion error in estimating New Deal debt increase during the depression under the Roosevelt Administration, the President omitted the New Deal guarantee of four or five billions in bonds of lending companies. We may expect respectable losses on these also. It is unfortunate that within ten days after that address the national debt should have jumped another billion. And this is not the last jump. From the high signs in the government skies I venture that by next July the increase under the New Deal will be not 9½ billion but 12 billion.

But now we come to the President's major defense for this gigantic spending and unpaid bills. That is the need to relieve the unemployed. I shall explore that subject, for there is no better example of the whole workings of the New Deal. Its organization is typical of the whole gamut of waste, folly, ineffectiveness, politics, and destruction of self-government. When in the face of a decrease in the unemployed the cost of relief rises from $1,100,000,000 to an appropriation of 4 decimal point 8 billions for a single year it is certainly reason for searching inquiry.

Incidentally, when I comb over these accounts of the New Deal my sympathy arises for the humble decimal point. His is a pathetic and hectic life, wandering around among regimented ciphers trying to find some of the old places he used to know.

Let me say one thing right at the outset. There is no disagreement upon the public obligation to relieve distress which flows from national calamity. The support of that comes from the conscience of a people. It comes from their fidelity to the Sermon on the Mount. The American people know that the genuine sufferers on relief are not slackers. They know the weary days of tramping the streets in search for a chance to work. They know the discouragement and despair which have stalked those homes. There is not a real man or woman whose heart does not warm to them, who will not sacrifice for them.

Some five years ago I stated that, "as a nation we must prevent hunger and cold to those of our people who are in honest difficulties." I have never heard a disagreement with that. And I wish to emphasize that there is no humor in relief. It is grim human tragedy.

I believe I can without egotism claim to have had some special experience in relief. At one time or another it became my task to organize and administer relief to over one hundred and fifty million people who had been reduced to destitution by war or by famine or by flood both at home and abroad. I gave some years to that service in the aspiration to save life, to allay suffering, to restore courage and faith in humanity.

It also became my duty in 1930 to see that relief was organized for our unemployed. Organization of relief upon a nation-wide basis was practically unknown in the world before those experiences. It therefore fell to me and my colleagues to pioneer in methods. We had to learn what basis would best and most sympathetically protect those in distress and still place the least burden on those who had to pay for it. I spent long, weary days listening to arguments whether to have direct money relief, or relief in kind, or public works, or made-work or "boondoggling," or centralized administration, or decentralized responsibility. We tried out these alternatives. Out of those poignant experiences we learned certain fundamentals. We quickly learned that there were four types of persons who rush into relief. There were the starry-eyed who periodically discover that relief is needed and that everything up to date is wrong. There were those whose major passion was sociological experiment upon a mass of distress. There were those who would make profit from misery. There were always those present who do not neglect the political possibilities of relief. But there were the sterling, solid men and women in every city and hamlet who willingly served and sacrificed.

We learned that relief was an emergency operation, not a social experiment; that the object was to serve the people in genuine distress and nobody else. We learned that the dreamers cannot effectually conduct the grinding tasks of relief; that politics must be shunned as a plague. We learned that centralized bureaucracy gives the sufferers more red tape than relief. We learned that we must mobilize on a voluntary basis the best hearts and brains of every community to serve their neighbors. We learned that there must be complete decentralization to them of both authority and administration. We did not have to learn that local self-government and local responsibility was the basis of American life.

In 1930 by co-operation with the States, we secured the creation of State committees of leading citizens. With them we secured the creation of similar committees in every city, town, and county where relief was needed. These committees had no politics. They were men and women experienced in large affairs, sympathetic, understanding of the needs of their neighbors in distress. And they served without pay. In those days one did not enter into relief of his countrymen through the portals of a payroll. American men and women of such stature cannot be had as a paid bureaucracy, yet they will serve voluntarily all hours of the day and defer their own affairs to night.

These committees used the existing officials; they engaged their own tested organizations; they employed their own trusted citizens. They had the complete authority to determine the methods best adapted to their neighborhoods. They knew the problem of the man next door better than anybody in Washington. They themselves determined for their locality what method was to be used. They adapted these needs to the individual families. Their stewardship was under the limelight of their own community. They gave spiritual aid and encouragement.

At the start the relief in 1930 depended upon private giving. As times became more difficult, the committees co-operated in the use of county and municipal funds; and as it became still more difficult many of the State governments provided them with funds. Finally, as State resources weakened, we provided Federal Government funds to be distributed to the State governments and by them redistributed to the local organizations. That we built up no bureaucracy is evident from the fact that although the government had many new emergency tasks, yet during the Hoover Administration the total number of all government officials decreased by ten thousand. That form of organization expressed in its noblest form the whole American ideal of local self-government, local responsibility, national cooperation, and the voluntary spirit of human service.

There was no important failure to provide for those in real need. There was no substantial complaint or suggestion of waste, politics, or corruption. Neither the Republican Party nor any of its agencies ever asked for votes or claimed that its administration reserved votes for it. That idea was repugnant to every decent sense of Americanism.

However, all this was forgotten on March 3, 1933. We may accept that the date of Creation was moved to March 4, and we may examine what sort of a world has been made.

At that moment good men appeared who were certain that before their advent everything was done wrong. Also came the visionaries, the profit-maker, and, above all, the politician. They all yearned to serve their fellowmen.

The whole relief work was promptly centralized from Washington. State and local organizations were dismissed or reduced to mere window dressing. A paid bureaucracy was spread over the land. The history of the last two and one-half years shows the floundering of this Administration. That needs no more proof than the buffeting of those in distress from FERA or PWA or its subsidiaries to EPW, then to SERA, then to CWA, partly to FRSC, then back to FERA, and over to WPA. It has been a sort of rain-maker's cabalistic dance. As each of these alphabetical organizations flares up in folly and waste its victims and its accounts have been buried by juggling of the alphabet. When they are all buried their spirit will live on as IOU. Now the Federal government disavows its responsibilities for all but 3,500,000 out of the 10,000,000 unemployed. But what of the tragic anxiety in this mass of people lest they may be left out in all this shifting? That reminds them to collect a little political influence that they may not be forgotten men.

From ample experience during my Administration we were compelled to the conclusion that Federal Public Works in these

times except in narrow limits do not secure enough jobs to justify them. Nor does employment seem the dominant idea in
the billions now being poured down such projects. Part of these
billions are going into wholesale sociological experiments. Most
of them are already demonstrated failures. Part of these works
are to take the government into business competition with the
citizen. The government pays no taxes. The Treasury pays the
losses. The constant threat of them retards enterprise and therefore jobs. One of the ideas in these spendings is to prime the economic pump. We might abandon this idea also for it dries up
the well of enterprise.

One department of these works is of interest to the farmer.
The reports of the Reclamation Service show new expansions
begun in the past three years which in capital and interest will
cost over $800,000,000 to complete. We in the Far West like
it. At the same time the farmer is being paid to let land lie idle.
It lacks some element of horse sense. But we have been governed by paradoxes and contraries and complexes ever since "the
mechanics of civilization came to a stop." The New Dealers
told us we were hungry because we had too much food and the
way to repletion was through scarcity. Perhaps this reclaimed
land will enable us some day to improve that third-class diet
which we encourage today with scarcity, increased cost of living, and taxes.

There is something for thought also in the recent protest of
the Democratic Mayor of Pittsburgh, who complains that "A
job in our city done under unemployment relief methods cost
$64,000, while the contract estimate was $18,000. This is typical of all projects to a greater or less degree." He further says
that "By its methods . . . it has created a blood clot in the ar-
teries of industry."

I do not wish to weary you with details. Anyway the taxpayer
had better not complain of these gigantic wastes. He will be
told he has murder in his heart through trying to starve his fellow citizens.

We may compare the most of these two forms of administration—the one founded on local self-government under the

glare of its local public opinion; the other being run by a political bureaucracy from Washington.

Statistics are dry subjects, but just now figures are the most important thing in our national life. The entire cost of relief to unemployment during the last year of the Republican Administration was about $1,100,000,000. That includes Federal, State, municipal, county and private giving. It includes Federal public works above normal and does not include relief to agriculture. The Federal overhead was not over $250,000 a year. The total number of paid Federal employees was less than two hundred.

Now let us examine the respective needs in these two periods. The average of the monthly figures of the American Federation of Labor shows 11,600,000 unemployed during the last year of the Hoover Administration. During the year of the New Deal ending this October the unemployed have averaged about 11,100,000. That was a decrease of the unemployment load by about five per cent.

Now let us note the increase in relief cost. However, the marvellous migratory habits of these relief funds from one place in the alphabet to another make them difficult hunting. But judging from Treasury and other statements the expenditures on all relief alphabets in the year ending last October for Federal, State, and local were over $3,500,000,000. This also includes Federal Public Works over normal, but does not include relief to agriculture. There were over 140,000 officials on the Federal payroll, not including the people on relief. The salaries of these officials alone must come to about $300,000,000 a year. It is easy to detect another $200,000,000 in pencils, typewriters, offices, automobiles, Pullman fares, etc., not to mention press releases. That is an overhead of four or five hundred million per annum. Some increase in relief was necessary, but an increase of 300 per cent in costs in the face of a 5 per cent decrease in unemployment load is significant. And the overhead amounts to nearly one-half the whole cost of relief three years ago.

In confirmation of this, I have inquired as to the figures of several cities and counties. To cite one of them, the number on relief increased 5 per cent, the cost 250 per cent. The others confirm these increases.

Every community has been forced to become a conspiracy to get their share from the Federal grab bag. And saddest of all, the responsibility of local self-government has been dulled; we are becoming a nation of prayer wheels directed to Washington.

We may well wonder why local organization of relief, consonant with the whole spirit of democracy, has been shifted to a Federal bureaucracy at Washington. Some part of it has to do with politics and yearning for sociological experiments. Jobs have been thereby found for over 140,000 new Federal officials. If it was decided to bureaucratize relief from Washington, then every call of good government demanded that the staff be selected by nonpartisan merit tests through the Civil Service Commission. But that service which has been built up over many years by every President was ignored and repudiated, and the spoils system substituted. You know and I know and the people know that this horde of officials has been appointed by the advice and consent of Democratic politicians.

The inevitable and driving purpose of any political bureaucracy is to use its powers to secure its jobs. The sudden appropriations to cities, counties, and states were singularly timed to elections. And this is not the only method of making politics out of human misery. Governor Smith has said that nobody shoots Santa Claus. But the people may learn that there are other things moving around in the dark besides Santa Claus.

One thing is certain. A mass of propaganda spreads over the country to the effect that relief to the unemployed originates with the New Deal and would end with the New Deal. Those in distress will not be misled. Whatever aid they receive comes not from any official or party. It comes out of the pockets of their fellow citizens. It will not end as long as there is need for any resources left.

Do you want more proofs of waste, folly, chiselers, and petty corruption? You know it in your own town, city, or village. Read your own newspapers, whose columns periodically reek with accounts of disorganization and waste. Their editorials cry to heaven against the use being made of relief for politics. If only the money taken from the taxpayers could go to those in distress there would be less cause for public indignation.

The administration of relief needs reform right now. It needs it in the interest of good government. It needs it in the interest of the eighty-five per cent of our citizens who have to pay for it. They include everybody who works. The cost of these wastes and follies is collected by hidden taxes in every package that comes from the store. Or worse, we are laying it onto our children by debt. Reform is needed in the interest of the fifteen per cent who are on relief, that they get better and more secure service. To the self-respecting Americans on relief these wastes and follies are a tragedy. They know it dissipates money they need. It delays their deliverance to a real job. The inspiration of relief comes from the heart, but its effectiveness must come from the head.

As the New Deal always demands alternative plans, I offer four:

1. Stop these wasteful Federal public works projects; confine them to projects which meet the needs of the nation.

2. Decentralize the administration of all other forms of relief. Turn them back to the States and local communities. Do it in joint co-operation with the governors, mayors, and county authorities. Enlist again the voluntary services of American men and women on a non-partisan basis. Give such responsible committees as they create the entire determination of how it should be done. Allot to the States less than one-half the present funds being spent in the relief. Require the local authorities to find from their local funds at least five per cent as check on waste. Require the State to do its share. Discharge most of the Federal officials connected with these relief agencies. Those in real need will be better cared for than they are today.

3. Do it now. That would go far to assure a clean election. But it is more than that. It would relieve human distress which suffers enough without the poison of politics in its bread.

4. We have a further obligation beyond relief to this ten million unemployed. True relief must come from honest pro-

ductive jobs, not from public funds. Those jobs would return quickly if the currency were stabilized and this torrent of unnecessary expenditure were stopped and the budget were balanced. That would recreate confidence in the future. It would relieve the threat of inflation which demoralizes all business and sets up false recoveries. It would start men building again for the future. It would bring into action the vast amount of improvement needed in housing and in machinery, now being worn out through seven years of obsolescence. It would set free the energies of new enterprise. These people on relief have suffered enough from having playboys take America apart to see how the wheels go round.

In conclusion, I should like to say a word to the young men and women among my listeners. Some of us have not much more span of life. We have seen America grow in greatness. Except the cost of war we have seen increasing security to the average man. Our interest is for those who will carry the burden and create the glories of America after us. We will continue fighting. But you have to live the years, you have to carry America on. It is your pockets into which the government will reach deeper and deeper if this goes on. It is you whose opportunities are being limited. I have but one suggestion. That you study the history of your country. That you survey its scene today. That you debate every phase of this government. That you carry this debate to every street corner, every schoolhouse, every shop, and every counting room. What you decide will be final for our country. You will have the burdens. And may the Divine Being guide you aright.

New Deal Agricultural Policies and Some Reforms

LINCOLN, NEBRASKA

[*January 16, 1936*]

I HAVE recently debated various realities of the New Deal at Oakland, New York, and St. Louis. I propose now to explore it further, particularly its agricultural policies and their effect on the whole people.

The New Deal has developed a new technique in debate. They set up a glorious ideal to which we all agree unanimously. Then they drive somewhere else or into the ditch. When we protest they blackguard us for opposing the glorious ideal. And they announce that all protestors are the tools of Satan or Wall Street. When we summon common sense and facts they weep aloud over their martyrdom for the ideal.

The New Deal explanations of their agricultural policies exceed thirty million words. You will not expect me to turn the light into every dark corner in thirty minutes. Some of the rugged prima donnas who have directed these policies have resigned and said worse things than I would say. One quality of the old Regulated Individualists was team work.

Right at the outset let us get some things perfectly clear. There is an agricultural problem. It concerns the entire nation. It concerns the happiness of 7,000,000 homes. Our country will not have reached either full moral or economic stature until confidence and hope shine in these homes. The problem is still unsolved.

Aside from its flagrant flouting of the Constitution the New Deal farm method had within it destruction both to the farmers and to the nation. A new program is necessary. It is now in the making. The nation has a right to insist that it must be effective and it must be based upon sound principles.

I shall debate the subject in five directions.

Part One will be the reasons why the farm question is of national interest. I hope this part will be emphatic.

Part Two is a few words upon the causes of the farmers' troubles. I hope this part will not wholly spoil the stock in trade of many politicians, for they have to live also.

Part Three is what the New Deal is doing to the farmer as a citizen, along with all other citizens. These are the things to avoid in the future. I hope this part will not be too sad.

Part Four is what the New Deal has done to the farmer in his farming business. This is also sad.

Part Five consists of some discussion of a new program. It may shock those who believe in doing nothing for human ills. It may shock those who believe that all healing medicine comes off the collectivist brew.

In all parts there are remarks on what the New Deal has been doing to the whole structure of human liberty and American institutions in the guise of farm relief.

Each part has unpleasant features to somebody. However, my position is such that approval by politicians and many others who live by the sweat of the farmers' brows is immaterial. If this country is to be saved as a decent place for the farmers' children and all our children to live in ordered liberty and faith of the future, we have a lot of unpleasant truth to face. In the long war for right thinking falsehood often wins the first battle. But truth always wins the last—if the nation survives in the meantime.

PART I

President Roosevelt on December 9, at Chicago, properly stated one reason why the plight of the farmer is an issue which concerns all of the American people. He said, "Farm prosperity cannot exist without city prosperity, and city prosperity cannot exist without farm prosperity." Every President since George

Washington, every public man, every economist and every school-teacher has said the same thing. It is vitally true, even if it is not news. But the President omitted to state other reasons why his farm policies are an issue vital to the whole American people.

The first is that the urgent need of farm relief has been used as a cover to impose the New Deal philosophy upon the American people. That is comprised of government by individuals in place of a government of laws. It comprises goosestepping the people under this pinkish banner of Planned Economy. That was tried under the NRA but the Supreme Court halted it early. It has had a longer march under the AAA. Step by step the New Deal Agricultural Policies advanced from cajolery with a gentle rain of checks to open coercion. Men who planted on their own farms and sold in their own way the product which God and their own labor give them could have been sent to jail for doing just that. That is not liberty. That is collectivism.

The second reason the President did not state was that those ideas of production control revolve upon planned scarcity instead of the plenty upon which America alone has made progress. To stop the production of 50,000,000 fertile acres is not progress. That also concerns the whole people. Civilization has made progress solely through producing more and more of varied things. The whole history of humanity has been a struggle against famine and want. Within only the last half-century America achieved a triumph in this age-long struggle by the creation of a system which at last can produce a plenty for a reasonable living for all of us. We have not solved the problem of its distribution, but in this plan of scarcity we are surrendering the very foundations of human hope.

The third reason was that the processing tax levied to support this program bore most heavily upon the 15,000,000 workers' homes. It was an undeserved burden to those women struggling to feed their men and their children. But the worst of that scheme was that it set boiling the witches' cauldron of class conflict of town against the farmers. This tax should never be revived.

PART II

The causes of the farmer's troubles must be honestly faced if we are to have common-sense remedy. Economic patent medicines require no diagnosis except decision that the patient is in pain.

The difficulties of our agriculture came mainly from the war and its hectic aftermaths. Wars always do that to the farmer. Demoralization lasted twenty years after the Napoleonic wars and a dozen years after our own Civil War.

I am glad that the President at last admits that the war had something to do with the farm depression. At Chicago, on December 9, 1935, he says, in referring to farm prosperity in the period before the war: "They were the last years before the world-wide disturbance, caused by the World War, took place in our economic life." I had been told so often by the New Deal that I did it that I had given up hope of salvation. I feel better.

The dislocation of wars and slumps hits the farmer harder than any other group. Farm prices are more sensitive to these shocks than wages and industrial prices. All parts of the economic system inevitably come back into balance with time. But farm recovery is longer drawn out. That is the higher economics of it.

The painful symptom of it appears in the farmer's pocket in the slump of purchasing power of his dollar. Many farmers cannot hold on against these delays in readjustment. I have held that we cannot see the capable and industrious driven from their homes during these periods if they want to make a fight for them. That is the humanity of it.

There is at least one hopeful aspect of these war causes of the farmer's difficulties. They do not last forever. Many of our measures can be of emergency character. Recovery will cure many difficulties—that is, if it is allowed by the New Deal to come.

When the world depression was turned, in June and July, 1932, agricultural prices rose in a start toward equality with industrial prices. The farmer's dollar improved more than 20 per cent. Prices were moving into a natural relation again. Then came the era of the Great Fear. Fright over the coming of the New Deal skidded the country into the money and bank panic. The President said "the mechanics of civilization had come to a dead stop." Many a driver who has had a bad skid thinks that. Then began the magic of the New Deal. And they repeated each mistake of the Farm Board and added a big idea. That big idea is that you can catch an economic force with a policeman.

Incidentally the culmination of that era of Great Fear is the convenient starting point for all of the President's comparative statistics. He chooses the low point of quotation induced by their own actions. If he would go back a few months into 1932, before the Great Fear started, he would find the prices were 80 to 100 per cent higher than those he quotes. And they were in 100-cent dollars. And even then they were only at the turning of the greatest depression in history. His quotations look like an effort to warm the nation over cold glass chunks in an illuminated grate.

PART III

Things have been done to the farmer by the New Deal which do not relate alone to agriculture.

Firstly, this torrent of wasteful spending, unbalanced budget and debt will be paid by the farmer as well as all others. It will blight all his days with anxiety. The farmer pays for it not alone in direct taxes, but hidden taxes are wrapped in everything he buys. The farmer in fact pays in larger measure than any other group because he buys not alone for his family but also for his farm and is less able than any other production group to mark up the prices of his products and pass these taxes on to the consumer. Moreover, about one-quarter of the $14,000,000,000 of probable increased New Deal debt will rest on the farm as a super-mortgage. Blessed are the young, for they shall inherit the national debt.

Secondly, the present policies of paying for the New Deal by credit inflation produce stock booms that are a great dole for the "money changers." President Roosevelt, on July 24, 1933, stated that we cannot attain prosperity "in a nation half-boom and half-broke." The New Deal has attained just that. That half-boom is on in the Stock Exchange, the farmers are half broke—and the 20,000,000 on relief are fully broke. These credit booms add little to farm prices. When they crack they throw the farmer in the ditch.

There is a thirdly, on currency policies. There is a fourthly, on making the farmers pay for a large part of the Social Security Act and receiving little benefits. There is a fifthly, on relief policies which make it impossible for farmers to get labor in the midst of unemployment. There is a sixthly and a seventhly, on some other white rabbits. All of them make farm thinking difficult and intense. I do not have the time to discuss them all now.

PART IV

If we are now to deal competently with farm relief we must examine the experience with the New Deal farm measures. There are proved dangers which must be avoided. In other words, what have these New Deal principles done to the farmer?

President Roosevelt on one occasion said: "I like to think of the AAA not as a temporary means . . . but as an expression of principle." From their practical works, irrespective of their words, the main principle is the economy of scarcity based on control of production enforced by telling the farmer what he can plant.

The largest justification has been that it has raised prices. Prices have improved. I leave you three thoughts on that subject: First: The inflation of the dollar, the drought, and world recovery would have made higher prices in any event. Second: *The Chicago Tribune* is authority for the statement that the farmer's income from many uncontrolled commodities has been greater in proportion than from those which have had the attention of the New Deal. President Roosevelt on May 30, 1935, prophesied that "if we abandon crop control wheat will immediately drop to 36 cents a bushel and cotton to five cents a pound."

He felt the same about hogs. I do not know how long a time there is in "immediately." It is more than a week. Third: At the same time another principle of the New Deal was to lift wages and industrial prices. The sum of these two principles is that the farmer has less to sell and pays more for what he buys. Labor pays for it in increased cost of living. By this device we have got the Economic Dog running around in circles chasing his tail.

We may explore the effect of the processing tax in case some one might suggest we try it again. In early 1933 President-elect Roosevelt expressed himself as horrified and directed the defeat of my proposal to the Democratic Congress to balance the budget by a manufacturers' sales tax of 2½ per cent. My proposal exempted food and cheaper clothing. We did that in order that we should not impose the burden upon the poor. Yet, as President Roosevelt, he places a manufacturers' sales tax of 25 per cent on pork, and 30 per cent on flour, both absolute essentials to the poor. That blow at the poor was no doubt softened by calling it a "processing" tax. The implication was that some wicked middleman would pay it. The housewife rebelled at this more abundant life. One result of it was that the consumption of food in 1935 fell below the worst year, 1932, by the product of over 15,000,000 acres.

We may explore what these New Deal principles did to our export and import market. You will remember that 1932 was the year when "it could not be worse." So we will take that worst year and compare it with the New Deal year of 1935. From that worst year exports of cotton have decreased 4,250,-000 bales; our grain 93,000,000 bushels; our animal products by 500,000,000 pounds. This is estimated to be the product of about 20,000,000 acres. But, worse than that, this greatest food-producing country on earth has imported this year about 100,-000,000 bushels of grain, 700,000,000 pounds of animal products, and increased its imports of vegetable oils to be used as substitutes by another 700,000,000 pounds. It would take another probable 15,000,000 acres to produce these imports. The Secretary of Agriculture says America must choose one of three courses in foreign trade. The three are various degrees of the theory of more industrial imports in order that the American farmer may sell more to foreign countries. But what he produced was a fourth choice; that is, to give the foreign farmer the American farmer's market.

From all this decrease in home consumption and shift in foreign trade the farmer has lost the market for more acres than the whole New Deal curtailment of 50,000,000 fertile acres. Is that not the principle of the Economic Dog chasing his tail?

On January 10 President Roosevelt declared himself in opposition to "shipping our soil fertility to foreign nations." The logical conclusion of all that is to stop exports altogether. There is a futility here somewhere. The idea is that we encourage imports of industrial products and create unemployment at home. We are told we must do this in order that the farmer may export his products. Now we are told that it is not to our advantage to export farm products at all. He overlooks the fact that we can manufacture synthetic fertilizers to any amount necessary to cover export of "soil fertility."

In May, 1932, when I vetoed a bill for reciprocal tariff treaties, I stated that most of such treaties would sacrifice the American farmer. The New Deal method of testing poison is apparently to make the nation swallow it. By just these reciprocal treaties the American market is today being opened to farmers of Cuba, Canada, Spain and Italy. Yet under these principles farmers are told they must allow fertile acres to be idle because there is no market for their products. It is very confusing. The Economic Dog whirls even faster under this stimulus.

We must explore as to where we get to when we start controlling crops. This principle of scarcity gets scarcer and scarcer. The moment one farm product was regimented, another had to be mobilized to prevent the farmers' energy from going into that. So we marched from seven controlled commodities in May, 1933, to five more in April, 1934, another in May, 1934, and finally we come to potatoes in 1935. Moreover, these measures are moving steadily to more and more coercion and less rain of checks—as witness the Cotton and the Potato Acts. As I read further and further into the 6,250 verboten words of the potato law, I realized that one of the impulses to cheerfulness was about to be mashed out of American life. The potato had yielded not only food, but it had radiated humor to our daily conversation. It was once the happiest of all the vegetables. Its life would have been saddened by the bootlegger, the passive resister, and the Federal inspectors. Confined to a package by law, its eyes would have been dimmed by the alphabetical revenue stamps it must bear.

One of the assured principles of New Deal farming is politics. One would think in the thunders of idealism that have accompanied Planned Agriculture it would be clean of politics. I have but one comment. That is to read two lines from a letter I hold written by a high officer in the AAA to a gentleman who spent his life in scientific work for the farmer and who was accepted for appointment in that service. It says, ". . . it will be necessary [for you] to secure political clearance, which means a letter of approval from the Democratic National Committee in California." The Department of Agriculture was wholly under merit service before this sort of idealist got it. The execution of these principles required 120,000 part- or full-time Federal officials. Their pay was assessed against the farmers. This new breed of middlemen every day tried hard to bring agriculture into balance with politics.

We may explore the effect of this economy of scarcity and crop control upon employment. For instance, the reduction of cotton by ten million acres is producing a hideous poverty in the share croppers of the South. It is creating unemployment all over the nation of some hundreds of thousands of agricultural laborers, railway men, and others who formerly lived by producing and handling the 20 million tons of agricultural products that could come from the acres forced to idleness.

And above all other consequences, the whole notion of regimenting the farmer under bureaucracy was the negation of the free American spirit. The system of scarcity was being applied to human freedom.

Does all this corroborate President Roosevelt's indication on

December 9 at Chicago that agriculture is "making great strides" toward a "balance either within itself or with industry and business"? If so, it was a juggler's balance.

Finally—Does anybody believe that this flimsy structure under agriculture, of regimenting men, of putting fertile acres out of action, of giving American markets to foreigners, and levying its cost on the poor would not have fallen of its own weight, even without the Supreme Court?

PART V

We may now explore some of the roads to relief.

And every country, including ourselves, has adopted measure after measure to protect the farmer and to speed a return to stability. Other nations tried most of the New Deal measures before the New Deal was born. From all this experience we should by now have learned some lessons in what is harmful, what is futile, and what will help.

We shall be less than intelligent, and we shall be heartless of the farmers' problems if we do not distill from this wreckage of these experiments some lessons in truth. And there have been aids to recovery extended to the farmer both at home and abroad which have been successful. The first group of these aids is: Increase consumption of food by restoration of employment. That can come only with a balanced budget, stable currency and credit. Give the farmer our own home market. Adopt such sane national policies as will again restore reasonable export markets. Out of this group of policies we can restore demand to many millions of fertile acres.

The second group of policies is: To retire submarginal lands where people cannot make a living. Do it in the more effective and humane way proposed by Secretary Hyde in 1932. Retard new reclamation projects until the land can be used.

A third group of policies is: Encourage co-operative marketing and those marketing agreements which contribute to prevent gluts in the flow to markets. The farm credit machinery established by Republican Administrations and improved by the New Deal should be still further improved.

But beyond these measures this farm situation is now one where still further emergency measures pending general economic recovery are necessary. They are doubly necessary as a new road must be built by which agriculture can get back on to solid ground from the quicksand of the New Deal. We shall need to open our minds to further experiment.

I suggest as one contribution to new methods that instead of trying to find a balance to agriculture by paying the farmer to curtail a crop, we should endeavor to expand another crop which can be marketed or which would improve the fertility of the soil. We import vast quantities of vegetable oils, sugar and other commodities. There are industrial products that could be introduced by the American farmer. We need to replenish our soils with legumes and restore coverages. If we include this suggestion with the policies I have already mentioned, which would recover our lost acres from foreigners, we would be able to employ more than all the acres put out of action by the New Deal. We would reverse this economy of scarcity to an economy of plenty.

This question of sustained fertility and better land use was brought to the forefront by former Governor Lowden in 1930. Nation-wide conferences under Secretary Hyde in 1932 further developed parts of this subject. The matter was still further advanced by the Republican side in the campaign of that year. These ideas have been further contributed to by many thinking men since that time. In order to secure these objectives I believe we must be prepared to subsidize directly such special crops until agriculture has again been brought into balance. At the end of such a road we could hope for a balanced agriculture in full production and increased fertility in our soils.

I am advised that it can be done within the spirit as well as the letter of the Constitution.

Since this paragraph was written these ideas have been discussed in Washington as a method of overcoming the debacle brought about by the New Deal. But if they are adopted it should be under certain fundamental safeguards. There should be no attempt to again impose New Deal ideas of controlling and regimenting the farmer or restricting production. He must be free of any restriction and control contracts. The farmer must be an entirely free man to use his own skill and judgment. The administration of these methods should be handled by the Land Grant Colleges in order to free agriculture of politics and the vast bureaucracy now loaded upon the farmer. This work should be co-ordinated by a non-political national board. The cost should be borne by the general taxpayer and not loaded upon the poorest of the country through some tax like the processing tax. Otherwise this method will again be a subterfuge of pinkish National Planning under another alphabet.

Somebody will shy at the blunt word "subsidy." And, in fact, the American people have been going all around Robin Hood's barn, rather than use it. Over a century ago we began it in canals and turnpikes, since then we have kept it up. Railroads, highways, ships and aviation, and silver mines and land reclamation —agriculture—we usually do it under some other name than subsidy. We had better begin to use straight words and we will act straight. A subsidy is a burden on the taxpayer, but it does not regiment or destroy the initiative or freedom of the receiver —it is to stimulate that.

In conclusion may I offer a word of personal emotion? It lies far beyond the land of economics. I have spent years in public service in many countries during this most fateful period of human history. I saw as few men the backwash of war upon the common man of these countries. I saw at first hand revolution creeping in under promises of relief from the agonies of war destruction. I have seen the insidious destruction of liberty by propaganda. I have seen suffering humanity sacrifice that liberty, the greatest of all human achievements, for an illusion of security. The farmers of Russia supported the Bolsheviki against the new-born Democracy on the promise of the land. Today they have the choice of Siberia or the collectivist farms. I have seen freedom, the most priceless heritage, torn from children that this generation might escape its responsibilities. I wish to say to you unhesitatingly that our country has been following step by step the road through which these millions of people in foreign countries lost their liberties. Our farmers have had that blessing of individual liberty in greater fullness in their lives than any other part of even our own people. It was the farmers who fired the first shot at Lexington. It must be the farmers of America who defend that heritage. I ask you to stop, look, and listen.

The Confused State of
the Union

PORTLAND, OREGON

[*February 12, 1936*]

PART I

IN LESS than a year our country must make a decision no less fateful than that which confronted Abraham Lincoln.

Since the Great War Liberty has fallen in a score of nations. In America where it blazed brightest and by its glow shed light to all others it is today impaired and endangered.

Again "we are . . . testing whether that nation or any nation so conceived and so dedicated can long endure."

When that test confronted Lincoln, he carried it to the people in national debate. No greater tribute can be paid him than that we shall devote this day of his memory to that high purpose.

If the truth and right decisions are to be found, this discussion must be held to the mold of courtesy, good humor, hard hitting, and above all to the intellectual honesty which Lincoln kept in all his fateful years.

Personalities and mud-slinging never clarified a national issue.

There has lately been a new avalanche of oratory on behalf of the "common people," the "average man," the "economic middle class," and the "rank and file." That is right. These are the people for whom America was made. They carry the burdens of America. They make its moral fiber. They are the people whose interest needs defense right now. Mr. Lincoln said the Lord must have loved them because he created so many of them. There are others who love their votes.

The President stated a month ago that the issue before us is "the right of the average man and woman to lead a finer, better, and happier life."

That is an objective to which we all agree. That is the ideal of Americans since it was first mentioned in the Declaration of Independence. That is not at issue. The issue is the New Deal methods and objectives which are destroying this very thing.

The issue is the attempt to fasten upon the American people some sort of a system of personal government for a government of laws; a system of centralization under a political bureaucracy; a system of debts; a system of inflation; a system which would stifle the freedom and liberty of men. And it can be examined in the cold light of three years' experience.

It would seem that since the Supreme Court decisions we have abandoned the issue of the More Abundant Life. That was found to contain many roads to trouble.

PART II

It is the actual State of the Union that I propose to discuss this evening.

The outstanding State of this Union at this hour is a state of confusion. Confusion in thought, confusion in government, confusion in economic life, and confusion in ideals. Few national problems have been really solved. I have time for only a few illustrations of this bewildering muddle which jeopardizes the liberty of a great people.

And the test of it all is, whether we are moving to the "finer, better, and happier life for the average man and woman."

The President in his message on the State of the Union seems to fear that fear is prevalent in the Union. He says, "The only thing we have to fear is fear." He finds malevolent forces creating fear. Just so.

The New Deal has been a veritable fountain of fear. The day after the New Deal was given life at the election of 1932 began the Great Fear which created the bank panic of March 4th. The stock boom today is not from confidence in the future; it is partly from fear of inflation. The unemployment of millions of men in the capital goods industries is due to fear of New Deal currency policies. It was the Supreme Court decisions crashing through New Deal tyrannies which brought a gleam of confidence from the fears that had retarded recovery. The guiding spirit of the alphabet has not been love. It has been fear.

The President in reporting on the State of the Union also found it alive with "money-changers," "seekers for selfish power," "dishonest speculators," "economic autocrats," and "entrenched greed."

However, that has points in confusing the public mind. Any judge of debate would admit it. It has merit as a call to class war, a red herring across the trail of failure, an implication that all opponents are defenders of evil, a claim that righteousness now has refuge alone in Washington, and an avoidance of facts and figures. It is not the mold of debate of Abraham Lincoln. It does not heal the wounds of the Nation.

In any event, in opposing the New Deal you did not know you were allied with those forces of darkness. You know it now.

No one defends such wickedness. But it happens that after three years of the New Deal the same men direct business today that were there three years ago. But what has become of the new laws designed to reform the wicked? We have seen no indictments except political oratory. That is confusing.

You will recall that three years ago the President gave the comforting assurance that "The money-changers have fled from their high seats in the temple of our civilization." It would appear that after three years of the New Deal they have all come back again with helpers. Also I had the impression that the New Deal had taken over the business of changing the money.

The human animal has many primitive instincts that morals, religion, and the law have not been able wholly to eradicate. He has two forms of greed—the greed for money and the greed for power. The lust for power is infinitely the worse. The greed for money can be curbed by law, but the greed for power seizes the law itself for its ends. At least the greed for money does not afflict us with fine phrases and slogans as to what is good for us.

The abuses of liberty by greed for money are weeds which grow in the garden of productive enterprise. If government is clean it can pull them up. The abuse of liberty by the greed for power is a blight that destroys the garden itself.

The President states ". . . In thirty-four months we have built up new instruments of public power. In the hands of the people's government this power is wholesome and proper." The President concedes that in other hands it would "provide shackles for the liberties of the people." That is confusion of dictatorship with democracy. The very origin of this Republic was in order that nobody should possess such power over the people.

These instruments of power march to the "finer, better, and happier life" under a banner of strange device—"Planned Economy." By this time you know this glittering phrase does not mean economy in government spending. It has proved to mean Politically Dictated Economic Life. It is of many battalions. We have seen so far Planned Industry, Planned Farming, Planned Government in Business, Planned Relief, Planned Credit, Planned Currency, and Planned Attack on the Constitution. And I might suggest two more. They are Planned Deficits and Planned Politics.

I need recall only those first two builders of confusion, the NRA and the AAA. These two Towers of Babel which the children of men built were also to reach to Heaven. The headlines tell us of the character of the bricks and the mortar. Must Legislation. No Debate. Personal Government by Proclamation. Ballyhoo. Codes. Factory Production Restricted. Competition Limited. Monopolies Created. Government Price Fixing. Increasing Costs. Increased Prices. Decreased Consumption. Increased Cost of Living. Strikes. Lockouts. Boycott. Coercion. Crack Down. Jail. Small Business Men Washed Out. Crops Plowed Under. Animals Slaughtered. Housewife Strikes. Consumption of Food Decreases. Nation Imports Foods. Farmers' Markets Given to Foreigners. Economy of Scarcity. Nation Gets Richer by Producing Less at Higher Costs.

Their language was confounded and they were scattered by the Supreme Court.

But a new confusion arises. The spokesmen of the administration talk of the resurrection of these theories as the basis of our future economic life. The President refuses to say that they are finished. On the contrary in his address of January 3, after asserting the success of New Deal measures, he says: "I recommend to Congress that we advance, that we do not retreat." My impression is that Napoleon used somewhat that expression when he was marching to Moscow.

The American people have a right to have this clarified. Has the President abandoned these theories or not?

The third battalion of confusion has been the spending, budget deficits, debts, currency, and credit. Within a month since the President's budget message it has become more confused by four or five billions more expenditures.

Those who judge progress by the size of figures will agree that great improvements have taken place in the National Debt since the Mechanics of Civilization came to a stop on March 4, 1933. During the Hoover Administration the debt increased about $1,250,000,000, after allowing for recoverable loans. That is only about 10 per cent of what the New Mechanics will accomplish. That increase will be about up to $14,000,000,000, less recoverable loans and plus large losses on guaranteed mortgages. The National Debt now bids fair to rise to a minimum of $35,000,000,000.

I note in the budget message President Roosevelt said, "The finances of the government are in better condition than at any time in the past seven years." You may remember the uneasiness of the decimal point which I mentioned some months ago. It has moved steadily to the left.

The New Deal could also report, "As a part of our fiscal policies we have set up 'Managed Credit' under the political seizure of the Federal Reserve System. We have set up 'Managed Currency' under political control of the value of the dollar. We have abandoned the gold standard. We have repudiated government obligations. We have made vast purchases of foreign silver at double the price of 1933. We are glad to say we have now enough foreign silver to plate all the spoons in the world."

Soon after assuming office three years ago President Roosevelt commented upon my partial failure to persuade a Democratic Congress to balance the budget. He said sternly: "Too often in recent history liberal governments have been wrecked on the rocks of loose fiscal policies. We must avoid this danger."

Those rocks are now looming up out of this fog. The nation has been steered into the dangerous channels of borrowing these vast deficits from the banks, by a huge cycle of bank credit inflation. That is printing-press credit. The charts of all history show this channel leads to currency inflation. Every democracy which entered these straits has been sunk.

The explosive forces of inflation are already being generated. That is easily proved. The average prices of industrial common stocks today are up to the level of 1926. But in 1926 there were no unemployed; today there are 10,000,000 unemployed. In 1926 our foreign trade was flourishing; today it is demoralized. In 1926 our budget was balanced, our currency was stable; today the budget is the worst unbalanced in history, the currency has its foundation in the will of one man.

The average price of industrial stocks has been restored to 1926, but have the real incomes of farmers and labor been restored to 1926?

We may well explore a little further as to what all this confusion of national finances means to the average man or woman. These currency and credit policies have driven men all over the nation into a scramble of buying equities to protect themselves. These policies have made a paradise for the speculator. He lives by shrewd anticipation in a land of confusion. Millions have been made in the stock market. Millions have been made by foreign speculators in silver. At the same time millions of Americans are tramping the streets looking for work. Speculation drains employment, it does not make it. Having opened the channels of greed, rightly the President may be worried over the greedy.

But worse than all that, out of these devaluation and inflation policies the cost of living inevitably and inexorably rises. The average man and his housewife will find these policies in every package they buy. They will find them in the decreased purchasing power of their insurance policy and their savings. Did it ever occur to American wage earners that the devaluation was a cut in wages? Some European statesmen were frank enough to say it when they did it. And on top of that somebody has to pay for this spending. Both we and our children will pay for these follies of our generation even if our liberal government escapes wreck upon the rocks of these loose fiscal policies. Does that point the average man to a "finer, better, happier life"?

The American people have a right to know and to know now what steps the President proposes to clean up this budget and money confusion. Unless this confusion can be quickly dissolved it will lead to one of the great tragedies of all humanity—inflation.

The fourth battalion of confusion is the administration of relief. Under that guise great sociological experiments have been undertaken. The government has gone into private business on a huge scale. These enterprises have created a million confusions and fears. Relief run from Washington and not from home has resulted in billions of waste spread over every town and country.

It has impaired self-reliance and morals both in individuals and in local government. The poison of politics is mixed in the bread of the helpless. The New Deal is optimistic that with relief under political control from Washington its dependents can be persuaded in their vote. But the ballot box is secret and the conscience of the average American man and woman may not be confused.

The New Deal is not confused in politics. National Planning has been a success in that field. But it is a moral confusion of every ideal of American government. For fifty years it has been an aspiration of America that our government officials should be removed from the political spoils system. The selection by merit through the Civil Service Commission was not alone to gain efficiency in government. Its purpose was to raise the morals of public life. It was to make impossible the bribe-taker, the invisible government of the greedy, and the corruption of elections. Since 1880 every President has steadily builded that service.

Let us examine the record. The Coolidge officials under the Civil Service were about 75 per cent. The Hoover increase was to over 81 per cent. The Roosevelt decrease has been to 57 per cent. This is exhibit A of New Deal idealism.

All this sometimes reminds me of the small girl who said, "Mother, you know that beautiful jug that you said had been handed down to us from generation to generation?" Mother replied, "Yes, Ann, what of it?" And Ann answered solemnly, "This generation dropped it."

But we may explore that still further. During the Hoover administration, despite the many emergency agencies needed to meet the depression, the total number of Federal officials was decreased by 10,000. But under the New Deal, part- or full-time political officials have been increased by over 335,000. In his Jackson Day speech the President urged committees of one to support the New Deal in the campaign. He has a good start with 335,000 committees—and their wives.

But the average man who does not get his feet into the trough has to carry these officials on his back.

We have started upon the road of business recovery. That began instantly upon the restoration of some degree of confidence by the Supreme Court. But it is a confused recovery. We have still 20,000,000 people on relief after three years. Our durable goods industries lag behind. That is where the bulk of the 20,000,000 on relief come from. Our construction industries depend upon long-term confidence. But long-term confidence is weak. By a confused currency, men do not have confidence in what $100 may buy five years hence.

Moreover, real and permanent recovery will not take place so long as every business man must make a blind bet on these confusions in Washington.

A balanced budget and a stable currency would put more men to work than the whole WPA. They need confidence, not confusion.

These gigantic plans of dictated economy were undertaken

without searching inquiry as to fact or experience. They were undertaken without even shaping on the anvil of debate. They were undertaken in disregard of the Constitution. They have been without adequate administrative checks and balances. They have been administered by political appointees of inadequate executive experience. Despite this horde of officials there is now disintegration and confusion in the halls of government.

The New York Times, a supporter of the administration, is the authority for the statement showing that the Resettlement Administration employs 12,089 Federal officials, that it is giving relief to 5,012 persons or families, that it costs $1,750,000 a month for the officials, and $300,000 a month for the relief. If that is true, each family head had $350 worth of Federal officials devoted to him each month to see that he got $60! He must be having a strenuous time keeping these officials busy.

We are deluged with inconsistencies in action and conflict in purposes. Statements, propaganda, and philosophy collide every day. Many are half truths and some are murky on that other half.

PART III

President Roosevelt has called upon the shades of his favorite past presidents to enliven the effervescence of righteousness which bubbles through intoxicaing waters of the finer life. He has at times recalled Jefferson, Jackson, Lincoln, and Theodore Roosevelt to justify this State of the Union. I have not noticed any call upon the shade of Grover Cleveland.

To clear up some confusion as to their views I may also summon the shades of these favorite presidents upon the same subjects.

First, Thomas Jefferson, who said, "Were we directed from Washington when to sow and when to reap we should soon want bread." Apparently this was forgotten when they created the AAA.

Jefferson also said, ". . . the principle of spending money to be paid by posterity, under the name of funding, is but swindling futurity on a large scale." That would seem even truer to the children of this generation.

President Jackson said, "All history tells us that a free people should be watchful of delegated power." He did not know what it was to watch perpetual motion in delegated powers.

Jackson also believed in "To the victors belong the spoils." He was contented by appointing 2,000 of his followers to office. After all, he had a moderate spirit.

Theodore Roosevelt said, "If a change in currency were so enacted as to amount to dishonesty, that is repudiation of debts, it would be very bad morally."

This quotation was not sent to Congress with New Deal currency bills.

And may I add one quotation from Daniel Webster, who says: "He who tampers with the currency robs labor of its bread. He panders indeed to greedy capital, which is keen-sighted and may shift for itself, but he beggars labor, which is unsuspecting and too busy with the present to calculate the future. The prosperity of the working people lives, moves, and has its being in established credit and steady medium of payment."

Theodore Roosevelt also made many remarks upon the Civil Service. For instance: "No question of internal administration is so important . . . as . . . Civil Service Reform, because the spoils system . . . has been for seventy years the most potent of all the forces tending to bring about the degradation of our politics." That is not often quoted out loud.

Theodore Roosevelt further said, "A broken promise is bad enough in private life. It is worse in the field of politics. No man is worth his salt in public life who makes on the stump a pledge which he does not keep after election. . . ."

There is more to that quotation, but I omit it lest it would create hard feelings.

The President quotes Josiah Royce. Perhaps he overlooked this remark from that philosopher: "The present tendency to the centralization of power in our national government seems to me, then, a distinct danger. It is a substitution of power for loyalty."

Just a quotation or two from Lincoln. He asked that President Polk answer certain questions, and said, "Let him answer fully, fairly, and candidly. Let him answer with facts and not with arguments. Let him remember that he sits where Washington sat, and so remembering, let him answer as Washington would answer."

That shows they used to treat Presidents less gently than we do.

Beyond all this there are more somber confusions. The ideals of liberty have been confused.

Behind all this is the great and fundamental conflict which has brought infinite confusion to the nation. That is the conflict between a philosophy of orderly individual liberty and a philosophy of government dictation.

Ten of the assaults upon liberty have already cracked against the Constitution of the United States. And has there been public outcry at their loss? There has been a lift to the soul of the Nation. Millions of average men and women have given thanks to the Almighty that the forethought of great Americans has saved for them freedom itself.

But the Court cannot deal with all the assaults upon the spirit of American liberty. It was the spirit of liberty which made our American civilization. That spirit made the Constitution. If that spirit is gone the Constitution is gone, even though its words remain. The undermining of local government by centralization at Washington, the spoils system, the reduction of Congress to a rubber stamp, these monetary policies—what of these?

The President implies he will not retreat, despite the decisions of the Court. We have heard mutterings that the Constitution must be changed, that it is outmoded, that it was useful only in the horse and buggy days. There was sinister invitation to Congress to "find means to protect its own prerogative."

No progressive mind will feel that the Constitution shall not be changed to meet the needs of changing national life.

But what is the change these men harbor in their minds? The American people have a right to know. They have the right to know it now.

Whatever that change may be, it must be clear of those confusions which impair the great safeguards of human liberty. There must never be confusion in the Bill of Rights, the balance of powers, local government, and a government of laws, not of men.

Do you not conclude that the State of the Union is one of confusion? Is this in the interest of the average man and woman?

Does this advance our children toward a "finer, better, and happier life"?

A great American once said in application to another crisis: "We have, as all will agree, a free government, where every man has the right to be equal with every other man. In this great struggle, this form of government and every form of human right is endangered if our enemies succeed. There is more involved in this contest than is realized by every one. There is involved in this struggle the question whether your children and my children shall enjoy the privileges we have enjoyed." That was Abraham Lincoln.

True Liberalism

COLORADO YOUNG REPUBLICAN LEAGUE,
COLORADO SPRINGS, COLORADO

[*March 7, 1936*]

PART I

THIS assembly marks the anxiety which stirs the nation. Never before have our young men and women so interested themselves in public questions.

It was not long since we fought a great war to "make the world safe for democracy." Hardly four years ago we accepted freedom as we accepted the air we breathed. No man thought our ideals were endangered in his lifetime. Yet now men freely propose how much of liberty we shall sacrifice. Certainly your freedom and your opportunities in life are being mortgaged.

Naturally I have been interested in the New Deal replies since I began discussion of these critical issues. The President said on Jan. 3, 1936: "We have been specific in our affirmative action. Let them be specific in their negative attack." I have tried to be obliging.

But they have made no answer to facts or chapters or verses given in proofs. They, however, are not taciturn as to personal remarks. I did note that one of the New Deal spokesmen in this debate seeks to justify the violation of their platform promises by claiming that I did not hold to our platform promises. There were thirty-nine promises in the Republican platform of 1928. Of these, thirty-seven were carried out even in depression by my administration. And those fulfilled promises included upholding the Constitution and the preservation of national honor. Two secondary promises broke against the obstinacy of a Democratic Congress.

I leave research into their platform promises to well-known Democratic leaders. The examination of spilt milk is of importance. It shows that certain people cannot be safely entrusted with the jug.

The New Deal was not included in the Democratic platform of 1932. But the interpretation of political forces does not rest alone upon platforms. It rests also upon a knowledge of the motives and aims of men and the forces they represent. Eight days before that election I stated that the real intention of these men was to tinker with the currency. I said their program would raise government expenditures to nine billion a year. I said it was their intention to put the government into business. I said it was their intention to undermine State and local government by centralization in Washington. I said it was their intention to regiment our people and undermine the American System with imported European philosophies. That was all vociferously denied. All those interpretations have come true except as to that nine billion—it was only 95 per cent correct.

During the past few months I have made some further interpretations of where we are now headed. I hear again from the New Deal spokesmen the old cat-calls of 1932—"creating fear," "creating fear."

The Formulas of Revolution

For many years I have studied the tactics and techniques in European countries by which Liberty has been dethroned and dictatorship erected by men greedy for power.

First they ascribed the tragic miseries of the times not to the Great War, where it belongs, but to some party or class. The great phrases born from the finest emotions of mankind were used to camouflage the greed for power. They made great promises. They demanded violent action against human ills that are only slowly curable. They claimed that sporadic wickedness in high places had permeated the whole system of liberty. They shouted new destructive slogans and phrases day by day to inflame the people. They implanted unreasoning hates in the souls of men. They first grasped at power through elections which Liberty provided. Then began the "must emergency instruments of power," "to save the nation." The first demands were powers of dictation over industry and agriculture and finance and labor. Legislatures were reduced to rubber stamps. Honest debate was shut off in the halls of deliberation. A powerful government propaganda was put on the taxpayers' bill, that hates and suspicions could be further inflamed. And all of these men insisted that civilization had begun all over again when they came into power.

In the final stages of European degeneration Liberty died from the waters of her own well. That was when the waters of free speech were poisoned by untruth. Then have followed the last steps to dictatorship, with suppression of freedom of speech, freedom of worship, of the courts, and all other freedoms. Men were goose-stepped in a march back to the Middle Ages.

Whether they know it or not, the New Deal has imitated the intellectual and vocal technique of typical European revolution. In the talking and legislative stages they made some progress. You will recollect also the claim that even civilization came to a dead stop on March 4, 1933.

But America has not reached these final stages. Thanks to a people of a great heritage, to the press and the radio, free speech still lives in America. I intend to use a little more of it tonight.

PART II

The American System of Liberty

My remarks tonight are addressed in large measure to the younger generation. It is you who will have to bear these increased burdens. It is you and your children whose opportunities are being limited.

But far beyond that, our immense objectives upon which depend the welfare of mankind require the faith, the idealism, the courage of youth that they shall not fail. This is more than an acceptance or a rejection of the collectivist ideas and blunders of the New Deal. You must carry forward. The problems of today are different from those of 3 years ago or 10 years ago.

But what sort of an America do we want? What should be our foundations? What should be our ideals?

Perhaps without immodesty I can claim to have had some experience in American life. I have lived all kinds of it. I have seen it in contrast with many countries. I lived my early boyhood on an Iowa farm. I lived it later as the ward of a country doctor in Oregon. I lived among those to whom hard work was the price of existence. The opportunities of America opened out to me the public schools. They carried me to professional training of an American university. I began by working with my own hands for my daily bread. I have tasted the despair of fruitless search for a job. I know now there was an economic depression either coming or going at that time. Nobody told me of it. So I did not have the additional worry of what the government would do about it.

But I have lived the problems of labor both as a workman and with the men who had to find the payroll. I have lived in the administration of industry with its problems of production and the well-being of men.

My profession took me into many foreign lands under many kinds of government, both of free men and of tyrannies. I saw the squalor of Asia, the frozen class barriers of Europe. I was not a tourist. I was associated in their working lives and problems. I had to deal with their social systems and their governments. And everywhere to the common people America was the hope of the world.

Every yearly homecoming was again to me a proof of the glory of America. I was each time refreshed by the sight of its less grinding poverty, of its greater kindliness and its greater spread of opportunity to the common man. It was more than that. It was a land of self-respect that comes alone from freedom of the spirit.

I participated on behalf of America in a great war. I saw untold misery and revolution. I have seen liberty die and tyranny rise. I learned of its unending calamities.

I have been repeatedly placed by my countrymen where I had need to deal with the hurricanes of social and economic destruction which swept the world. I have had every honor that any man could want, and I have seen the worst misery that men can produce.

These experiences with all these mighty forces which influence the destiny of humanity make for humility of conclusions. And I recount all this to give emphasis to one great conviction.

I believe in the American System of Liberty. I believe in it from thousands of experiences. I believe that upon its foundation is the one hope of the common man. It has faults. But it contains the only real ferment of progress.

There are other systems of Liberty. But at the heart of our American System is embedded a great ideal unique in the world. That is the ideal that there shall be an opportunity in life, and equal opportunity, for every boy and girl, every man and woman. It holds that they have the chance to rise to any position to which their character and ability may entitle them. That ideal is limited or ended if this nation is to be goose-stepped from Washington.

About every outstanding advance which has promoted the welfare of mankind in the last century has been born in countries of free men and women. The steam engine, electricity, automobiles, telephones, airplanes, radio, free schooling, the great advances in biology, are but part of them. I might include the adding machine but its present use by the New Deal raises doubts as to its contribution to the welfare of mankind.

On the other hand almost every one of the world's mistakes has its origin in personal government. Violation of treaties, great wars, persecution of the Jews and other religionists, and so on down to the fantastic laws by a Must Congress, and the slaughter of pigs.

YOUTH AND AMERICAN LIBERTY

American young men and women should have the right to plan, to live their own lives with just one limitation—that they shall not injure their neighbors. What they want of government is to keep the channels of opportunity open and equal, not to block them and then charge them for doing it. They want rewards to the winners in the race. They do not want to be planed down to a pattern. To red-blooded men and women there is joy of work and joy in the battle of competition. There is the daily joy of doing something worth while, of proving one's own worth, of telling every evil person where he can go. There is the joy of championing justice to the weak and downtrodden. These are the battles which create the national fiber of self-reliance and self-respect. That is what made America. If you concentrate all adventure in the government it does not leave much constructive joy for the governed.

In economic life there is but one hope of increased security and comfort for the common man, of opportunity for all. That is to adopt every labor-saving device, every discovery, every idea to reduce waste and the cost of producing goods. We must work our machines heartlessly but not our men. Thereby goods can be sold cheaper and more people can buy. That is the only sure road to a job for every man. It is the only road to restored employment. That production of a plenty can spring alone from the initiative and enterprise of free men. That is no system of robbery. It is action for the common service. That is destroyed at once by the grotesque notion that government shall limit production.

We cannot operate this world of machines and men without leadership. Competent leadership can come only by the rise of men and women in a free society by the impulse of their own ambition, character, and abilities. That leadership cannot come by birth, or by wealth, or be nursed like queen bees. That leadership cannot be chosen by bureaucrats. It comes from the ambition of free men and women against the polishing-wheels of competition. It comes in a system of rewards. America should not be divided into the "haves" and "have nots," but into the "doers" and the "do nots."

There are those who scoff at individual liberty as of no consequence to the poor or unemployed. Yet it is alone through the creative impulses of free and confident spirits that redemption

of their suffering must come. It is through them alone that social security can be attained. Our job is not to pull down the
great majority but to pull up those who lag behind.

PART III

BUSINESS AND AMERICAN LIBERTY

And at once we come to the relation of government to economic life. I have discussed many of its phases elsewhere. On
this occasion time permits me to refer only to the relations of
government to business. For in this field lies a large part of the
choice that youth must make.

We have three alternatives.

First: Unregulated business.

Second: Government-regulated business, which I believe is
the American System.

Third: Government-dictated business, whether by dictation
to business or by government in business. This is the New Deal
choice. These ideas are dipped from cauldrons of European
Fascism or Socialism.

UNREGULATED BUSINESS

While some gentlemen may not agree, we may dismiss any
system of unregulated business. We know from experience that
the vast tools of technology and mechanical power can be seized
for purposes of oppression. They have been used to limit production and to strangle competition and opportunity. We can
no more have economic power without checks and balances than
we can have political power without checks and balances. Either
one leads to tyranny.

And there must be regulation of the traffic even when it is
honest. We have too many people and too many devices to allow them to riot all over the streets of commerce. But a traffic
policeman must only enforce the rules. He will block the traffic
if he stands on the corner demanding to know their business and
telling them how to run it.

THE AMERICAN SYSTEM OF REGULATION

I am one who believes that the only system which will preserve liberty and hold open the doors of opportunity is government-regulated business. And this is as far from government-dictated business as the two poles. Democracy can regulate its citizens through law and judicial bodies. No democracy can dictate and survive as a democracy. The only way to preserve individual initiative and enterprise is for the government to make the same rules for everybody and act as umpire.

But if we are to preserve freedom we must face the fact that ours is a regulatory system.

And let us be definite once and for all as to what we mean by a system of regulation. It looms up more clearly against the past three years.

1. A great area of business will regulate its own prices and profits through competition. Competition is also the restless pillow of progress. But we must compel honest competition through prevention of monopolies and unfair practices. That is indirect regulation.

2. The semi- yet natural monopolies, such as railways and utilities, must be directly regulated as to rates to prevent the misuse of their privilege.

3. Banking, finance, public markets, and other functions of trust must be regulated to prevent abuse and misuse of trust.

The failure of the States, particularly New York, to do their part during the boom years has necessitated an extension of Federal action. The New Deal regulations of stock and security promotion in various aspects have the right objectives. They were hastily and poorly formed without proper consideration by Congress. But they point right.

4. Certain groups must be appropriately regulated to prevent waste of natural resources.

5. Labor must have the right to free collective bargaining. But it must have responsibilities as well as rights.

6. At one time we relied upon the theory of "shirt sleeves to shirt sleeves in three generations" to regulate over-accumu-

lations of wealth. This is now guaranteed by our income and inheritance taxes. Some people feel these taxes take the shirt also.

But there are certain principles that must run through these methods.

1. The first principle of regulation is the least regulation that will preserve equality of opportunity and liberty itself. We cannot afford to stifle a thousand honest men in order to smother one evil person.

2. To preserve Liberty the major burden of regulation must fall upon the States and local government. But where the States hopelessly fail or when the problem grows beyond their powers we should call upon the Federal government. Or we should invoke the machinery of interstate compacts.

3. Regulation should be by specific law, that all who run may read. That alone holds open the doors of the courts to the citizen. This must be "a government of laws and not of men."

4. And the American System of Liberty will not function solely through traffic policemen. The fundamental regulation of the nation is the Ten Commandments and the Sermon on the Mount.

Incidentally, the government might regulate its own business by some of the standards it imposes on others.

There are certain humanities which run through all business. As we become more experienced, more humane, as conditions change, we recognize things as abuses which we once passed over. There are the abuses of slums, child-labor, sweated hours, and sweated wages. They have been diminishing for decades before the New Deal. They have not been solved yet. They must be solved. We must not be afraid to use the powers of government to eliminate them.

There will be periodic unemployment in any system. It is even so in the self-declared economic heavens of Socialism and Fascism. With common sense we could provide insurance programs against it. We could go further and prevent many causes of depressions.

Out of medical and public-health discoveries we have in

eighty years increased the number of people over sixty years of age from four per cent to eight per cent. That imposes another problem upon us.

This American System has sprung from the spirit of our people. It has been developing progressively over many generations. However grave its faults may be they are but marginal to a great area of human well-being. The test of a system is its comparative results with others and whether it has the impulses within to cure its faults. This system based on ordered liberty alone answers these tests.

The doors of opportunity cannot be held open by inaction. That is an ideal that must be incessantly fought for.

These doors are partly closed by every gentleman who hatches some special privilege. They are closed to somebody by every betrayal of trust. But because brickbats can be used for murder we do not need stop building houses. These doors are partly shut by every needless bureaucrat. And there is the tax collector. He stands today right in the door.

Every new invention, every new idea, every new war shifts and changes our economic life. That greatest instrument of American joy, the automobile, has in twenty years shifted regulation in a hundred directions.

Many obstructions and abuses have been added by the New Deal. Many of them are older but no worse. While the inspiration to reform comes from the human heart, it is achieved only by the intellect. Enthusiastic hearts have flooded us with illusions. Ideals without illusions are good. Ideals with illusions are no good. You may remember that youth with a banner of strange device. Was it "Excelsior" or was it "Planned Economy"? He froze to death.

PART IV

GOVERNMENT–DICTATED ECONOMIC LIFE

Young men and women have grave need to look into this New Deal alternative to our American System.

If any one does not believe there is a bite in that innocent term

"Planned Economy," he might reread this paragraph from one of the leading New Deal spokesmen:

"It is . . . a logical impossibility to have a *planned economy* and to *have business operating its industries,* just as it is also impossible to have one within our present *constitutional* and *statutory structure.* Modifications in both, so serious as to mean *destruction* and *rebeginning,* are required."

That is involved language but if it means anything it means that both private business and the Constitution must be modified so seriously as to mean destruction and rebeginning.

The President, far from repudiating these ideas, has continuously supported "Planned Economy." On one occasion he said, ". . . All of the proposals and all of the legislation since the fourth of March have not been just a collection of haphazard schemes but rather the orderly component parts of a connected and logical whole."

The Supreme Court has removed some ten of these component parts. And rather than have the score raised to thirteen before an election we have seen three more quietly removed. However, if the New Deal is re-elected they will be found to have a lot of spare parts.

Do not mistake. The choice is still yours. But the New Deal has no choice. The New Deal is committed to drive ahead for government dictation of our economic life. It is committed by a thousand statements, by a thousand actions. It is committed by the supporters upon whom it is dependent.

The President assures them "we will not retreat." They did mention a breathing spell. A spell is a very limited period.

I have spoken at length upon these subjects elsewhere, but I may remind you of a few examples of the choice that the New Deal offers to youth. Under that "connected and logical whole" a man could be fined and sent to jail for starting a new business of his own; for refusing to sell his own products as directed; for not reducing his production; for increasing his production if his energies found a market; for selling at prices below his competitors; or for having 101 gold dollars.

Also you might note that when you ask the man with a profit

and loss motive for a job, he asks just one thing, "Can you do the job?" When you ask the government for a job, your ability is second to your politics, your delivery of votes, and your affiliations generally. That is not equality of opportunity.

And what of this managed currency and this managed credit, which threaten Liberty and opportunity with the poison of inflation? What of this governmentally raised cost of living? What of all this continued waste and folly wrought in the name of relief? What of the folly of these purchases of foreign silver? What of the debauchery of the Civil Service and the politics in relief?

What of the taxes that will ooze from this spending and debt all your lives?

Do not mistake. The new taxes of today are but part of them. More of them are as inevitable as the first of the month. The only alternatives are repudiation or inflation. No matter what nonsense you are told about corporations and the rich paying the bill, there will be two-thirds of it for the common man to pay after the corporations and the rich are sucked dry.

Taxation enslaves as well as dictatorship. Every increased dollar in taxes is a limitation upon your opportunities. It means you have to work that many days more for the government instead of for your own advancement. Your fireside talks in the future will be with the tax collector.

And where do we get to after all this attempt to supplant the American System? At the time of the election day in 1932 the American Federation of Labor reported 11,600,000 unemployed. Today, after three years of the New Deal, they report 11,600,000 unemployed. To get these people back to their jobs was the outstanding job of our government. It was the excuse given for all these doings. But the grim fact remains that it has failed in its primary purpose. And fifteen billion dollars will be added to the national debt before the New Deal is over.

PART V

What Is Real Liberalism?

We hear much as to who is a Tory, a Reactionary, a Conservative, a Liberal, or a Radical. These terms when used honestly reflect an attitude of mind. The political use of them was imported from England. They do not fit well in America. However, they have certain advantages. You can elect yourself to any one of these groups if you say it often enough. If you do not like anybody you can consign him to the one which is most hated by your listener.

Taking a compound of definitions coming out of Washington, the impression would be that the Tories do the money-changing. The Reactionaries are members of well-warmed and well-stocked clubs. The Conservatives are greedily trying to keep their jobs and their savings. The Liberals have the exclusive right to define the opinions of others. The Radicals do not know what to do but do it in every direction.

As a matter of serious fact, these terms have been used mostly for camouflage and for political assassination.

The natural choice of youth is toward true liberalism. True liberalism seeks all legitimate freedom first, in the confident belief that without such freedom the pursuit of other blessings is in vain. Liberalism is a force true of the spirit, proceeding from the deep realization that economic freedom cannot be sacrificed if political freedom is to be preserved.

It is a false liberalism that interprets itself into dictation by government. Every step in that direction crushes the very roots of liberalism. It is the road not to liberty but to less liberty. The spirit of liberalism is to create free men. It is not the regimentation of men. It is not the extension of bureaucracy. You cannot extend the mastery of government over the daily life of a people without somewhere making it master of people's souls and thoughts.

Today, however, the term Liberal is claimed by every sect that would limit human freedom and stagnate the human soul

—whether they be Fascists, Socialists, Communists, Epics, or New Dealers.

This misuse of English political terms is used to cover the confusion of thought that pumps from the New Deal. Yet our American problems cut squarely across such muddy classifications.

If an open mind, free to search for the truth and apply it in government, is liberal, then you should be liberal.

If belief in open opportunity and equal opportunity has become conservative, then you should be conservative.

If belief that this can be held only in a society of orderly individual initiative and enterprise is conservative, then you should be conservative.

If opposition to those things which abuse and limit equal opportunity, such as privilege, monopolies, exploitation, or oppression whether in business or in government, is liberal, then you should be liberal.

If opposition to managed economy whether of the Socialist, Fascist, or New Deal pattern is Tory, then you should be Tory.

If the humane action to eliminate such abominations as slum squalor, child labor, and sweated labor, to give greater protection from unemployment and old age is radical, then you should be radical.

If the use of all the powers of the government to relieve our people from hunger and cold in calamity is radical, then you should be radical.

If belief in the old-fashioned virtues of self-reliance, thrift, government economy, of a balanced budget, of a stable currency, of fidelity of government to its obligations is reactionary, then you should be reactionary.

If holding to the Bill of Rights with its safeguards of the balance of powers and local government is Tory, then you should be Tory.

If demand that change in the Constitution be by open submission to the people and not by subterfuge constitutes reaction, then again you should be reactionary.

If demand that we have a government of laws and not of

bureaucrats is conservative, then you should be conservative. If you agree with all this, then you have shed yourselves of many "isms" or you have melted them into plain Americanism.

If you add to that a belief in decency of Americans, a conception of spiritual prosperity, and a faith in the greatness of America, you will have lifted these realities to the realms of idealism.

But it all sums up to this—whether the choice of youth will be to carry on that liberty for which Americans have died upon a thousand battlefields.

PART VI

EXPANDING OPPORTUNITIES OF YOUTH

I hear much that new opportunity for youth is gone. It occurs to me that for 150 years God-fearing people under the blessings of freedom built up quite a plant and equipment on this continent. It teems with millions of farms and homes and cattle and pigs, despite the AAA. There are railroads, highways, power plants and factories, stores and banks, and money-changers. There are towns and magnificent cities. There are newspapers, colleges, libraries, orchestras, bands, radios, and other noises. It is very sad, but did it ever occur to you that all the people who live in these houses and all those who run this complicated machine are going to die? Just as sure as death the job is yours. And there are opportunities in every inch of it.

The New Deal would dim your dreams of new adventure by telling you that there is nothing to do any more but run the old plant. The President on one occasion stated: "Our industrial plant is built. . . . Our last frontier has been reached. . . . Our task now . . . is the sober, less dramatic business of administering the resources and plants already in hand, etc." That no doubt excepts the new government plants.

As a matter of fact, science and invention during even these troubled years since the war have given us further mighty powers of progress. These inventions will create a thousand new frontiers. You have the blood and the urge of your American forebears. You are as good stuff as they. You are better trained and equipped than they were. I have no doubt of your character and your resolution. I know American youth is champing at the bit to take advantage of an opening world. From that, if we preserve the American System of liberty, we could have a century of glorious opportunity to every young man and woman. We could have a century of unparalleled progress to the nation.

Are Our National Problems
Being Solved?

FORT WAYNE, INDIANA

[April 4, 1936]

PART I

THE essence of a free government is debate. The problems of America are not the private property of those temporarily in office. Informed public opinion is often surprisingly quickly transformed into action.

Since last October I have debated a number of our most urgent national problems. I have reviewed results. I have suggested methods of solution.

As answer the New Deal subordinates have loosed a smoke screen of personalities and have begun to fire the squirt guns of propaganda. These are not answers that add to understanding. They are not the bold answer of responsible leaders expounding their point of view and offering their solutions. And slogans do not even pinch-hit for facts.

The most dangerous invasions of liberty by the New Deal have not been in the economic field as violent as they are. The Supreme Court can check that. The corruption of clear thinking is in the long view far more insidious and destructive to the safeguards of America.

Civilization has advanced only whenever and wherever the critical faculty in the people has been free, alive, and unpolluted. It slumps whenever this is misinformed, suppressed or intimidated. That is the most certain lesson in history. They who have the thirst for power over the daily lives of the people, in order to protect themselves from the political consequences of their actions, are driven irresistibly and without peace to a greater and greater control of the nation's thinking.

Those who seek for power thus move easily from propaganda to raucous denunciation. From that it is but a step to intimidation. And we witness today the seizure of private communications of innocent persons and the press. That is gross violation of the spirit of the Bill of Rights. But Americans are not easily intimidated. A number of the unterrified have taken to sending me pungent telegrams, expressing the prayer that some New Deal agency will seize them and commit every word of them to memory. This may be the modern method of the Constitutional right of petition—at least of bringing petitions under the eyes of the New Deal.

PART II

There are some phases of these so-called answers in this debate to which I wish again to refer.

There is an elaborate phantasmagoria to which the New Deal spokesmen seek to give life with their pulmotor of propaganda. That relates to the situation in the country when they came into power on March 4, 1933.

Mr. Roosevelt is anxious that the American people shall believe that the nation was "in ruins" when he took office. From the panic of bank depositors which greeted his inauguration he concludes that the Republicans did it.

That incident is still used to justify his abandoned promises. It is still used as the excuse for the attempt to transform the fate of a nation. We may, therefore, explore a little further into this particular question.

I hardly need restate the fact, now well established by disinterested economists the world over, that America was shaking itself clear of the depression, under its Republican Administration, in June–July, 1932. The whole world started forward. Prosperity had actually swung around the corner and was on its way up the street of our national life when it encountered the change in national policies. After Mr. Roosevelt's election in 1932 we alone of all great nations were set back. Most other nations continued forward.

The causes which produced that skid in national progress are now a matter of documented public record available to everybody.

I may mention just one incident. On February 17, 1933, fifteen days before Mr. Roosevelt's inauguration, it had become apparent that a panic was inevitable unless Mr. Roosevelt would co-operate to allay fear. I, as President of all the people, addressed to Mr. Roosevelt as President-elect of all the people a personal appeal in my own handwriting which was delivered personally to him by a trusted messenger. It contained these words:

A most critical situation has arisen. The major difficulty is the state of public mind . . . a statement by you upon two or three policies of your administration would restore public confidence . . . by the removal of fear.

With the election there came the natural and inevitable hesitation. . . . A number of discouraging things have happened on top of this. . . . The breakdown in balancing the budget. . . . The proposals for inflation . . . the publication of R. F. C. loans [by the Democratic Congress] . . . a state of alarm . . . rapidly reaching a crisis . . . flight of capital . . . foreign withdrawals of gold . . . hoarding. It is obvious that you . . . are the only one who can give prompt assurance that there will be no tampering or inflation of the currency, that the budget will be unquestionably balanced.

But no such assurance was forthcoming. In a word I asked that the whispers of speculators and others that Mr. Roosevelt did not intend to keep his campaign promises should be stopped by an emphatic public confirmation of those promises. That those speculators and insiders were right was plain enough later on. This first contact of the "money changers" with the New Deal netted those who removed their money from the country a profit of up to 60 per cent when the dollar was debased.

The urgent necessity for the President-elect to make such

a statement to stop the panic was urged by others including the Advisory Council of the Federal Reserve Board and by responsible newspapers. The usual reply is that the President-elect had no responsibilities until March 4th. There are a dozen answers to that. One is that every American citizen has a responsibility. Another is that as President-elect he had not hesitated on December 29, 1932, to take the unprecedented responsibility of ordering the Democratic Congress to oppose the steps I had taken to balance the budget.

Having got the nation into that hole, the Administration showed great determination and speed in getting us out. For this latter they deserve credit.

That unnecessary bank panic created a temporary slump in the upward movement of farm and other prices and employment. And we listen every day to the New Dealers chant like a Greek chorus of the doleful bottom from which they started.

Some of their spokesmen are so tragic as to announce that the "tramp of revolution" was in the air. Those young men have yet to learn that bank depositors even in a panic have not been known to lead revolutions. A sane people with a heritage of orderly democracy do not revolt by violence. America had no thought of Revolution. But revolution was in the minds of the Brain Trust. They had nothing else on their minds. However, they did deeply touch the national funny-bone.

These men did use the occasion to grasp for power. They did try to impose a new system on the American people. For months they called it the Roosevelt Revolution. They liked that word Revolution for quite a while! The implication of that thrilling heroic word has now been softened to the soothing idea of a more abundant life.

PART III

What interests a great nation is the route to safety and prosperity for all the people. To find that route we must have an understanding of the obstructions which detour us from national progress. On these questions we may have widely differing points of view and we may hold these differences honestly.

Obviously the immediate problem was the depression. And here if we are to have national understanding we must enter for a moment on higher economics even if it is dull.

Depressions are not new in human history. All of them are preceded by wars or inflation or booms with sprees of speculative greed. When they are world-wide that makes them worse. No government can legislate away the morning after any more than it can legislate away the effect of a tornado—not even the New Deal.

The real cure of depressions is in prevention of their causes. That is one of the greatest of all human problems, and I believe it can be largely achieved. But let me say bluntly that when one is upon us there is only one road to recovery.

Fictitious values must come down. Wild stock promotion must be liquidated. Wreckage must be cleared away. Get-rich-quick ideas must evaporate. Life must be put on a saner and simpler basis. People just have to rearrange the furniture of their minds. Costs must be reduced that prices may be reduced and thus more people can buy. Thereby there is more consumption, more production, more jobs. It takes time. It takes patience. It takes courage. Losses are inevitable.

Ending the misery of unemployment comes at once when these obstructions are eliminated. In a free country everybody goes to work to solve his own problems. The sum of all these efforts makes the movement upward just as inexorable as the movement downward. That is the higher economics of it.

But this depression had two features different even from other great depressions of history. Our banking system was not organized to meet such shocks, by its very decentralization. The whole world was tormented by social unrest and economic panaceas.

Our government had in the past never taken action of any great importance in depressions or panics, no matter how much the losses or suffering. There were three alternatives in front of us. We could let the depression liquidate itself out with all the dangers and suffering. We could adopt the methods later attempted by the New Deal. These have proved wrong ever since they were tried by Emperor Diocletian. And he was about the last of the Roman emperors.

We chose a new alternative. We determined that the government should help protect the people from storm—that it should assist recuperative forces. I held that it must see that food and shelter were given to those in distress. I held that government must inspire co-operation among the people to protect themselves. I held wages should not decrease more than the reduction in the cost of living. I held we must put before the people the shield of government credit to prevent panic and lessen bankruptcy. Above all, I held that we must maintain that Gibraltar of all confidence—the financial integrity and honor of the Federal government. That involved balancing the budget, keeping a true ring in the American dollar. I held we should co-operate with foreign nations in their efforts to prevent destruction and promote recovery. I held that we must protect our American institutions from social unrest and passions. I held that government must cling to certain principles of American liberty fought for in this land for 160 years.

Under these policies economic forces turned upward in July, 1932.

Then arrived the New Dealers with their point of view. There was a youngster once who told his father that the teacher wanted him to bring to school simple statements of the Einstein theory and of the New Deal. Father said, "We will begin with the Einstein theory, that is easier."

Mr. Roosevelt's campaign for election was based upon the implication that the depression was caused by me personally. That is a great compliment to the energies and capacities of one man. From this point of observation they got the conclusion that depressions could be easily cured by the magic of spending, priming the pump, tinkering with currency and credit, artificially increasing prices. They limited production in both farm and factory to create artificial profits. They imposed higher costs on industry and thus forced up prices. They adopted the curious concept of economy of scarcity. And all the time they were trying to change the American system to match the Middle European ideas. Public confidence in the long future was thus dominated by fear. From it all they slowed down the natural forces of recovery which were in motion. Thereby they greatly retarded recovery. And the price of that is infinite misery and anxiety to those whose jobs have been delayed.

The Supreme Court in effect wiped off this fantasy of scarcity through the NRA and AAA decisions. It removed obstacles and confusions. It restored confidence in our institutions. The natural forces of recovery now again move forward.

The nation needs recovery beyond all conception. One practical reason is that people think more clearly with the aid of black ink rather than with red ink or the short-pay envelope. And incidentally, the New Deal does not fail to remember that Chanticleer crowed each morning and claimed credit for the rising sun. You remember "we planned it that way."

But the result of the New Deal policies which remain has been to give us a ragged picture of recovery. We witness the increase in the market value of corporation common stocks from about 30 billions at the time of the election in 1932 to about 60 billions today. That is about 100 per cent. There are said to be about 8,000,000 different common stockholders. There are also about 8,000,000 farmers. I have not noticed any thirty billion rise for these farmers. There are more unemployed. The temple of finance seems more comfortable today than the temple of labor. Or the temple of Agriculture. Anyway, money-changers have got more jobs than the forgotten man.

PART IV

And continuously, day in and day out, before and even since his inauguration, and in the evening by the fireside, Mr. Roosevelt has condemned with great bitterness the policies and methods of the last Republican Administration. And that has become another chant of the Greek chorus. That chorus was louder under the artificial lights of promise than it is now in the daybreak of performance.

And the saddest blow of all is that certain New Dealers now

arise and say that I was the father of the New Deal. Omitting their monetary and spending debauch, about all the agencies they will have left after the Supreme Court finishes cleaning up their unconstitutional actions will be the institutions and ideas they got from the Republican Administration.

The reaction to those decisions is likely to be a new series of propaganda entitled the new book of Martyrs.

We have now lived through three years of Mr. Roosevelt's administration. It would now seem fair for me to ask the following questions.

Did this Administration keep the promises upon which it was elected?

Has it solved our great national problems?

Some of the multitude of New Deal policies have been right. The American people do not expect policies undertaken to reach 1000 per cent batting average. But a baseball statistician says their batting average on promises has been .033. On major policies it has been .030. On the Constitution it has been .006.

In other addresses I have debated many phases of these questions. I may quickly summarize those discussions. And to do it I must use figures and statistics. Demagoguery abhors arithmetic except when it adds zeroes to its expenditures.

UNEMPLOYMENT

You will remember Mr. Roosevelt's assurances of quick restoration of employment. The New Dealers said every one was to be at work on Labor Day, 1933. The Federation of Labor now reports 12,600,000 unemployed as against 11,600,000 which they reported when Mr. Roosevelt was elected.

Whatever these disputed figures are, they do not measure the full story. When this Administration increases government expenditures by three or four billions a year over the Republican Administration, they buy cement and a thousand things which create jobs. But these men are as much on the government payroll as if they were on the WPA. In that light we have many more men out of real permanent jobs. That is a pitiful result from three years' colossal expenditure of public money for priming the pump.

It has given employment to about 300,000 new political officials to work the pump handle. They use only one hand at the handle and pull voters with the other.

The first job of the nation is to get these self-respecting people back to real jobs. That will come about when sound economic policies for handling this depression are restored and not before.

May I ask, has the problem of unemployment been solved?

RELIEF

Mr. Roosevelt severely criticized the Republican methods of organizing relief. Great politics was made out of human misery. The New Deal jerked the administration of relief from the hands of devoted men and women of each community, where responsibility had been lodged by my Administration. That destroyed local concern to neighbors. That undermined the sense of responsibility in local government. Our national morning prayer is now directed to the Federal Treasury. I have shown in a former address that the expenditure including Federal, State, and local was raised from $1,100,000,000 per annum up to over $3,500,000,000 per annum. Of this between $400,000,000 and $500,000,000 is overhead for this Federal political machine. And there are about the same number of people on relief.

That the health and strength of the people were maintained by local administration is demonstrated by every statistical service. Infant mortality, for instance, was less in 1932 than ever before or since.

The present Federal Relief Administration should be dissolved. The new appropriation of one and a half billions should be allocated to a restored local administration. Those in distress would be better served—and with less politics in the bread.

Has the relief problem been solved?

REDUCTION OF EXPENDITURES

You recollect that Mr. Roosevelt promised the voters to reduce government expenses by 25 per cent. The idea that this could be done was no doubt based upon the savings proposed by my Administration and rejected by the Democratic Congress. They did not emphasize the origins of their story at that time. The last Republican Administration spent less than three and one-third billions per annum after deducting recoverable loans and statutory debt retirement, and including postal deficit. The Roosevelt Administration on the same basis is today spending double that sum. That is about 100 per cent up instead of 25 per cent down.

May I ask, has the problem of government expenditures been solved?

BALANCING THE BUDGET

During that campaign Mr. Roosevelt laid much emphasis on immediate balancing of the budget. Yet the budget deficits in Mr. Roosevelt's Administration have increased year by year. Before these four years are over, after deducting recoverable loans, the total increase in the National Debt will exceed twelve and a half billions. This compares with less than one and a third billion after deducting recoverable loans during the last Republican Administration. That Republican increase of about 10 per cent of New Deal practice was bad enough. But it at least has the merit of being a residue after continuous battle with a Democratic Congress to keep it down.

May I ask, has the budget problem been solved?

CURRENCY

Mr. Roosevelt, four days before the election in 1932, said in effect that the gold clause was more than a contract, that it was a covenant.

What was that covenant? It was "payable in gold of the present weight and fineness." That was repudiated.

Why was the Republican Administration right in its battle to hold to that covenant? First it was to uphold the national honor. And there are practical reasons which can be shown now not in theory but in fact.

The dollar was devalued to 59 cents for the expressed and deliberate purpose of artificially raising prices. If that works the cost of living will rise up to 60 per cent. The consequence is that devaluation is a continuing and subtle reduction of wages and salaries. These never keep pace with rising costs of living. If they are right it is a reduction in the purchasing value of every insurance policy and every savings bank deposit. It is a transfer of values from corporation bondholders to corporation stockholders. There are 63 million life insurance policies, secured by bonds, while there are said to be 8 million stockholders. It injures every educational and hospital endowment. All this is a method of redistributing the hard-won savings of the forgotten man.

The President said in excuse that there was not enough gold to pay everybody who held gold obligations. You might as well say there are not enough coffins to bury the people all at one time.

Do not think I am advocating the return to the 100-cent dollar. It is too late.

But we do not have even a fixed 59-cent dollar. We have the black magic of managed currency. From that springs instability and lowered confidence in the future. That means fewer jobs for the unemployed.

May I ask, has the problem of a stable currency been solved?

The Credit System

The battle by the Republican Administration to sustain the banking and credit structure of the country was violently criticized in the campaign of 1932. Among strong words were "highly undesirable," "wholly unnecessary," "muddle," "government-created credit," "dangerous evil." There were no hard words left to me to use. The Republican Administration did boldly adopt unprecedented measures for placing the shield of federal credit in front of industry and agriculture. We did employ the Federal Reserve System to replenish the credit drained by the collapse in Europe. We did strengthen the gold reserves. We created the National Credit Association, and the Reconstruction Finance Corporation. We set up the Agricultural Credit Banks, the Home Loan Banks. We strengthened the Land Banks. We reformed the Bankruptcy laws so as to permit orderly adjustments between debtors and creditors.

These measures saved ten thousand institutions. They served to protect millions of men on their jobs and millions of the farm population from foreclosure. They guarded insurance policies and savings from destruction.

Despite its criticisms of these agencies and ideas the New Deal has used and expanded every one of them. They now choose to forget where they come from. But far from these sound measures we are today in a morass of printing-press credit. Beyond it the doors to the temples of speculation have been opened wide and handsome. We are again back to the job of getting rich quick.

But I ask, has the credit problem been solved?

BUREAUCRACY

In the 1932 campaign Mr. Roosevelt said:
"Abolish useless commissions and offices."

Let us explore a little. Despite the emergency agencies of which they complained the Republican Administration reduced the total of officials by 10,000 in the four years of the last Republican Administration. The New Deal by full- and part-time jobs has increased them by 325,000. Some thirty or forty new agencies of government have been created. And further 81 per cent of all federal officials were under the merit system when the Republican Administration left office. Today they are 57 per cent only.

And political bureaucracies have one positive conviction. It is that the Government should pay all their expenses including the expenses of their re-election.

May I ask, has the problem of bureaucracy been solved?

MONOPOLIES

You remember that promise so often repeated by Mr. Roosevelt in 1932—"Impartial enforcement of the Anti-Trust Laws to prevent monopoly," etc. You also remember that statement of the President—"History will record the NRA as the most important and far-reaching legislation ever enacted." Everybody knows the NRA piled up the most gigantic monopolistic practices since Queen Elizabeth. They restricted production, fixed prices, and brought destruction to small business men.

Time and again the last Republican Administration refused to listen to the siren of these NRA ideas. But no better proof is needed that competition was maintained by the Republican Administration than the orgy of monopolistic practices which broke loose on its abandonment by the New Deal. Today we have before us the full import of the NRA: It was framed on the exact pattern of Mr. Mussolini. And now Mr. Mussolini discloses that it is but the first step to complete Socialism. He has taken over the monopolies for the Government. And we are promised that the NRA will be born again in America.

May I ask, has the question of monopoly been solved?

TARIFF

You will remember Mr. Roosevelt's promises of "immediate" "drastic" reductions of the tariff. When Mr. Roosevelt made those promises I said that if protection to American industry and agriculture was taken away "Grass will grow in the streets of a hundred cities, a thousand towns; the weeds will overrun the fields of a million farms." At that time I believed in promises, so I was wrong about that grass. They have not dared to carry out those promises. On the other hand, they have in fact increased the tariffs by devaluation of the dollar. They continue to nibble them through secretly made treaties.

Tariff making by Congress has always been a sorry spectacle. Many duties are always made too high. Democrats as well as Republicans alike, log roll into that position. But the last Republican Administration established a new and vital reform in tariff making. We gave the first effective powers to the bipartisan tariff commission to lower or raise the tariffs on a proper basis. All proceedings were to be open to public hearings and in judicial form. The orgy of greed and privilege which surrounded constant change by Congress was at last done away with. This policy gave reality to the aspiration of progressive men over half a century.

But the New Deal has sidetracked this Commission. It has been replaced by the secret determination of tariffs in back rooms without public hearings, through so-called reciprocal tariff negotiations. Men are deprived of their livelihood by secret covenants secretly arrived at.

There is no greater exhibit of personal government in the whole New Deal. That is not democracy. However, if you contemplate welcoming a prodigal son you can get a fatted calf from Canada.

But has the tariff problem been solved?

AGRICULTURE

In the campaign Mr. Roosevelt promised a plan that would solve the most difficult of all problems, the restoration of agriculture. The principles he stated in his campaign had no resemblance to the plan he adopted as President.

Mr. Roosevelt bitterly denounced the methods of the Farm Board. That Board did make a valiant attempt to serve the farmer. It did cushion many blows which saved him hundreds of millions. From its experience the Board evolved more promising plans. These plans were rejected. The New Deal however did adopt every one of the discarded experiences of the Farm Board and added the joy of telling the farmer what to plant.

The regimentation of the farmer has failed. And so after three years we start all over again. And this time the New Deal goes back to the Republican ideas of 1932 for part of their program.

Some of the results of Mr. Roosevelt's plans still linger. The American farmer's export market has been given to foreigners. His domestic market has been reduced. The greatest food-producing nation in the world had been made partially dependent upon foreigners for its food.

May I ask has the agricultural problem been solved?

SOCIAL SECURITY

Mr. Roosevelt promised much—his administration has legislated much on social security. It points in the right direction. We should be in sympathy with legislation to protect old age and unemployment. And the methods adopted by the New Deal will need mighty revisions to make them do what is promised.

But the social security of the common man has received disastrous blows from the New Deal. These blows far transcend any gains he might get from the Social Securities Act. The first social security is a productive job. These government policies which keep 12,000,000 men walking the streets are neither economic nor social security.

Will the New Deal say that this stupendous squandering, this inevitable increase in taxes, do not diminish or undermine the economic security of the common man?

President Roosevelt answers this when he said:

"Taxes are paid by the sweat of every man who labors. . . . Workers may never see a tax bill but they pay in deductions from wages and increased cost of what they buy." Perhaps they will solve the old-age problem through earlier mortality of the taxpayer from worry.

And now will they say that the devaluation of the dollar and the inevitable effect on wages and insurance and savings contribute to the social security of the common man and his wife? And his children?

May I ask has the problem of economic security been solved?

OTHER PROBLEMS

There are a host of other problems.

Has the railway problem been solved?

Banking reform better than the Republican proposals was

promised. About the only reform effected is the political control of credit. But has the banking problem been solved?

And there is the foreign trade problem. If our trade were critically examined and adjustments made for devaluation and price changes, it would show little improvement from that worst year of 1932. In any event has it been solved?

And there is the stabilization of international currency upon which the expansion of farmers' markets greatly depends. The Republican negotiations were repudiated. But has the problem been solved?

And there is industrial peace. Let us look at the record. During the three depression years of the last Republican Administration less than 16 million man days were lost in strikes and lockouts. About 54 million were lost in the first three years of depression under the Roosevelt Administration.

Has the problem of industrial relations been solved?

There is another phase of this national discussion. That is the New Deal habit of offering great nebular objectives and promises without telling the method to attain them. It makes easy and soothing oratory. There are certain objectives upon which we would all agree. I should like to see every American have a safe job which supported his family in complete comfort and security. I should like to see him own his own comfortable home or farm. I should like him to have a vine, a fig tree, a radio, an automobile and all the other gadgets. I want to see him protected in old age. I want to see his children given just as much education as they can take. I want them to be surrounded with every public protection including good government. And above all I want to see every American free from oppression and fear of the future.

Probably two-thirds of American families have these things now. That is more than in any other nation. We want them all to have these blessings.

May I ask will the New Deal methods so far demonstrated take us to those ends?

Time prevents further exploration.

I have from time to time suggested progressive solutions to

many of these problems. But here let me add that when a man is about to drive over a precipice the first constructive suggestion is to tell him to stop.

And I would be glad if the thinking American people would soberly consider if the Republican Elephant, even though he has made mistakes, is not far more surefooted toward recovery and progress than the bounding white rabbits of the New Deal. I recommend that magician's animal as the symbol of the New Deal party. It travels in uncertain directions at high speed. It multiplies rapidly.

PART V

There is one issue that transcends all others. That is the issue of American Liberty. In the last campaign we charged these men with the intention to introduce these foreign creeds of Regimentation, Socialism, and Fascism into America. They denied it. No proof is needed after three years of these attempts at so-called Planned Economy; this government in business; this breaking down of constitutional safeguards by centralization of power; this reduction of Congress to a rubber stamp; this substitution of personal government of men for government of laws; and these attacks upon the Constitution.

The American people have a right to know and to know now whether the New Dealers will abandon these attacks upon the American system. They should stand up and repent or they should defend their intentions.

This economic system will change with time. The Constitution will change.

But there are the immutable principles of ordered Liberty that cannot be allowed to die in America. From that alone can come economic security and prosperity. That made the character and self-respect of Americans. For in Liberty is the spirit of independence. Independence among nations, yes. But there is far more than that. From ordered Liberty comes personal independence. That was the American dream. That was given us by the God of our fathers.

An American Platform

PART I

IN ADDRESSING an organization of women let me say at once that I have never believed the understanding of governmental problems differed in women and in men. But many years of observation have taught me that women have a keener perception of morals in government. They have a greater conscience in national ideals.

During the past year I have devoted myself to debate and the exposure of the New Deal for what it really is. I have done so solely because the republic is in great peril. These men have set forces in motion which unless they be stopped will lessen the living and happiness in every cottage. They will shrink the chance in life of every boy and girl.

I have offered constructive American alternatives. The President recently in addressing the youth of our nation advised them "to dream dreams and see visions." I have advised them to wake up.

The radio has carried these speeches into tens of millions of homes. The newspapers have printed them in tens of millions of copies. Thousands and thousands have written, opening their hearts to me, in passionate cry that we quicken this attack.

But the exposure of the New Deal is only one-half of the battle. The people are rightly demanding to know what we propose to do.

The Republican Convention will assemble in a few weeks. The Republican Party is the only available instrumentality through which an aroused people can act. The Democratic Party is imprisoned by the New Deal. We should dismiss all factional issues and invite those Democrats who feel as we do to join us in faith that we have but one purpose—that is to place the republic on the road to safety. The platform must be more than a party platform. It must be a platform for the American people. Upon the determinations of the Convention will depend the fate of a generation.

The bare planks in the platform can only be composed on a sheet of paper. They should be composed in the fighting words which the times demand. But behind these words must be the determination to restore American liberty and to revitalize American life.

Nor can we define our problems in the vague and distorted phrases of conservatism, liberalism, or radicalism. Those expressions mean nothing unless you precisely define them each hour. Our job is bigger than dialectics.

It would be far better that the party go down to defeat with the banner of principle flying than to win by pussyfooting.

PART II

The grim danger that confronts America is the destruction of human freedom. We must fight again for a government founded upon ordered individual liberty and opportunity that was the American vision. If we lose we will continue down this New Deal road to some sort of personal government based upon collectivist theories. Under these ideas ours can become some sort of Fascist government. In that case big business manages the country for its financial profit at the cost of human liberty. Or we can become some sort of Socialist state. In that case everybody gains as much as his greed for political power will bring him at the total loss of his liberty. I do not know whether Socialism or Fascism is the greater evil. I do know they are not the American dream. They have become the world's nightmare.

The President may deny that he intends to travel into a collectivist desert. But his policies are driving the people there. And many of his advisers glory in the progress already made.

In another sixty days the New Deal party will convene in this city, where American Liberty was first proclaimed. After Christianity, that was the greatest light which has ever flashed over the human horizon.

I trust those gentlemen will bare their heads before Independence Hall. Under the invisible presence of the men who founded a nation that liberty might live, they should apologize to the American people. Instead they will produce splendiferous alibis. But the spirits of Washington, Jefferson, Hamilton, Adams, and Franklin will judge their promises and their stewardship. These spirits may well wonder whence came these men, that they dare walk in such precincts.

The Republicans have not only to shake off these forces, we have to remove all abuses of liberty whether they were born before or since the New Deal.

Let me say this: The whole of economic argument, the whole of statistical evidence, the whole social argument becomes barren unless it is tested in terms of human beings.

This is a nation of men, women, and children, not a nation of railroads, machines, or land or economic abstractions. We must visualize it as a nation of homes. Indeed, most problems of government are an enlargement of the problems of every household.

To restore liberty and progress the Republican Party must furnish the country a program which covers:

A restoration of morals in government.

A revival of confidence and courage in the destiny of America.

Real policies of economic and social regeneration in place of the New Deal extravaganzas.

Realistic, drastic, and immediate reforms.

PART III

IMMEDIATE REFORMS

There are five horsemen of this new Apocalypse. They are Profligacy, Propaganda, Patronage, Politics, and Power. Their other names are Pork-barrel, Poppy-cock, Privilege, Panaceas, and Poverty.

As a result, after three years the number of unemployed is about as great as it was at election day in 1932. The agricultural problem is still unsolved. The business world has little confidence in the good intentions, or the sanity, or the integrity of our government.

There are certain steps that should be taken at once. I may summarize specific reforms I have already mentioned in public addresses.

This cataract of wasteful expenditure should be stopped. The budget must be balanced. The increase in debt must be ended. The gold standard should be re-established. These futile purchases of foreign silver should cease. The laws authorizing the President to inflate the currency and to gamble in foreign exchange should be repealed. Tinkering with credit inflation must be ended. We must stamp out that train of gunpowder. It leads to an explosion of inflation which itself alone would destroy any democracy. Genuine banking reform must be achieved. This horde of political locusts should be driven away. The spoils system should be extirpated once and for all. The Civil Service should be restored.

Return the administration of relief again to State and local non-partisan committees of leading citizens. Give them such Federal subsidy as meets the need of the unemployed. Take the favoritism of politics out of the bread of relief. By wise use of tariffs protect our farmers from this flood of imports. By wise use of subsidies find employment for our surplus acres in products we can use and can export. Restore foreign trade. Take the handcuffs off honest business. Stop the attempts to suppress free opinion. Obey the Constitution. Change it when necessary, but obey it. Give us a government of laws and not of men.

PART IV

ECONOMIC AND SOCIAL REGENERATION

These are but the first moves to get these 12,000,000 people back into productive jobs, to make secure the farmer's livelihood and the ability of business to expand its payrolls. Beyond this, the Republican Party must present policies of social and economic regeneration.

The test of the welfare of the nation is the way the average man and woman must live, the conditions under which they work, the way they raise their children, the way they conduct their government. The concern of every decent man and woman is to lift these standards. The impulses to social welfare must come from the human heart, but its realization can come only from the intellect.

America was the first nation to question that the poor must be always with us. But unless these New Deal economic policies are reversed there will be only increased poverty.

ECONOMY OF PLENTY

The party should pledge itself to reverse the whole New Deal planned scarcity into an economy of plenty. When that is done we have to put in motion those economic forces that will secure wider diffusion of this plenty. The notion that we get richer and more prosperous by producing less is about as progressive as a slow-motion film run backwards.

DISTRIBUTION OF PROPERTY

The party should stand for a constantly wider diffusion of property. That is the greatest social and economic security that can come to free men. It makes free men. We want a nation of proprietors, not a state of collectivists. That is attained by creating national wealth and income, not by destroying it. The income and estate taxes create an orderly movement to diffuse swollen fortunes more effectively than all the quacks.

THE GOVERNMENT AND BUSINESS

The American system is a system of regulated business and compulsory competition. When government dictates to business or goes into business it has gone into the business of coercion and tyranny. It slows down production and employment and makes poverty. But the consciousness of inner rectitude which goes with this New Deal greed for power leads to visions of loveliness that can bewilder a people into the jumping-off place.

If we are to preserve democracy we must make the government the umpire of business. If the New Dealers would go to a few baseball games they would learn that the umpire cannot play on the team and be an umpire. Bad business practices can be ruled off the field. But who is to umpire if the umpire is to pitch?

If the present powers of the Federal Government or the states are inadequate to protect the people from exploitation or monopoly and to prevent waste of natural resources, the Republican Party should have no hesitation in proposing constitutional authority to secure these powers.

The party must assure the country of more national resistance against high-pressure groups who would secure special privilege to the prejudice of the country as a whole. They have a right to present their needs and views. But the modern pressure tactics will disintegrate this democracy unless there is courage to resist them.

There are a multitude of other economic and social questions the sane solution of which means added security and added comfort to every home. The important thing is that the Republican Party must deal with them with forthright decision and with an open vision which befits a progressive nation.

I have discussed many of these questions elsewhere. There are three which are of special interest to women to which I might refer again.

CHILD LABOR

Every decent American agrees upon the abolition of child labor. Republican Presidents have progressively mobilized opinion against it. We did in twenty years decrease the number of children under sixteen in industry—that is, outside of farming, from about 900,000 to less than 200,000 at the last census report in 1930. That was a decrease in proportion of about 70 per cent in twenty years. The President said that under the codes child labor went out in a flash. It was mostly a flash in the pan.

The Republican Party must pledge that it will really be done.

OLD AGE PENSIONS

Many states under normally Republican governments have given old age pensions for years. We should approve of Federal subsidy to the states to strengthen and unify their efforts. The contributory pension part of the social security acts will require radical revision. It covers only 50 per cent of the people. This revision must be done in justice to the farmers if for no other of many reasons. The farmers are omitted from its benefits, yet they will be called upon to pay. The reason is that the support of the scheme is a charge upon wages and industry which will sooner or later be passed on to the consumer. It will eventually add 5 to 10 per cent to the cost of living. The farmer will be paying as much as the worker and get nothing. The Republicans must find a sane plan of old age pensions.

HOUSING

I have for years been promoting better housing. The last Republican administration established the Home Loan Bank system and the R.F.C. provisions for slum clearance. That was the first governmental effort to better the financing of home building. The whole New Deal housing set-up needs reorganization. We must get the government out of the home

mortgage foreclosing and house-renting business and give a
genuine impulse to better homes.

PART V

NEW MAGIC FROM THE NEW DEAL

Since I last discussed these questions the New Deal has
brought forth another new magic formula to reach the millennium. On April 25 President Roosevelt said: "Reduction
of costs of manufacture does not mean more purchasing power
and more goods consumed. It means just the opposite." The
President elaborates its benefits and implies it is the base of
his slogan for '36. If this word "opposite" means anything,
then this statement says that "increased costs of manufacturing
means increased purchasing power and more goods consumed."
Most of the world has been under an illusion about this up
to now. We had all thought that the way to enable the people
to buy more was to use every art of technology and government
to reduce costs and therefore prices, provided we held up wages
and incomes to farmers and others. We had relied on such
experiences as the automobile. We got about two-thirds of the
world's automobiles because the production costs and, therefore,
prices were brought down into reach of 20,000,000 families.

At least we now know why the New Deal has imposed all
their different devices of debts, taxes, restriction of production,
juggling with currency, and a score of other methods of artificially forcing up costs and prices. The magic formula may
also explain why we still have 12,000,000 unemployed. Certainly there is no joy for the consumer in this return again to
Planned Scarcity.

If I were writing a bill of rights for women I should include
something about her rights as a consumer. The woman does
most of the buying. She has to make things go around. She
has to do most of the saving. She has to protect the future.
These artificial increases in the cost of living all decrease the
amount she can purchase and save.

What of those women who must eke out the reduced buying power of these magic formulas?

Doctor Kemmerer, speaking in New York City a month ago, said: "We have already set into operation powerful inflationary forces which when they have ultimately worked out their influence on commodity prices will probably result in giving us a cost of living approximately double what it is today."

Over 40,000,000 women are the beneficiaries of life-insurance policies alone. Sixty-five per cent of all savings accounts are in the names of women. There are some 63,000,000 women and girls in the United States. We have been accused of a few forgotten men, but the New Deal has forgotten all the women. Lincoln said, "Don't swap horses in the middle of the stream." A school for Democratic ladies is repeating that advice. They should be sure it is a horse. My belief is that it is a white rabbit.

PART VI

Moral Regeneration in Government

The Republican Party must face tasks beyond economic and social regeneration. These are tasks of moral regeneration. The Republican Party was born to meet a moral issue.

A nation is great not by its riches or buildings or automobiles but through the character of its people. The fibres of that are work, thrift, piety, truth, honesty, honor and fidelity to trust. I emphasize this before a group of American women because it is at the knees of American womanhood that the men of America have generation by generation learned these standards.

The first standard bearer of these virtues must be its government and public officials. But there is apparently a New Deal in virtue.

Every spread of bureaucratic control that makes men more subjective or dependent on government weakens that independence and self-respect. National stamina suffers by encouraging parasitic leaners whether on doorposts or governments. There is self-respect and dignity that marks free men.

Honor in public life begins with political parties. The people must depend upon political parties to carry out their will. When men are elected to high office on certain promises and those promises are cynically broken, how may we expect a citizen to feel the obligation of a promise and good faith?

There are standards of intellectual honesty in government. Framed propaganda and perverted figures mislead the thinking of the people. Pressures upon the press lead down the same dark alley. That is salesmanship, not statesmanship.

There are standards of gentlemen in government. The seizure by the government of the communications of persons not charged with wrong-doing justifies the immoral conduct of every snooper.

There are standards of financial honor in government. The New Deal devalued the dollar. Thus it repudiated the covenants of the government to those who had entrusted it with their savings. Senator Carter Glass on April 27, 1933, rightly said: "To me it means dishonor; in my conception it is immoral." If a private citizen had repudiated 41 per cent of his debt to the grocer by just telling him it was off, at least he would be removed from his church. He also would be expelled from Wall Street. The government cannot restore the dollar, but do such transactions build character in a people?

The New Deal administration ordered every citizen to bring in his gold coin and receive $20.00 an ounce for it under penalty of jail. At the very time citizens were bringing in the small funds that many of them held against a rainy day, our government was paying $35.00 an ounce to foreigners to purchase gold. If a private person were to coerce his neighbor into selling him something for less than it was worth, he would be sent to jail. If financial honor does not rest in the government, can we expect it in the people?

The Republican Party has never dishonored the government promise to pay. We must demand a return to financial honor in government.

THE SPOILS SYSTEM

There is a gigantic question of morals in this spoils system. President Theodore Roosevelt said:

"The man who debauches our public life, . . . by the corrupt use of the offices as spoils . . . is a greater foe to our well-being as a nation than is even the defaulting cashier of a bank, or the betrayer of a private trust."

Recently I had opportunity to observe comparative morals in the spoils systems by a contrast between Tammany Hall and the New Deal. In a Tammany-dominated borough in New York in early 1933 before the New Deal, there were about 11,000 persons on relief. Tammany had appointed about 270 additional officials under their particular spoils system to manage a relief at a cost of under $30,000 a month for the officials. This job was taken away from wicked Tammany influence and directly administered by the New Deal. At a recent date there were in the same borough 2000 Federal officials appointed under the New Deal spoils system at a cost of $300,000 per month for salaries to manage 16,000 persons on relief. Tammany may learn something new in the spoils system. It was only 10 per cent efficient. And the same thing is going on all over the country and you know it.

Can the American people be bought with their own money?

And does any one seriously believe that when practically all of the people on relief over the whole country register Democratic that they are Democrats? We know thousands do not intend to vote the Democratic ticket. Does the action taken by these people to protect themselves from their own government make for character building and morals?

Does it improve national morals and character in our people when they see huge sums being rushed into politically important districts two jumps ahead of an election?

FIDELITY TO PUBLIC TRUST

There is no fidelity higher than that owed by public officials to the Constitution and the safeguards of liberty in our government. That extends far beyond the letter of the law. It must be supported in spirit. Anything less is betrayal of trust if this republic is to live.

When the New Dealers' Convention meets near Independence Hall they will no doubt summon with powerful oratory over a hundred broadcasting stations the shades of that heroic Continental Congress. I trust at that moment the American people will remember what the New Deal has done to the Congress of the United States in these recent years.

The independences of Congress, the Executive, and the Supreme Court are the pillars at the door of liberty. For three years we have not had an independent Congress. We have not even had a good debating society. We have had a rubber stamp applied by presidentially inspired gag rule. That is not fidelity to the spirit of the Constitution.

For the first time in American history the word "must" has been directed to an independent arm of the government by the Executive. The NRA was enacted by the House of Representatives in six hours. The AAA was given eight hours.

These measures would have gone far to transform the whole of America into a Fascist state if they had not been set aside by the Supreme Court. Yet they had been operated for months in violation of the whole foundation precepts of democracy. Small business people have been penalized, people lost their jobs, and a thousand discouragements loosed in violation of the Constitution.

Great groups of people receiving some special privilege have been built up. When this privilege is denied by the courts then the New Deal has sought to incite these people against the court as a public enemy.

The parliamentary principle of control of the purse has saved liberty a hundred times over these last 300 years. It has saved the people from injustice in taxes many thousand times. So little is the New Deal Congress interested that it made only casual inquiry into what would be done with a whole 4 billion 800 million dollars in one lump.

There is also that gigantic secret fund of $2,000,000,000, which was slipped to the President to operate in foreign exchange or to support government bonds on the market. Why, for the first time in American history, is there secrecy in government expenditures? Manipulation to support market quotations is properly prohibited to Wall Street under the Securities Act. There is little point of taking sharp practices out of private life and putting them into government. Is that a training in morals?

We have worried much in our history over the independence of the Supreme Court. We have more cause to worry over the independence of Congress. Congress has delegated its conscience.

If we examine the fate of wrecked republics the world over and through all history, we will find first comes a weakening of the legislative arm. It is in the legislative halls that liberty has committed suicide. For two hundred years the Roman Senate lingered on as a social distinction and as a scene of noisy prattle after it had surrendered its real responsibilities to personal government.

Sea lawyers may argue that these things do not constitute a violation of oath of office. Right-thinking people will hold that they are a breach of public trust.

PART VII

I want to see not only the restoration of liberty, not only economic recovery, not only solution of economic and social problems, not only a regeneration of morals in government—I want to see recovery of sturdiness, of courage and of faith in America. There is in every race some quality distilled from its racial life. Ours was the spirit of independence, of self-reliance, of devotion to duty in men and women. I have here a quotation from some country paper. I regret I have mislaid its source—but it breathes with honest Americanism.

"We [Americans] have been historically a self-reliant, vigorous, assertive people. We refused to stand for tyrants or tyranny in whatever form. We have depended on ourselves. We created our own opportunities. . . . We were not deterred by difficulties or defeated by disaster. We were resilient, courageous, fearless. We sought new worlds to conquer, obstacles to surmount, and success to attain. As a people we were firm, courageous, unconquerable. And now what are we? We want things done for us. We flinch or cave in in the face of opposition. We lack forthrightness and nerve to oppose things that are wrong."

The New Deal has not done all that, but some of it. We have for four years listened to a continuous defamation of everything that has gone before. Honest achievement of men has been belittled and attributed to improper motives. Things embedded in our patriotism are smeared with contempt. We are told we must surrender liberty for economic security. We are told that the frontiers of initiative and enterprise are closed. We are told that we are in ruins and we must begin anew.

People speak less today of the greatness of America. Pride in her achievement is weakened. There is doubt of her destiny.

We think of ourselves as poor and helpless. Yet with only 6 per cent of the population in the world we have more youth in schools of higher learning than all the other 94 per cent. We have more laboratories dragging new secrets from nature than all the others put together. We have more developed mechanical power than all of them. We can produce more food and clothes and iron and copper and lead and coal and oil than any other country in the world. We now have nearly two-thirds of all the automobiles, radios, and bathtubs in the world. We have a larger proportion of people who own their own homes and farms than has any other nation. In a generation we raised the purchasing power of wages by 30 per cent and we knocked two hours off each working day. This has been achieved under private enterprise and free men. They could do even more in another generation. Women have ever taken a larger view of life than men. It is now the life of America that is in question.

Our trouble today is moral as well as economic. Is it not time we jerk ourselves out of this, and clean out the high priests of these heresies? Should we not defy a few Brain Trusts and restore the national virtues of thrift and honor and hard work?

Then the greatness of America will shine again.

The Road to Freedom

REPUBLICAN NATIONAL CONVENTION,
CLEVELAND, OHIO

[*June 10, 1936*]

IN THIS room rests the greatest responsibility that has come to a body of Americans in three generations. In the lesser sense this is a convention of a great political party. But in the larger sense it is a convention of Americans to determine the fate of those ideals for which this nation was founded. That far transcends all partisanship.

There is a moral purpose in the universe. There are elemental currents which make or break the fate of nations. Those forces which affect the vitality and the soul of a people will control its destinies. They far transcend the importance of transitory even though difficult issues of national life.

I have given about four years to research into the New Deal, trying to determine what its ultimate objectives were, what sort of a system it is imposing on this country.

To some people it appears to be a strange interlude in American history in that it has no philosophy, that it is sheer opportunism, that it is a muddle of a spoils system, of emotional economics, of reckless adventure, of unctuous claims to a monopoly of human sympathy, of greed for power, of a desire for popular acclaim and an aspiration to make the front pages of the newspapers. That is the most charitable view.

To other people it appears to be a cold-blooded attempt by starry-eyed boys to infect the American people by a mixture of European ideas, flavored with our native predilection to get something for nothing.

You can choose either one you like best. But the first is the road of chaos which leads to the second. Both of these roads lead over the same grim precipice that is the crippling and possibly the destruction of the freedom of men.

Which of these interpretations is accurate is even disputed by alumni of the New Deal who have graduated for conscience's sake or have graduated by request.

In Central Europe the march of Socialist or Fascist dictatorships and their destruction of liberty did not set out with guns and armies. Dictators began their ascent to the seats of power through the elections provided by liberal institutions. Their weapons were promise and hate. They offered the mirage of Utopia to those in distress. They flung the poison of class hatred. They may not have maimed the bodies of men but they maimed their souls.

The 1932 campaign was a pretty good imitation of this first stage of European tactics. You may recall the promises of the abundant life, the propaganda of hate.

Once seated in office the first demand of these European despotisms was for power and "action." Legislatures were told they "must" delegate their authorities. Their free debate was suppressed. The powers demanded are always the same pattern. They all adopted Planned Economy. They regimented industry and agriculture. They put the government into business. They engaged in gigantic government expenditures. They created vast organizations of spoils henchmen and subsidized dependents. They corrupted currency and credit. They drugged the thinking of the people with propaganda at the people's expense.

If there are any items in this stage in the march of European collectivism that the New Deal has not imitated it must have been an oversight.

But at this point this parallel with Europe halts—at least for the present. The American people should thank Almighty God for the Constitution and the Supreme Court. They should be grateful to a courageous press.

You might contemplate what would have happened if Mr. Roosevelt could have appointed enough Supreme Court Justices in the first year of his Administration. Suppose these New

Deal acts had remained upon the statute books. We would have been a regimented people. Have you any assurance that he will not have the appointments if he is re-elected?

The succeeding stages of violence and outrage by which European despotisms have crushed all liberalism and all freedom have filled our headlines for years.

But what comes next in the United States? Have the New Dealers dropped their ideas of centralization of government? Have they abandoned the notion of regimenting the people into a Planned Economy? Has that greed for power become cooled by the resistance of a people with a heritage of freedom? Will they resume if they are re-elected?

When we examine the speeches of Tugwell, Wallace, Ickes and others, we see little indications of repentance.

Let me say this: America is no monarchy where the Chief of State is not responsible for his ministers. It has been traditional in our government since the beginning that the important officials appointed by the President speak in tune with his mind. That is imperative if there is to be intellectual honesty in government. President Roosevelt finds no difficulty in disciplining his officials. Witness the prompt dismissal of those who did not publicly agree with him. The President will not discharge these men on whom his New Deal is dependent. No matter what the new platform of the New Deal party may say, the philosophy of collectivism and that greed for power are in the blood of some part of these men. Do you believe that if re-elected they intend to stand still among the wreckage of their dreams? In the words of Mr. Hopkins, perhaps we are too profanely dumb to understand.

PART II

So much for the evidence that the New Deal is a definite attempt to replace the American system of freedom with some sort of European planned existence. But let us assume that the explanation is simply hit-and-run opportunism, spoils system, and Muddle.

We can well take a moment to explore the prospects of

American ideals of freedom and self-government under that philosophy. We may take only seven short examples:

The Supreme Court has reversed some ten or twelve of the New Deal major enactments. Many of these acts were a violation of the rights of men and of self-government. Despite the sworn duty of the Executive and Congress to defend these rights they have sought to take them into their own hands. That is an attack on the foundations of freedom.

More than this, the independence of the Congress, the Supreme Court, and the Executive are pillars at the door of freedom. For three years the word "must" has invaded the independence of Congress. And the Congress has abandoned its responsibility to check even the expenditures of money. They have turned open appropriations into personal power. These are destructions of the very safeguards of free people.

We have seen these gigantic expenditures and this torrent of waste pile up a national debt which two generations cannot repay. One time I told a Democratic Congress that "you cannot spend yourselves into prosperity." You recall that advice did not take then. It hasn't taken yet. Billions have been spent to prime the economic pump. It did employ a horde of paid officials upon the pump handle. We have seen the frantic attempts to find new taxes on the rich. Yet three quarters of the bill will be sent to the average man and the poor. He and his wife and his grandchildren will be giving a quarter of all their working days to pay taxes. Freedom to work for himself is changed into a slavery of work for the follies of government.

We have seen an explosive inflation of bank credits by this government borrowing. We have seen varied steps toward currency inflation that have already enriched the speculator and deprived the poor. If this is to continue the end result is the tears and anguish of universal bankruptcy and distress. No democracy in history has survived its final stages.

We have seen the building up of a horde of political officials. We have seen the pressures upon the helpless and destitute to trade political support for relief. Both are a pollution of the very fountains of freedom.

We have seen the most elemental violation of economic law and experience. The New Deal forgets it is solely by production of more goods and more varieties of goods and services that we advance the living and security of men. If we constantly decrease costs and prices and keep up earnings the production of plenty will be more and more widely distributed. These laws may be restricted in new phrases but they are the very shoes of human progress. We had so triumphed in this long climb of mankind toward plenty that we had reached Mount Pisgah where we looked over the Promised Land of abolished poverty. Then men began to quarrel over the division of the goods. The depression produced by war destruction temporarily checked our march toward the Promised Land.

Then came the little prophets of the New Deal. They announce the striking solution that the way out is to produce less and to increase prices so the people can buy less. They have kept on providing some new restriction or burden or fright down to a week ago.

Can Democracy stand the strain of Mother Hubbard economics for long?

At least it has enabled the New Deal to take a few hundred thousand earnest party workers to the Promised Land. It takes the rest of us for a ride into the wilderness of unemployment.

Any examination of the economic muddle of the past three years shows the constant thread of price fixing, restriction of production and drive against small business. That is the soul of monopoly. That has maintained from the NRA to the last tax bill. These are old tricks, not new disguises, which put shackles upon the freedom of men.

In desperate jumping from one muddle to another we have seen repeated violation of morals and honor in government. Do I need recall the repudiation of obligations, the clipping of the coin, the violation of trust to guard the Constitution and the coercion of the voter? When the standards of honor and morals fail in government they fail in the people.

There are some moral laws written in a Great Book. Over all there is the gospel of brotherhood. For the first time in the history of America we have heard the gospel of class hatred preached from the White House. That is human poison far more deadly than fear. Every reader of the history of democracy knows that is the final rock upon which all democracies have been wrecked.

There is the suggestion in the Gospels that it is the meek who will inherit the earth. That disinherits the New Dealers. There are recommendations to righteousness for righteousness' sake only. I will not elaborate that.

If all this is the theory and practice of Muddle where has it brought us, even now? We have spent $15,000,000,000 more than the last Republican Administration. We have a debt ten billions greater than even the great war debt. After three years we still have the same number of unemployed that we had at the election of November, 1932. These actions are bringing injury to the well being of people it purports to serve. It has produced gross reactionarism in the guise of liberalism. And above all the New Deal has brought that which George Washington called "alterations which may impair the energy of the system and thus overthrow that which cannot be directly overthrown."

Republicans! After a hundred and fifty years, we have arrived at that hour.

PART III

The New Deal may be a revolutionary design to replace the American System with despotism. It may be the dream stuff of a false liberalism. It may be the valor of muddle. Their relationship to each other, however, is exactly the sistership of the witches who brewed the cauldron of powerful trouble for Macbeth. Their product is the poisoning of Americanism.

The President has constantly reiterated that he will not retreat. For months, to be sure, there has been a strange quiet. Just as the last campaign was fought on promises that have been broken, so apparently this campaign is to be slipped through by evasion.

But the American people have the right to know NOW,

while they still have power to act. What is going to be done after election with these measures which the Constitution forbids and the people by their votes have never authorized? What do the New Dealers propose to do with these unstable currencies, unbalanced budgets, debts, and taxes? Fifty words would make it clear. Surely the propaganda agencies which emit half a million words a day could find room for these fifty. I noticed they recently spent three hundred words on how to choose a hat. It is slightly more important to know the fate of a nation.

PART IV

You have the duty to determine the principles upon which the Republican Party will stand. You make the laws of the Party. Whether it is within the Party or a government, our system is a government of laws and not of men. This Party holds its promises.

The immediate task is to set the country on the road of genuine recovery from the paths of instability. We have enough inventions and enough accumulated needs to start the physical rebuilding of America. The day the Republican Party can assure right principles we can turn this nation from the demoralization of relief to the contentment of constructive jobs. Herein —and herein alone—is a guarantee of jobs for the 11,000,000 idle based upon realities and not on political claptrap. In the meantime the Party which organized efficient relief of the unemployed three years before the New Deal was born will not turn from those in need. That support to distress comes from the conscience and sympathy of a people, not from the New Deal.

Four years ago I stated that the Republican Party must undertake progressive reforms from evils exposed by the boom and depression. But I stated our first job was to restore men to work. The New Deal has attempted many reforms. They have delayed recovery. Parts of them are good. Some have failed. Some are tainted with Collectivist ideas. That task must be undertaken anew by the Republican Party.

A new danger is created to the Republic in that the swing

from the foolishness of radicalism will carry us to the selfishness of reaction.

The Republican Party must achieve true social betterment. But we must produce measures that will not work confusion and disappointment. We must propose a real approach to social ills, not the prescription for them, by quacks, of poison in place of remedy.

We must achieve freedom in the economic field. We have grave problems in relation of government to agriculture and business. Monopoly is only one of them. The Republican Party is against the greed for power of the wanton boys who waste the people's savings. But it must be equally adamant against the greed for power and exploitation in the seekers of special privilege. At one time I said: "We can no more have economic power without checks and balances than we can have political power without checks and balances. Either one leads to tyranny."

The Republican Party must be a party which accepts the challenge of each new day. The last word in human accomplishment has not been spoken. The last step in human progress has not been made. We welcome change when it will produce a fairer, more just, and satisfying civilization. But change which destroys the safeguards of free men and women is only apples of Sodom.

Great calamities have come to the whole world. These forces have reached into every calling and every cottage. They have brought tragedy and suffering to millions of firesides. I have great sympathy for those who honestly reach for short cuts to the immensity of our problems. While design of the structure of betterment for the common man must be inspired by the human heart, it can only be achieved by the intellect. It can only be builded by using the mold of justice, by laying brick upon brick from the materials of scientific research; by the painstaking sifting of truth from the collection of fact and experience. Any other mold is distorted; any other bricks are without straw; any other foundations are sand. That great structure of human progress can be built only by free men and women.

Here in America, where the tablets of human freedom were first handed down, their sacred word has been flouted. Today the stern task is before the Republican Party to restore the Ark of that Covenant to the temple in Washington.

Does this issue not transcend all other issues? Is it not alone the ground of Republican unity but unity beyond all partisanship?

PART V

The gravest task which confronts the party is to regenerate these freedoms.

There are principles which neither tricks of organization, nor the rigors of depression, nor the march of time, nor New Dealers, nor Socialists, nor Fascists can change. There are some principles which came into the universe along with the shooting stars of which worlds are made, and they have always been and ever will be true. Such are laws of mathematics, the law of gravitation, the existence of God, and the ceaseless struggle of humankind to be free.

Throughout the centuries of history, man's vigil and his quest have been to be free. For this the best and bravest of earth have fought and died. To embody human liberty in workable government, America was born. Shall we keep that faith? Must we condemn the unborn generations to fight again and to die for the right to be free?

There are some principles that cannot be compromised. Either we shall have a society based upon ordered liberty and the initiative of the individual, or we shall have a planned society that means dictation no matter what you call it or who does it. There is no half-way ground. They cannot be mixed. Government must either release the powers of the individual for honest achievement or the very forces it creates will drive it inexorably to lay its paralyzing hand more and more heavily upon individual effort.

Less than twenty years ago we accepted those ideals as the air we breathed. We fought a great war for their protection. We took upon ourselves obligations of billions. We buried our sons in foreign soil. But in this score of years we have seen the advance of collectivism and its inevitable tyranny in more than half the civilized world. In this thundering era of world crisis distracted America stands confused and uncertain.

The Whig Party temporized, compromised upon the issue of slavery for the black man. That party disappeared. It deserved to disappear. Shall the Republican Party deserve or receive any better fate if it compromises upon the issue of freedom for all men, white as well as black?

You of this Convention must make the answer.

Let us not blink the difficulties. Throughout the land there are multitudes of people who have listened to the songs of sirens. Thousands of men, if put to the choice, would willingly exchange liberty for fancied security even under dictatorship. Under their distress they doubt the value of their own rights and liberties. They do not see the Constitution as a fortress for their deliverance. They have been led to believe that it is an iron cage against which the wings of idealism beat in vain.

They do not realize that their only relief and their hope of economic security can come only from the enterprise and initiative of free men.

Let this convention declare without shrinking, the source of economic prosperity is freedom. Man must be free to use his own powers in his own way. Free to think, to speak, to worship. Free to plan his own life. Free to use his own initiative. Free to dare in his own adventure. It is the essence of true Liberalism that these freedoms are limited by the rights of others. Freedom both requires and makes increasing responsibilities. There is no freedom in exploitation of the weak and in the dead hand of bureaucracy.

There's something vastly bigger than payrolls, than economics, than materialism, at issue in this campaign. The free spirit of men is the source of self-respect, of sturdiness, of moral and spiritual progress. With the inspirations of freedom come fidelity to public trust, honor and morals in government. The social order does not rest upon orderly economic freedom alone. It rests even more upon the ideals and character of a people.

Governments must express those ideals in frugality, in justice, in courage, in decency, and in regard for the less fortunate, and above all in honor. Nations die when these weaken, no matter what their material prosperity.

Fundamental American liberties are at stake. Is the Republican Party ready for the issue? Are you willing to cast your all upon the issue, or would you falter and look back? Will you, for expediency's sake, also offer will-o'-the-wisps which beguile the people? Or have you determined to enter in a holy crusade for liberty which shall determine the future and the perpetuity of a nation of free men? That star shell fired today over the no man's land of world despair would illuminate the world with hope.

In another great crisis in American history, the founder of this Republican Party, Abraham Lincoln, said: "Fellow citizens, we cannot escape history. We . . . will be remembered in spite of ourselves. No personal significance or insignificance can spare one or another of us. The fiery trial through which we pass will light us down in honor or dishonor to the latest generation. . . . We—even we here—hold the power and bear the responsibility. We shall nobly save or meanly lose the last, best hope of earth. . . . The way is plain . . . a way which if followed, the world will forever applaud."

Republicans and fellow Americans! This is your call. Stop the retreat. In the chaos of doubt, confusion, and fear, yours is the task to command. Stop the retreat, and turning the eyes of your fellow Americans to the sunlight of freedom, lead the attack to retake, recapture, and reman the citadels of liberty. Thus can America be preserved. Thus can the peace, plenty, and security be re-established and expanded. Thus can the opportunity, the inheritance, and the spiritual future of your children be guaranteed. And thus you will win the gratitude of posterity, and the blessing of Almighty God.

Gold Plank in the
Republican Platform

TELEGRAM TO CHESTER ROWELL
CALIFORNIA DELEGATION

[*New York, June 11, 1936*]

The text of Herbert Hoover's telegram demanding a gold plank in the Republican platform and received by Chester Rowell, chairman of the California delegation, follows:

I HAVE your telegram requesting my views upon the nature of the currency plank in the platform. They are as follows. They are some things on currency that must be remembered.

1. The term "sound money" was polluted by its being used to mislead the people by the New Deal. It is a weasel word.

2. So-called managed currencies will be managed by politicians and subject to pressures of demagoguery or special interest. There can be no economic stability in that quarter.

3. The New Deal devaluation to 59 cents when it becomes fully effective will reduce the purchasing power of 60,000,000 insurance policies and 20,000,000 savings bank deposits by 60 per cent. It will to a lesser extent reduce all wages and salaries. The Republican Party should guarantee that there will be no further devaluation.

4. A large part of our unemployment is due to lack of long-term confidence and consequently long-term capital for new enterprise and permanent improvement. These people cannot be returned to work and the farmers given a full market until that confidence is restored. That can only be fully restored by a currency convertible into gold.

5. The world for years has been engaged in a gigantic trade war using managed currencies and currency depreciation as principal weapons. The farmer's export market and his relief from imports cannot be fully assured until there is international currency stability. Putting up tariffs to meet manipulations of foreign currencies is an endless job. There must be restoration of currency stability by agreement and America must lead.

6. There can be no currency stability with a continued unbalanced budget and the constant danger of the inflation to meet Government deficits.

7. Foreign silver purchases and Presidential powers over inflation are intolerable afflictions added to managed currency. Therefore, it seems to me the course to pursue is:

(*A*) Repeal all Presidential powers over currency.

(*B*) Guarantee that there will be no further devaluation.

(*C*) Seek international agreement to stabilize currencies.

(*D*) Resolutely determine to restore gold convertibility of the currency, either in coin or bullion, as may be determined wise at the earliest practicable moment.

Reform in the Administration
of Relief

WOMEN'S CONFERENCE ON CURRENT PROBLEMS,
NEW YORK CITY

[*September 23, 1936*]

I HAVE been asked to speak for a few moments upon the administration of relief. And discussion of relief is not a part of life that can be lightened with humor.

Having one time and another organized relief of unemployment or famine caused by war or depression in some twenty-three nations I can at least speak with some familiarity of its problems. And these occasions have raised every aspect of administration that haunts us today.

Let me repeat at the outset the enlarged view of governmental responsibilities of this nation to which I gave expression six years ago. I then said: "As a nation we must prevent hunger and cold to those of our people who are in honest difficulties." That primary duty still holds. Relief must go on so long as there is need for it.

There are two parts to this responsibility. The first and transcendent one is the humane obligation to our fellow men and women in distress. This implies not alone the provision of a living but it implies organizing that individual helpfulness which gives hope, courage and self-respect.

The other responsibility is to execute this task without waste, for other human beings must toil and make sacrifice to provide relief.

In all this task we must have not alone conscience and heart but also intellect.

Relief Under Bureaucratic Organization

There are different ways of organizing and administering relief. We cannot contemplate nation-wide calamity as a permanent part of the life of the country. Therefore national relief from calamity is by the nature of things an emergency matter. There is not, nor can there ever be, a generation-trained politically independent bureaucracy waiting to administer it.

Even the best of bureaucracy free from politics can operate only in a world of checks and balances tangled with red tape. It must at least be governed with desk-made standards and rules which wind down a long cone from the top. Its final expression to the individual in distress is bound to be limited and ill adapted to the varied individuals and their poignant needs. And all the faults of bureaucracy are multiplied a thousand times when it is chosen by the political chairman and not by merit. A thousand new and malignant forces inevitably arise.

I do not need to point out that in every part of the country the columns of the newspapers, thousands of knowing citizens and the people on relief cry out against some form of waste, injustices or petty corruption or politics.

I realize full well the suffering that comes in these times. I realize the difficulties of large relief measures spread over a nation—I will not elaborate or emphasize the details of failure. I do wish to see these national duties better done.

The Present Experiment in Relief

In the nation-wide debate going on over the needed reform of relief administration, two alternatives are constantly set up. One is Federal centralization under Federal political bureaucracy. The other is local responsibility under local political officials. The defense made by the present method appears to be that the local political pot is the blackest. They claim that where that sort of decentralization has recently taken place it has proved incompetent and heartless. Whether this is true or not, these are the alternatives. What is overlooked is that political and centralized direction of relief of any kind will be wasteful and otherwise objectionable.

The only remedy lies in nonpolitical direction. It lies in completed decentralization of administration into the hands of the leading men and women of each State and community.

ORGANIZATION UNDER LOCAL RESPONSIBILITY

That basis of quick and effective local nonpolitical administration exists in America to a greater degree than anywhere else in the world.

One of the crowning glories of American life is the natural leadership in every community. That is the product of a democracy which in its very functioning is based upon voluntary action and co-operation. In every community there are from a dozen to a thousand men and women who have greater abilities than any bureaucracy. They have devotion and willingness to render such public service. They are sympathetic and understanding. In them their community has confidence. They are not politicians. They have their own jobs. But they will defer their own affairs till night and give their daytime free to assist their fellow townsmen. They will meet a community emergency without flagging. That has been tested time and time again.

This was the basis of organization for three years—1930, 1931, and 1932. At that time when it was my duty to see that relief to unemployment was assured, we spread over the country a network of local volunteer committees free from political domination. As the need of relief increased, the number and authority of these committees were extended until there were over 3000 of them. They were co-ordinated under State-wide committees by the national Director of Relief. They used existing organizations and the local authorities. This committee structure hired such paid staff as they required. The committees received no pay. Citizens of the type needed for such administration require no pay. They did the work with a minimum of administrative machinery and a maximum of volunteer service. They found jobs for the unemployed. They created a spirit in the community that held people from being discharged. They co-ordinated municipal, county, State and Federal, and private funds. They knew their own people and the needs of their localities. They were able to act without red tape. They determined whether relief was to be applied by cash, or in kind, or by work relief, as the immediate local need required. They gave particular solicitude to children. They gave encouragement and hope. They were doing neither politics nor social reform. They were taking care of distress.

From 1933, that organization was replaced or reduced to a façade by Federal centralization. We have now had time to measure the relative merits of the two methods. That is, of decentralized local administration in the hands of leading citizens or Federal centralization under politically selected bureaucracy.

COMPARATIVE COST

There is the question of comparative costs.

The finance of the relief of 1930–32 was secured by adaptations as needed of:

Contributions from county and municipal governments and personal sources. State grants-in-aid. Distribution of Farm Board commodities, Federal Public Works and R.F.C. loans to the States (really grants-in-aid).

The requirement of local and State contributions was a guarantee of economy. It was a challenge of local responsibility. It kept self-respect in both givers and receivers. The grants-in-aid were based on need, not upon political advantage or political pressures.

The unemployed today are said to be about the same as in 1932. The relief numbers are about the same today as they were 1932. The 1932 abnormal Federal, State, and local expenditures for unemployment relief and Federal public works totaled about $1,100,000,000. It is true that local resources were diminishing. Increases in Federal grants-in-aid were inevitable. But the cost of the various present branches of relief is now somewhere near $3,500,000,000 yearly. It is obvious that the major burden must now be carried by the Federal Government. It is my own opinion that one-half of this sum given by grants-in-aid to such administration as that of 1932 would attain greater benefits to those in distress. One indication is the cost of overhead. The former organization set up a volunteer Director of Relief Activities and an inspection service to see that the people were cared for. There were a few Federal officials to allocate funds. The total increase in Federal staff then cost less than $250,000 per annum. Today, the overhead is between three and four hundred million dollars for all kinds of relief activities.

For many years before 1930 I directed relief work for even larger numbers of destitute by relying upon the devotion of leading citizens. It was done for less than 3 per cent for overhead.

THE COMPARATIVE RESULTS TO THE UNEMPLOYED

The dominant question of all questions is not costs but results. Did this sort of administration of relief by sympathetic highly qualified groups of citizens that prevailed from 1930 to 1932 care for the deserving people who were in need? No human system of organization is perfect. But read the press of those years. It discloses that, aside from the sporadic accidents of any system, there were no criticisms for relief failure. No one starved. There were no daily headlines of fraud. There was much appeal for funds and painting of the need, but no painting of failure to provide. In the Presidential campaign of 1932, every charge that human ingenuity could invent was brought. And yet relief was scarcely discussed. Not a single charge against relief was made of politics, of waste, of corruption, or of failure to prevent hunger or cold.

Public health records are also a useful test. Undernourishment and cold are at once expressed in terms of increased disease and mortality. A study of the insurance, public health, and other statistics will show the surprising result that the population was in better physical health in 1932 than even during the boom year of 1928. The most illuminating figures are those of infant mortality which show that 1932 was the lowest in all American history. And remember, this was the third full year of depression. That the infant mortality has been rising since the relief was taken from local administration and centralized under political Washington is shown in the Public Health indexes:

1928	6880 deaths per 100,000
1929	6730 deaths per 100,000
1930	6460 deaths per 100,000
1931	6170 deaths per 100,000
1932	5760 deaths per 100,000
1933	5810 deaths per 100,000
1934	5990 deaths per 100,000

(Later years not available)

The Larger Aspects of Comparison

But there are more fundamental and more far-reaching effects involved than mere efficiency.

A whole gamut of governmental economic, social, and moral questions are now concentrated upon relief.

The sense of community responsibility has been turned to greed for Federal money. To protect themselves in an equal share of relief funds many a community has joined in a vicious scramble to get what it can from the Federal grab-bag. What some mayor or Congressman grabbed for his locality has become a claim for re-election. While the Federal debt is increasing there are States and municipalities which pride themselves that they are not increasing, or may even be reducing, their debts and expenses.

There are labor shortages in the face of large numbers on relief. The destitute cling fearfully to a certainty rather than lose their hold on a great Federal machine. Numbers of people are being thus reduced to a sort of numb dependency. There is less local effort to place people in jobs. Local public opinion to correct failure and wrong is less effective.

Today instead of sympathy for the unemployed and the destitute there is a growing resentment. The real sympathy from the national heart flows far more truly through personal leadership in the community than through Federal agents.

There is a spiritual loss in all this which cannot be estimated. Instead of building up the solicitude of neighbor for neighbor, instead of building the responsibility of good neighbors among men and women, we are cultivating hardness for the destitute, we are undermining self-respect of men and women. We are creating contempt for government.

One need of the nation today is a recall of a spirit of individual service. That spirit springs from the human heart, not from politics. Upon that spirit alone can this democracy survive. No greater call to service could be made than to remobilize local administration of relief.

Reform in Some Federal Taxes

DENVER, COLORADO

[*September 30, 1936*]

I SHALL not discuss political issues tonight, but no doubt any form of public expression can be distorted as politics except crooning. What I have to say at this moment is merely objective sociology and economics. If you get political emotions out of it then that is the product of your mind, not of mine.

I propose to talk on probably the most universally disagreeable subject in the world. That is taxes. The metal mining industry throbs with these pains—prospectors, miners, engineers, managers and operators all included. Being naturally a humane person I shall hold it to twelve minutes.

And I shall limit myself also to one segment of the tax structure. That is the corporation taxes, the estate taxes, and the income taxes. And I shall confine myself to Federal Taxes. Much could also be said upon the bad habits of States and municipalities. But I do not wish to be too dismal all at one time so I will not bring that up.

I shall limit myself still further to discussion only of the economic and social effects of the method and not the volume of these·taxes. Therefore, do not get any pleasurable anticipations that I am going to·demand reduction in taxes. That is not possible until the budget is balanced. Furthermore, the principle of making people pay according to their means is right. My administration having more than doubled the upper brackets of the income tax and the estate taxes up to 55 per cent, no one will accuse me of wanting to give relief from the burden of government to those classes of the destitute.

Indeed, having teeth pulled is necessary but the technique of the dentist may add grief to the nth degree and may injure the patient for a long time.

Let me say one thing about taxes in general. It has been a sort of theory that taxes should not be used to effect social or economic ends. That idea has been more honored in speech than in action, as witness the tariff ever since George Washington. Moreover, all taxes are an economic and social burden no matter how light they may be. But when taxation rises to the volume of from 15 per cent to 20 per cent of the national income, then the method of them may powerfully advance or retard social or economic forces no matter how they are levied. We might just as well frankly face the fact and try to direct them first into the least damage, and second, into producing the most benevolent effects possible.

CORPORATION TAXES

One of the distinguishing features of the recent corporation tax is its tax on undistributed profits. That in fact often becomes a tax upon such profits as are applied to other more useful national purposes than dividends to stockholders. The theoretical purpose is to impale the few tax dodgers who have not been impaled already upon the barbs of many entanglements. But by this law barriers are erected which stop the honest and necessary activities of a multitude of honest men.

There is no better instance of this than the metal industry. The continuation of our metal supply and the expansion of the industry rest to a considerable degree upon the new discoveries and energies of the prospector and small operator. They are seldom able to develop and equip their discoveries without some initial outside capital. Ninety-nine times out of a hundred these men must put their ventures in corporate form in order to define the interests and liabilities of themselves and those who find the money. Certainly this sort of corporation is not the manufacturer of evil or monopoly.

Every prospector or operator puts up a temporary plant and tries to make the mine pay its way to proved value or to determine the more efficient equipment. No prospector or operator can secure adequate capital for final equipment on reasonable terms until this is done. If the prospector or operator is forced to seek the whole of his ultimate capital requirements before this proof, it either kills his enterprise or hands him over to the promoter.

· Any one familiar with the growth of the West knows the mining industry has created and expanded from plowing in its own profits. Nor can it be done any other way. But the new law steps in and says that if you use your profits to prove and build up this business you must pay the government up to over 40 per cent on these profits. That is a tax of up to over 40 per cent upon improvements which give men jobs.

Furthermore metal mining in the early stages happens to be the most speculative of all business. On balance, more money goes into this stage of the industry than ever comes out.

If the government is going to take up to 40 per cent of the temporary profits from each ultimate failure, as well as the successes, the miner does not stand a dog's chance.

Somewhat the same situation applies to large low-grade deposits. Many of them which have been made successful industries by plowing in the profits of the first unit would never have started had they tried to find all the capital at once.

Here again this tax up to 40 per cent on profits becomes a tax on improvements that would give men jobs.

This taxation favors the big mining corporations. These concerns already have capital reserves; they can secure capital on easy terms. They can take up a dozen prospects and write off the losses against profitable ones.

Much the same situation exists in all the smaller units of business generally. They have been made from plowing in profits. Without doing that they would never have dodged infant mortality.

But there is even a wider point of view than this. I sometimes wonder if it ever occurred to anybody that one of the important things that makes jobs and increases national assets is expansion or improvement in plant or production. That should surely be our social and economic purpose. In that light it might be a sane thing for the government to reverse itself and say four things to the people.

First, that if you will expand or improve your equipment and production we will give you a reasonable exemption from corporation taxes on all the profits you expend that way. And I mean every form of corporation taxes, including the so-called normal tax on profits. But this exemption should be limited to the amount of profits plowed in for the purpose.

As a matter of fact, it would make more jobs than all the boondoggling of the nation—and they would be honest jobs. And it would increase the national assets and not deplete them.

There is another factor here beyond the desirability of encouraging new enterprise and expansion. Our tax-laws in reality allow nothing for obsolescence. I am aware of the allowances for depreciation but that does not cover obsolescence. Depreciation implies wearing machinery out. Obsolescence means the good machinery that needs to be thrown away to allow the installation of new inventions. Obsolescence has become a far greater element in industrial management during recent years, for invention proceeds at a tremendous pace. Machinery and equipment are today seldom worn out. They are discarded for something better. It is in the national interest that this should be done, since industry is not serving the public unless it is up to date. It is only thereby that we lower costs of production and prices, and thus improve the standard of living. Therefore freedom from corporation taxes on profits set aside for these purposes would be just common sense.

Second, it has been already pointed out that there are times when every business will lose money. It is at just such times that they cannot secure capital. If they have cash reserves they can hold staff and workmen together until things improve. The copper-mines of the West would have all closed down if they had not had reserves. In fact, the industries of the United States spent billions of their reserves doing that very thing in this depression. If they have been forced to pay out all their profits in dividends to stockholders in good times, bad times will mean vastly increased bankruptcy and many more workers on relief.

Would it not seem common sense to allow some further ratio of profits to be accumulated in every business against such contingencies? That is the greatest employment insurance that can be built up. And it is built up not at the cost of taxpayers but at the cost of stockholders.

Third, there is another complexion of all this. Our industry tends to become inflexible and static. There are forces in it which work far more powerfully in that direction than do monopolies upon which it is usually blamed. We do not get the decrease in price levels that increasing efficiency should produce. If we are going to stifle the opportunity of new men to go into industry or of industry to expand, then competition is still further stifled. But by reversing this and applying such pressures for competition as increased improvements and expansion of plant, we can produce more competition and lowering of prices in a day than all the anti-monopoly legislation will produce in a year.

Fourth, one effect of the new law will be the expansion of bonded debt of corporations who are forced to pay dividends on one hand and borrow money for improvements on the other. That is the advantageous thing to do under this new law but that increases overhead and renders such business less able to meet shocks.

Finally, after reasonable exemptions from all corporate taxes are given for these items—profits plowed into expansion and improvements, profits set aside against rainy days, profits set aside for depreciation, depletion and obsolescence—then if the corporation did not pay out the balance in dividends, it could well be construed as trying to avoid taxation. And I have no sympathy whatever with any such action.

To review for a moment: this method of catching tax dodgers seems clearly to penalize and embarrass our real economic needs. It tends to stifle honest enterprise, to lessen national assets, to help the powerful instead of the weak, to cost men jobs and take away much of their protection. By restricting improvement it diminishes competition. Yet we could entirely reverse these tendencies. The government would in the end get more taxes. It would give the small man a better chance.

Estate Taxes

Now we come to an even more dull segment of this address. That is the estate taxes. Very few miners leave taxable estate when they are done mining. But the effect of these taxes is important from a wholly different point of view.

Luck and genius create large fortunes. But the inheritance of great economic power by descendants is not consonant with a free people. We used to rely upon the incompetence of the descendants to dissolve these accumulations. But the old formula of shirt sleeve to shirt sleeve in three generations is impeded through the erection of two or three generation trusts which are about as bad as the old law of primogeniture. We abolished that long, long ago.

No doubt estate taxes do drive for the distribution of oversized fortunes but they could be made to do a better job. I will not go into that intricate question. But we could amply protect widows and children.

At the same time we could dissolve any inheritance of important economic power if we intelligently reform these taxes. In any event, not many of you will ever be subjected to the worries of large inheritance if you stay in the mining business.

Income Taxes

I now come to the income tax. There is more excitement in this for at some time in every miner's life he meets this head-on. Or at least he hopes to. Our worst efforts in governmental methods are applied to the income taxes. They contain a multitude of injustices; they do not levy the tax upon its true focus of ability to pay. They have proved to stimulate a host of damaging social and economic forces. They are unbelievably complicated. They offer vast opportunity for evasion. They are a torment and a terror to the honest citizen. And again I am not contending for reduction in the amount of the tax but for better method of application.

From our experience particularly during the depression we can appraise at least two features that badly need reform to stop costly wastage.

First we attempt to tax capital gains and we allow deduction of capital losses. No matter how complicated we make the industry of tax evasion, my observation is that in the long run the Government loses money on this tax because more people can conjure up more losses than the Government can conjure up new rules which locate their profits. But of far more importance than this we here place a dam against the free movement of property. The citizen refuses to sell real estate or mines or investments because of the huge tax on any increase in value. We create shortages of securities, and we accentuate booms and slumps. It makes for vicious speculation. It is today contributing to a new stock boom.

Second. We are about the only nation which allows tax exemption for Federal, State, and municipal bonds. Thus we create a wholesale sanctuary from taxation for large incomes. Those men who devote their incomes to building up the country and giving employment pay great taxes.

Worse, still, the exemption of government securities prevents the United States from installing a system of collecting income tax at its source. That is, having the normal tax collected and remitted to the Government by those who pay, instead of those who receive. That simplified idea is used by every other civilized government but because of tax-exempt securities we cannot work it. Our government in order to collect the income tax must pry into the detailed income of millions of people. If we collected at the source the government would only need pry into the detailed accounts of less than 15 per cent of the income taxpayers, that is, those who must pay more than the so-called normal tax. And it would help keep track of the super-tax payers also.

We will never clean all this up until we have the courage to pass a constitutional amendment abolishing all tax exemptions on government securities. But all this is a dull subject up to the moment when the income tax agent begins to pry into your affairs. Of all branches of mathematical science there is none that has bred more human emotion than this.

There is a lot more I could say on all these taxes, but if we could get these reforms the government revenues would be much larger, the results would be more constructive and less destructive, the taxpayer much less annoyed, employment greater, and life generally would be sweeter.

Intellectual Dishonesty in Government

PHILADELPHIA, PENNSYLVANIA

[*October 16, 1936*]

PART I

I PROPOSE to discuss the New Deal morals in arithmetic. Another title might be "Government by Deception." A subtitle might be "Intellectual Honesty in Political Campaigns." And I may say at once that the loss to this nation by the corruption of public thinking is far greater than the waste of public money.

To illustrate this subject I shall examine two speeches of President Roosevelt which relate to government expenditures. And I shall explore some of the published accounts of the Government. I choose these samples because figures are given, and there is something to get hold of besides Utopia. There is something we can test for old-fashioned integrity. The first of these speeches was at Pittsburgh in October, four years ago, when he was running for President. The second was at Pittsburgh two weeks ago, when he was defending what he had done in the meantime. And I shall at the end of this examination give you a constructive suggestion.

In that Pittsburgh speech of four years ago Mr. Roosevelt said that the Republican spending was "the most reckless and extravagant pace I have ever been able to discover in the statistical record of any peacetime government anywhere, any time." That speech showed high artistry in denunciation. It showed high imagination in figures. He exhausted the hard words of the political vocabulary—"desperate," "futile," "false," "pretty picture," "shocking," "unreliable," "spendthrift," "gamble," "bankruptcy," "prodigality," "extravagance," "muddle," "appalling." All that in one single speech. And all this was applied to an increase of the national debt during the last Republican Administration of something over 3 billions without deducting recoverable loans. Mr. Roosevelt having exhausted these words on 3 billions what is there left to us to use on his ultimate 14 billions?

He denied Republicans any mercy from the fact that Federal revenues had precipitously dropped off by 2 billion through a world-wide calamity. He denied us any quarter because we had placed humanity first in the American budget and spent and loaned public funds to a people in distress. Now he claims a patent on that idea. He gave us no credit marks for fighting a Pork Barrel Democratic Congress to get a balanced budget. He has patented many improvements on that barrel. With solemnity he promised to save 25 per cent a year from expenditures of the government and to at once balance the budget. And he tearfully appealed to the woman in her home struggling to balance her budget. And he vigorously asserted he would never conceal anything.

In reply at that time I corrected these misstatements. But misrepresentation can only be washed up in the laundry of time. That laundry is working.

Mr. Roosevelt in the 1936 model Pittsburgh speech naturally omitted correction of his inexactitudes of four years before. He now dismisses his own immensely greater deficits and all the evidences of his wastes and follies by the pious remark that for him and his supine Congress to have balanced his budget would "have been a crime against the American people." Thus he changes the rules between these two innings.

PART II

The President in this last Pittsburgh speech implies delicately that he brought about recovery from the depression. His minions of course shout it.

We can examine this also for a moment. The origins of this depression are agreed on by almost every economist, every scholar, every informed statesman in the world. It was the inexorable and inevitable world-wide aftermath of the World War. Its causes lay in the pit of destruction dug by the most titanic struggle in which humanity has yet engaged. Our own credit inflation contributed to our own difficulties. But this depression began in other countries before it touched the United States. No man or no government brought about that depression. Governments could do much to protect their citizens, their citizens' institutions and their savings from its blasts. But its sweep was as inexorable as a Caribbean hurricane.

Likewise the recovery from this depression was not the work of any one official or government or all of them. Recovery was the invincible result of a billion of human beings on the seven continents struggling to repair the breaches in their daily lives. Governments could aid their citizens in recovery; by foolish action they could retard it.

That the beginnings of recovery were world-wide, including the United States in the spring of 1932, is recognized by almost every economist, every scholar, every informed statesman. That was nine months before Mr. Roosevelt ever came to the Presidency. And in many of these countries without the interferences of New Deals recovery has marched further and faster than in the United States.

Mr. Roosevelt naturally does not emphasize the fact that at his election the United States alone faltered in the world wide march of Recovery. He does not recall that the American bank panic was a panic of fear that he would not keep his campaign promises, particularly as to the currency. He does not mention that in the dark days of European panics Republican policies had twice or thrice prevented the spread of these panics to the United States. He does not mention all his delays on recovery that were removed by the Supreme Court.

He paints a poignant picture of the difficulties of the country resulting from the bank panic which marked his inauguration day of 1933. He implies that the people were in danger of starving, that riot was in the air. Mr. Roosevelt does not mention that due to a Republican administration which had first put humanity first there had not been starvation in the previous three years of the depression. He does not mention that there had not been hunger riots in that four years and there had been no industrial riots.

And today he lays his claims to re-election upon the improvement in the country from the bottom of that ditch. He quotes a vast amount of figures to prove that. Those figures would look different if they were drawn before his election and were increased in accordance with his own devaluation of the dollar. He now claims political reward for that unnecessary forcing of the country into the ditch of panic. I am reminded of the boy who murdered his father and mother, then appealed to the judge not only for acquittal but for future support on the ground he was an orphan.

The President illustrated his views of this period by recounting a story of a nice old gentleman who fell off the dock in 1933 and was rescued. The gentleman was effusive in thanks but three years later he complained that he had lost his hat.

I have some inside information about that incident. The old gentleman was surreptitiously pushed off the dock in order that the hero could gain the plaudits of the crowd as a life saver.

With apologies to Governor Smith may I not suggest that Santa Claus has turned into Chanticleer whose crow each morning claims credit for the rising sun?

In the Pittsburgh speech two weeks ago the President develops the idea of a baseball scoreboard and sets certain figures upon it for the fans to look at. For instance, he said that the last Republican Administration had increased the National Debt by over 3 billions. He admitted that he had already increased it by 13 billions. But he claims a deduction of 6½ billions from his increase because of the bonus and for recoverable loans. Any umpire would call that statement out on three strikes of which one was a foul.

Strike one: He deducts the present recoverable loans from his debt. But he misses the opportunity to be intellectually honest and likewise deduct from the last Republican Administration over 2 billion of recoverable loans. They were handed to him, largely collected by him and spent by him. Second, no publication of the United States Government warrants Mr. Roosevelt's valuation of 5 billion on recoverable assets, especially when we consider the enormous hidden losses in the New Deal guaranteed loans. The third strike is that the debt for veterans was not paid off. It was merely borrowed from the banks and has yet to be paid off. Incidentally he did not include the further increase of debt he is piling up. Thus the score of Republican increase in taxpayers' debt is 1 billion not 3 billions. His own score on the same basis will be about 10 billions not 6½ billions. If such an unmoral scoreboard had been put before any baseball game in the country the manager would be driven off the field.

In this 1936 speech the President made the statement that between 1920 and 1930 8 billions of money out of American pockets had been sent to foreign countries and used by them to give employment to their citizens. He says that most of that money is gone for good. He implies that it was taken away from American workmen and given to foreign workmen. That reflects mostly upon my predecessors in office, including President Wilson. But I shall not let that smear rest upon them. President Roosevelt did not mention that this money was borrowed by foreigners on interest and was not gifts. He does not mention that it was borrowed from private Americans and not from our Government.

I have had each of these foreign borrowings which were offered to the American public carefully traced. I am informed their total was 7 billions, not 8 billions. That is, however, an error of only 12½ per cent and we can let that pass. Of these 7 billions that are supposed to be lost, 2 billions have become due and have been paid in full. Three billions are not yet due but interest and amortization are being met regularly. The remaining 2 billions are partly in default but are being salvaged as the world recovers. The net result is that this is an error of about 87½ per cent.

But even that is not the whole story. It is an economic fact that loans to foreigners must ultimately be transmitted in goods, services, or gold. Gold was probably not shipped. Therefore these private loans made employment of American workmen and American farmers in producing this amount of goods. In fact, those private loans contributed greatly to full employment in the United States during the whole decade of the 20's when unemployment existed in practically every other country in the world. President Roosevelt's statement is the more astonishing as he has himself advocated the loaning of money to foreigners, including Russia, thus to create markets for products of American shops and farms. He created the so-called Export Banks for this exact purpose. But in his case he has placed the risk on the taxpayer and not upon the private banker.

But still more interesting in this connection is the fact that Mr. Roosevelt has automatically and without consent of these private American citizens cancelled 41 per cent of these debts from foreigners. He did that when he devalued our dollar. He made the foreigners a gift of about 3 billions of dollars from American pockets. Before the dollar was devalued these people had to spend 41 per cent more gold or its equivalent in goods to the United States to meet their obligations than they have to send today. And I may add that this cancellation of foreign debts applies also to the 11 billions of war debts owed the American people. Here the President made a present to foreigners of another 4 billions of American dollars.

PART III

But this juggling with the scoreboard has not been confined to evanescent public speeches. It has gone far deeper than that. The American people over the years have rightly held implicit confidence in their government accounting. Before the New Deal we plodded along under the old religion in accounting methods. The Federal Government just put down all the money spent on one side of the ledger and every cent taken in on the other side of the ledger, and called it a day with either a surplus or a deficit.

The New Deal quickly introduced an entirely new system of double bookkeeping. "Emergency" or "Recovery and relief" expenditures on one side were separated from "General" or "ordinary" or "routine" expenditures on the other.

Such double bookkeeping never has been used for honest purposes by governments. Its very motive is intellectual dishonesty. That is pernicious deceit.

Mr. Roosevelt in this 1936 Pittsburgh speech implies that his gigantic increase in expenditures during the past four years has been necessitated by relief in some form.

You may, however, be surprised to know that a large part of the burden the people have willingly assumed for relief was used in hundreds of millions of reckless increase of ordinary routine expenses of Government.

The waste has been bad enough. But morally worse has been a continuous juggling with this double bookkeeping to cover this up.

But the New Deal has a great sorrow to hide. You remember Mr. Roosevelt promised that he would reduce expenses 25 per cent. The skeleton of that promise has rattled in the New Deal closet until they have tried to quiet it by juggling the double books.

To show how this is done I shall need to engage in some comparative figures. Figures are hard to listen to, but generalizations and political verbiage do not clarify the public mind. As a part of this laundry job I shall quote the publications of his Treasury Department and tell you the page.

On July 15 of this year of 1936, three months before the coming election, Mr. Roosevelt's Treasury Department published a handy table for New Deal orators giving many figures. They show New Deal expenditure on all accounts for three years were something over 23 billions 300 millions. Of this sum they claim the regular ordinary routine expenditures of the government were only 3 billion 100 million in the fiscal year 1934; they were 3 billion 720 million in 1935, and 3 billion 920 million in 1936 if we omit the bonus.

The real total expenditures of both kinds of books are now

about 9 billions a year. You might think that these figures show that the ordinary routine cost of the government is under 4 billion and the government spending will return to that figure when the unemployment emergency is over. Perhaps it is hoped you will think so until after this election. Presently I shall convey the sad news to you that the continuing regular expenses even if everybody gets a job will be more than 6 billions a year.

A searching examination into the thousands of pages of details in the Budget report which the public seldom reads shows several moral stains in these statements of regular expenses that need the laundry of truth.

They have three formulas for making these expenditures look less than they are—

Formula No. 1. The Roosevelt Administration has made some beautiful economies by just omitting certain items from its regular expenditures before it comes to the totals announced to the people. They appear only in an appendix. For instance, the expenditures for government trust accounts and for the District of Columbia paid by the residents have been deleted from totals under President Roosevelt. Also one-half the necessary annuity payment of $100,000,000 into the Veterans Bonus Fund was just omitted in the years 1934 and 1935. That had to be paid later on. These items make their spending for 1934 look less by $188,000,000. It makes 1935 look $213,000,000 less than the fact. It makes the 1936 expenditures look better for the New Deal by $238,000,000. This is one of the easiest methods of reducing government expenses yet discovered. You just don't put them in before you announce the total—and there you are.

Formula No. 2. It has always been a rightful principle of government accounting under the old commandments to pay all receipts or all final recoveries from revolving accounts into the Treasury. Then Congress appropriates them out and thus holds control of the expenditures. But the Roosevelt administration has improved this greatly. They now deduct certain receipts from expenditures before they come to the totals which are announced to the public. I knew a man once who was afraid of his wife and who went on a holiday that the family really couldn't afford. But he reported his expenses to her after deducting the business bills he collected en route. The New Deal has done some surprising sleight-of-hand with this line of arithmetic. In 1935 over $180,000,000 of the expenses were written off this way before the totals of expenditures were given to the public. In 1936 apparently over $500,000,000 of expenses are got rid of this way before we come to the final sum that is announced to the people. This is a good method of simplifying things. If they continue this long enough, we may have no expenses left. But puny sums like these mean nothing.

Formula No. 3. And this is a much more potent formula for juggling scoreboards. In the days of the old-time arithmetic the President and the Director of the Budget yearly fought each of the federal bureaus over every item of expenditures. Congress fought at the items and finally made a detailed appropriation for each of them, down to the salary of every clerk. The money could be used for no other purpose. That was the open budget openly arrived at.

But Mr. Roosevelt obtained many billions of lump appropriations from Congress to spend about any way he liked under the sympathetic title "relief and recovery." This method has enabled great results in saving through juggling. For these lump sums for relief were used in large quantities for regular ordinary expenses. It does make the regular expenditures reported to the people look less. It makes that Pittsburgh speech of four years ago look good to Democratic orators. But it conceals a vast rise in the regular routine expenses of the government. It enables it to be done without the consent of Congress. This should interest the people who thought they were making gigantic sacrifices for relief and that the administration was at the same time economizing wonderfully on old regular expenditures. This should also interest the people on relief who did not get the full money the people through Congress voted them. At this point we get to the real nubbin of morals in double book-keeping. We can make this all clear by specific examples.

The 1935 Annual Report of the Treasury on page 11 proudly

published the General or ordinary Expenditures of the Department of Commerce as only $10,967,000. That looks pretty good. It looks like a 75 per cent reduction from the last Republican administration. But let us search the record.

If we refer to the middle pages of the budget report for 1935 among the fine print we find that the Shipping Board has been transferred with all its assets to the Commerce Department. But behold, the sum of $21,600,000 was realized from the assets of the Shipping Board and cold-bloodedly deducted from the total expenses of running the Commerce Department for that year. That was the application of Formula No. 2 which I gave you.

But we find Formula No. 3 also applied. If we search we will find that $10,197,000 expenses of the department were paid out of "recovery and relief" funds. They are for items which were in Republican administrations considered simply the necessary running expenses of the government—such as building lighthouses, surveying the country, taking care of the fish, etc. They are not emergency outlays. Among these items I notice that even the propagation of fish has now in part become a matter of "relief and recovery." I have no doubt that the fish are working hard for recovery. Judging by the time between bites they haven't got far. But I am in favor of any effort on their part. And there are other items in this case which I will not tire you with. It is enough to show that the regular expenses of the Commerce Department are about four times the amounts shown in the report I have cited.

However, this is nothing in a land of billions. With this comforting thought we ought to explore more important jungles.

On page 10 of Mr. Roosevelt's 1935 Treasury Report the National Defense figure is given as $533,000,000. I was much interested in that figure, for in the last full Republican year of 1932 the combined expenditures of the War and Navy Departments, similarly omitting non-military expenses, were $712,-000,000. The Roosevelt figure was made to look like an economy of about $178,000,000. Here at once we had a 25 per cent reduction as promised at Pittsburgh four years ago. I felt sad over my failure to have discovered such a possible economy.

But when I searched to find how Mr. Roosevelt had accomplished it I found he had used Formula No. 3. Over $176,-000,000 in these military expenditures had been transferred to "relief and recovery" or "emergency." But more than that, there is a curious item of $102,000,000 which was deducted from the War Department expenditures for outstanding checks that had not been cashed. So we find that the whole expenditure on National Defense in 1935 was $278,000,000 greater than you might think from that page to which I referred. I might mention that the future military expenditures will exceed a billion a year under the New Deal.

It is a happy government that can in these days make the people believe it has reduced the military spending. That stroke of genius was attained by charging it to "relief" or "recovery." I recommend the method to the governments of Europe. It looks like disarmament and it creates greater military strength.

For another exhibit of genius in making reductions in the Ordinary or routine spending we can take the Department of Agriculture. In the last full Republican year of 1932 under the old religion in bookkeeping this department cost $318,900,000. The New Deal gives the General Expenditure for 1935 as $62,-036,000. You might think this was a gigantic reduction of over 80 per cent. But let us explore it.

If we read the fine print in the middle pages of that Budget volume attentively, we find that in 1935 by the use of economy Formula No. 3, $413,000,000 was charged to "Recovery and Relief" or "Emergency." Don't think this included the AAA. It did not. That cost $743,000,000 more. These transfers to relief include not only big items but little items like chasing bugs and moths.

There is sport in this bookkeeping jungle. It has been a function of the Federal Government for many years to chase the "Gypsy and Browntail Moths." The Republicans pursued these moths over many years at a cost of about $600,000 per annum. And in the old-fashioned way we charged it off and called it a day.

But in 1934 the New Deal at once effected a great economy.

The general or ordinary expenditure of this bug chase is now shown in the accounts as only $151,903. That was a grand economy of about 75 per cent. But behold you find printed in fine italics that Relief or Recovery or Emergency was charged with $1,490,000 for those moths. Thus the cost of the chase had really increased by 150 per cent.

Then we come to the chasing moths in 1935. Here we do still better. The ordinary or routine cost was only $9,503. That was an economy from the Republican Administration of about 99 per cent. You might think the moth had nearly died. But sad to relate, he was still flitting about and had to have money from relief to the extent of $382,000.

But worse is to come in 1936. Now we take the moth partly off relief. So according to the budget they increase the "regular," "ordinary," "routine" cost of this sport up to $395,000, from the low of $9,000 the year before. It is still a 30 per cent economy from that Republican $600,000. But this strictly humanitarian administration got also $2,900,000 Relief for the poor moth, and the chase finally shows an increase of 550 per cent over the wasteful Republicans. Yet the published ordinary general expenditures still look like that Pittsburgh 25 per cent reduction.

We can explore the Forest Service. In Republican administrations it cost about 20 million a year to look after the government trees. All this was just running expenses. In 1935 Mr. Roosevelt's accounts purport that it cost only $12,180,000 for ordinary expenditures. But if you look closely you will find $7,700,000 more was charged to "relief and recovery" or "emergency," which keeps the trees in about the same style they were accustomed to.

So these moral aberrations in accounts go, great and little. I have not the time to explore the other many parts of the government. But in this limited area I have pointed out about $900,000,000 juggles for 1935 alone. Only a congressional investigation could really determine the whole facts.

And there is another department in this juggling on which I might pause a moment. That is the political department. Not content with juggling their accounts to make them look better through the spectacles of that Pittsburgh speech of four years ago, they also go back and juggle the Republican expenditures and publish these juggles for comparison. In their Treasury statement of July 15, 1936, they dress the expenditures of the Republican administration in their two new styles "Regular" on one hand and "Relief" or "Emergency" on the other. They give the so-called "Regular" expenditures of the last full Republican year of 1932 as over 4 billion. But they faked their own rules. As an example, in their own years they charge highways and trails of different sorts to relief and recovery. But in recasting Republican accounts they call these items regular or ordinary expenditures. That alone makes a little difference of about 200 millions. Altogether they juggle their own juggling rules so as to make so-called regular Republican expenditures look 6 or 8 hundred millions to the bad.

Thus the Republican regular expenditures are juggled up and the New Deal regular expenditures juggled down. And Presto! The New Deal regular expenditures for the first full New Deal year of 1934 are a billion less than the Republican. You as well as the New Deal orators can see that plainly from Mr. Roosevelt's scoreboard.

And let me say right now: to present hypocritical, misleading figures is a new deal in American public life. It is not American. If you want to know my private opinion of these methods of government bookkeeping I refer you back to President Roosevelt's vocabulary I quoted early in this address.

If an income taxpayer or any corporation kept books like this administration, that is if they showed similar morals in juggling their accounts, they would be put in jail.

I ask you, is this the sort of example for a great government to set for its people?

PART IV

THE REAL EXPENDITURE UNDER THE NEW DEAL

But there is a question here more important than bookkeeping for political purposes. That is misleading the people through implication as to what their expenditures are likely to be for the future.

Now let us examine this question a little. Over the last eight years of Republican administrations and honest accounting the ordinary running expenses never varied much from 3⅔ billions. That is, if you exclude honestly those expenditures forced by relief against the depression. And everything was in that sum— debt redemption, post office deficit and trust accounts. The impression Mr. Roosevelt seeks to convey by the accounts is that his ordinary expenditures of government outside the bonus are still running at less than 4 billions per annum.

To indicate what they really are I will give you an estimate of what the ordinary routine expenses of the Federal Government will be if the New Deal is continued. That is, suppose we attain prosperity so that there is no longer need for unemployment relief, what are we still faced with? That gives them the best of it, for the unemployed will likely be with us all the days of the New Deal, although I hope not. This estimate is based upon stripping the jugglery off of every department and agency and then taking into consideration the New Deal's positive commitments. That estimate shows the regular running expenditures of this Government have jumped to about 6 billions per annum. That is an increase of 2⅓ billions from the Republican base of 3⅔ billions. And mind you that does not include relief.

More Taxation

The New Deal claims that there will be no need for increased taxes, that the budget will be balanced by increased prosperity. And this statement opens another field of intellectual dishonesty.

The government income for 1936 was about 4 billion after we omit repealed taxes. That leaves a deficit of two billion for regular running expenses even without continued unemployment relief. Present taxes may stretch up another $500,000,000 or even a billion with full prosperity. And it still leaves a huge deficit.

Those taxes are as inevitable as the night. But in the meantime the New Deal has a disingenuous solution. The administration apparently intends to treat the repayment of recoverable loans as revenue and to claim a balanced budget. If you borrow money from your bank and loan it to a friend, and ultimately your friend repays, then you would be well advised to pay off the bank. It is only a New Deal mind who would consider you had a raise in salary.

That is going on this minute.

CONCLUSION

In conclusion let me say: the morals of our people and intellectual honesty in public discussions should be cleaned of pollution from their government.

At the outset I stated I would give you a constructive suggestion. Therefore you should:

1. Resume congressional control of spending by the election of Republican Congressmen and Senators.

2. Drive these expenses down toward the Republican levels, balance the budget, put back the integrity of the government accounting, and above all restore truth and morals in government by the election of those honest gentlemen, Alfred Landon and Frank Knox.

This Challenge to Liberty

DENVER, COLORADO

[*October 30, 1936*]

PART I

WE ARE near the end of this debate. More than in any election for two generations we are voting on the direction which American civilization will take.

The press and the radio have been alive with discussion. It is not alone public men and women who are engaged in this debate. It is between the farmers in the field, the workers at the bench, the women in their homes, the men in their offices. They have met at the store, at the filling station and the street corner. It is a magnificent thing that a whole people should engage in this discussion. For such debate is the most precious safeguard of free men that the world has yet discovered.

A whole people with the ballot in their hands possess the most conclusive and unlimited power ever entrusted to humanity. If that power is exercised rightly, then America will prosper morally, spiritually, and in its daily occupations. If it is exercised under the spell of hate or selfish purpose or under intimidation it will drive this nation upon the rocks of destruction.

These issues are too great and the stakes too large for us to examine these questions in any mean or smearing fashion. I have said the problems we face penetrate to the very center of economic, social, and governmental life. The only field which we have not entered in this debate is the field of sportsmanship. I could wish we had some of that in the campaign.

If the Republic is to head in the right direction we must get at the real issues. We must dismiss the shadow boxing of a political campaign. We must dismiss secondary questions of governmental policy. We must strip our problems down to the great issue before the country.

Speaking just four years ago tonight in closing the Presidential campaign of 1932, I said:

"This campaign is more than a contest between two men. It is more than a contest between two parties. It is a contest between two philosophies of government. . . .

"We must go deeper than platitudes and emotional appeals of the public platform in the campaign, if we will penetrate to the full significance of the changes which our opponents are attempting to float upon the wave of distress and discontent from the difficulties we are passing through."

That night I spoke for the regeneration of the American System—the American plan of true liberalism in contrast with the philosophy of the New Deal—and I continued: . . . "you cannot extend the mastery of government over the daily life of a people without somewhere making it master of people's souls and thoughts. . . . Every step in that direction poisons the very roots of liberalism. It poisons political equality, free speech, free press, and equality of opportunity. It is the road not to more liberty but to less liberty. True liberalism is found not in striving to spread bureaucracy, but in striving to set bounds to it. True liberalism seeks all legitimate freedom first in the confident belief that without such freedom the pursuit of other blessings is in vain."

And in that address four years ago I said:

"The spirit of liberalism is to create free men; it is not the regimentation of men."

PART II

Through four years of experience this New Deal attack upon free institutions has emerged as the transcendent issue in America.

All the men who are seeking for mastery in the world today are using the same weapons. They sing the same songs. They all promise the joys of Elysium without effort. But their philosophy is founded on the coercion and compulsory organization of men. True liberal government is founded on the emancipation of men. This is the issue upon which men are imprisoned and dying in Europe right now.

The rise of this issue has dissolved our old party lines. The New Deal repudiation of Democracy has left the Republican Party alone the guardian of the Ark of the Covenant with its charter of freedom. The tremendous import of this issue, the peril to our country has brought the support of the ablest leaders of the Democratic Party. It is no passing matter which enlists side by side the fighting men who have opposed each other over many years. It is the unity demanded by a grave danger to the Republic. Their sacrifice to join with us has no parallel in American history since the Civil War. There run through my mind great words from the Battle Hymn of the Republic:

... "in the watchfires of a hundred circling camps
They have builded them an altar."

I realize that this danger of centralized personal government disturbs only thinking men and women. But surely the NRA and the AAA alone, should prove what the New Deal philosophy of government means even to those who don't think.

In these instances the Supreme Court, true to their oaths to support the Constitution, saved us temporarily. But Congress in obedience to their oaths should never have passed these acts. The President should never have signed them. But far more important than that, if these men were devoted to the American system of liberty they never would have proposed acts based on the coercion and compulsory organization of men.

Freedom does not die from frontal attack. It dies because men in power no longer believe in a system based upon Liberty.

Mr. Roosevelt on this eve of election has started using the phrases of freedom. He talks sweetly of personal liberty, of individualism, of the American system, of the profit system. He says now that he thinks well of capitalism, and individual enterprise. His devotion to private property seems to be increasing.

He has suddenly found some good economic royalists. And he is a staunch supporter of the Constitution. Two days ago he re-dedicated the Statue of Liberty in New York. She has been the forgotten woman.

Four years ago we also heard many phrases which turned out not to mean what they were thought to have meant. In order that we may be sure this time will Mr. Roosevelt reply in plain words:

Does he propose to revive the nine acts which the Supreme Court has rejected as invasions of the safeguards of free men?

Has he abandoned his implied determination to change the Constitution? Why not tell the American people before election what change he proposes? Does he intend to stuff the Court itself? Why does the New Deal not really lay its cards on the table?

But their illegal invasions of the Constitution are but the minor artillery with which this New Deal philosophy of government is being forced upon us. They are now using a more subtle and far more effective method of substituting personal power and centralized government for the institutions of free men. It is not by violation of the Constitution that they are making headway today. It is through taking vast sums of the people's money and then manipulating its spending to build up personal power. By this route relief has been centralized in their hands. By this route government has entered into business in competition with the citizen. In his way a score of new instruments of public power have been created. By this route the ordinary functions of government have been uselessly expanded with a double bookkeeping to conceal it. Public funds are used right and left to subsidize special groups of our citizens and special regions of the country. At public expense there is a steady drip of propaganda to poison the public mind.

Through this spending there grows a huge number of citizens with a selfish vested interest in continuing this centralization of power. It has also made millions of citizens dependent upon the government.

Thus also have been built huge political bureaucracies hungry for more power. This use of money has enabled the independence of members of Congress to be sapped by the pork barrel. It has subtly undermined the rights and the responsibility of States and local governments. Out of all this we see government daily by executive orders instead of by open laws openly arrived at.

The New Deal taxes are in forms which stifle the growth of small business and discourage new enterprise. By stifling private enterprise the field is tilled for further extension of government enterprise. Intricate taxes are interpreted by political bureaucrats who coerce and threaten our business men. By politically managed currency the President has seized the power to alter all wages, all prices, all debts, all savings at will. But that is not the worst. They are creating personal power over votes. That crushes the first safeguard of liberty.

Does Mr. Roosevelt not admit all this in his last report on the state of the Union: "We have built up new instruments of public power" which he admits could "provide shackles for the liberties of the people." Does freedom permit any man or any government any such power? Have the people ever voted for these shackles?

Has he abandoned this "new order," this "planned economy" that he has so often talked about? Will he discharge these associates of his who daily preached the "new order" but whom he does not now allow to appear in this campaign?

Is Mr. Roosevelt not asking for a vote of confidence on these very breaches of liberty?

Is not this very increase in personal power the suicide road upon which every democratic government has died from the time of Greece and Rome down to the dozen liberal governments that have perished in Europe during this past twenty years?

PART III

I gave the warning against this philosophy of government four years ago from a heart heavy with anxiety for the future of our country. It was born from many years' experience of the forces moving in the world which would weaken the vitality of American freedom. It grew in four years of battle as President to uphold the banner of free men.

And that warning was based on sure ground from my knowledge of the ideas that Mr. Roosevelt and his bosom colleagues had covertly embraced despite the Democratic Platform.

Those ideas were not new. Most of them had been urged upon me.

During my four years powerful groups thundered at the White House with these same ideas. Some were honest, some promising votes, most of them threatening reprisals, and all of them yelling "reactionary" at us.

I rejected the notion of great trade monopolies and price fixing through codes. That could only stifle the little business man by regimenting him under his big brother. That idea was born of certain American Big Business and grew up to be the NRA.

I rejected the schemes of "economic planning" to regiment and coerce the farmer. That was born of a Roman despot fourteen hundred years ago and grew up into the AAA.

I refused national plans to put the government into business in competition with its citizens. That was born of Karl Marx.

I vetoed the idea of recovery through stupendous spending to prime the pump. That was born of a British professor.

I threw out attempts to centralize relief in Washington for politics and social experimentation. I defeated other plans to invade State rights, to centralize power in Washington. Those ideas were born of American radicals.

I stopped attempts at currency inflation and repudiation of government obligation. That was robbery of insurance-policy holders, savings-banks depositors and wage earners. That was born of the early Brain Trusters.

I rejected all these things because they would not only delay recovery but because I knew that in the end they would shackle free men.

Rejecting these ideas we Republicans had erected agencies of government which did start our country to prosperity without the loss of a single atom of American freedom.

All the ardent peddlers of these Trojan horses received sympathetic hearings from Mr. Roosevelt and joined vociferously in his election. Men are to be judged by the company they keep.

Our people did not recognize the gravity of the issue when I stated it four years ago. That is no wonder, for the day Mr. Roosevelt was elected Recovery was in progress, the Constitution was untrampled, the integrity of the government and the institutions of freedom were intact. It was not until after the election that the people began to awake. Then the realization of intended tinkering with the currency drove bank depositors into the panic that greeted Mr. Roosevelt's inauguration. Recovery was set back for two years, and hysteria was used as the bridge to reach the goal of personal government.

PART IV

I am proud to have carried the banner of free men to the last hour of the term my countrymen entrusted it to me. It matters nothing in the history of a race what happens to those who in their time have carried the banner of free men. What matters is that the battle shall go on.

The people know now the aims of this New Deal philosophy of government.

We propose instead leadership and authority in government within the moral and economic framework of the American System.

We propose to hold to the Constitutional safeguards of free men.

We propose to relieve men from fear, coercion and spite that are inevitable in personal government.

We propose to demobilize and decentralize all this spending upon which vast personal power is being built. We propose to amend the tax laws so as not to defeat free men and free enterprise.

We propose to turn the whole direction of this country toward liberty, not away from it.

The New Dealers say that all this that we propose is a worn-out System; that this machine age requires new measures for which we must sacrifice some part of the freedom of men. Men have lost their way with a confused idea that governments should run machines. Man-made machines cannot be of more worth than men themselves. Free men made these machines. Only free spirits can master them to their proper use.

The relation of our government with all these questions is complicated and difficult. They rise into the very highest ranges of economics, statesmanship, and morals.

And do not mistake. Free government is the most difficult of all government. But it is everlastingly true that the plain people will make fewer mistakes than any group of men no matter how powerful. But free government implies vigilant thinking and courageous living and self-reliance in a people.

Let me say to you that any measure which breaks our dykes of freedom will flood the land with misery.

The Social Field

In the field which is more largely social our first American objective should be the protection of the health, the assurance of the education and training of every child in our land. We want children kept out of our factories. We want them kept in school. We want every character-building agency to surround them, including good homes. Freedom can march only upon the feet of educated, healthy and happy children.

We want a land of health, and greater recreation for everybody. We want more opportunity for the creation and care of beauty and those things which satisfy the spirit.

The Economic Field

In the field which is more largely economic our first objective must be to provide security from poverty and want. We want security in living for every home. We want to see a nation built of home-owners and farm-owners.

We want to see their savings protected. We want to see them in steady jobs.

These are the first economic securities of human beings.

We want to see more and more of them insured against death and accident, unemployment and old age. We want them all secure.

The American system of liberty has driven toward these ideals for a century and a half. We realize that one-quarter of our people are not able today to have the standards we desire. But we are proud of a system that has given security and comfort to three-quarters of our families and in which even the under quarter ranks higher than that of any nation in the world.

National wisdom and national ideals require that we constantly develop the economic forces which will lift this one-quarter of our people. It requires that we at the same time attain greater stability to employment and to agriculture in the other three-quarters.

This is no occasion to elaborate the details of a program. But surely we must dump the whole New Deal theory of restriction of production, of code monopolies, of constantly higher prices for manufactured goods. We must reject their currency and credit policies, which will repeat our calamities of booms and depressions with greater heights and depths. We must reduce spending and amend the forms of taxation which now destroy enterprise and employment. We hold over-swollen fortunes must be distributed through pressure of taxes.

We hold the first essential is to improve constantly our machines and methods. That will create plenty and make it cheaper. That will enable the under quarter of our people to obtain more goods. Thereby we give increasing employment to everybody. We hold that this can be done only by private industry and not by government. We hold it can be done only by rewarding men for skill and merit. We hold it can be done only through the energizing force of competition.

We hold that we must direct the mind of the nation to the elimination of wastes. There is waste in this government. There is waste in natural resources. There is waste in production and distribution. There is waste in labor conflicts. There is the worst of all waste in human beings. If we turn national effort to this instead of listening to ways to get something for nothing, we will attain not only security, but we will also raise comfort to levels never before envisioned. And above all we can do it and be free.

It may be that some super mind can tell us what to do each day for our own good or can even force us to do it. But we haven't seen any indication of such mind among the New Dealers. This country moves forward because each individual of all these millions, each thinking for himself, using his own best judgment, using his own skill and experience, becomes expert in bettering his family and his community. To do that they must captain their own souls. No man will be the captain of his own soul if a Tugwell manages it for him.

Doubtless some one will at once arise and shout wicked capitalism, laissez-faire, special privilege, or wolfish individualism. These are the illuminated pumpkins of tomorrow night's New Deal Hallowe'en.

We hold a rule of free men which overrides all such nonsense. That is, free men must have equal rights and equal opportunities. For that the government must be the vigorous umpire. But we want a Judge Landis, we do not want a Simon Legree.

You might think that reform and change to meet new conditions of life are discoveries of the New Deal. Free men have always applied reform. We have been reforming and changing ever since George Washington. Democracy is not static. It is a living force. Every new idea, every new invention offers opportunity for both good and evil.

We are in need of reform every day in the week as long as men are greedy for money or power. We need a whole list of reforms right now, including the reform of these people who have created a gigantic spoils system as a method of seizing political power.

PART V

Many of the problems discussed in this campaign concern our material welfare. That is right. But there are things far more important to a nation than material welfare. It is possible to have a prosperous country under a dictatorship. It is not possible to have a free country. No great question will ever be settled in dollars and cents. Great questions must be settled on moral grounds and the tests of what makes free men. What is the nation profited if it shall gain the whole world and lose its own soul?

We want recovery. Not alone economic recovery. We must have moral recovery. And there are many elements in this.

We must re-establish truth and morals in public life. No people will long remain a moral people under a government that repudiates its obligations, that uses public funds to corrupt the people, that conceals its actions by double bookkeeping.

We must have government that builds stamina into communities and men. That makes men instead of mendicants. We must stop this softening of thrift, self-reliance and self-respect through dependence on government. We must stop telling youth that the country is going to the devil and they haven't a chance. We must stop this dissipating the initiative and aspirations of our people. We must revive the courage of men and women and their faith in American liberty. We must recover these spiritual heritages of America.

All this clatter of class and class hate should end. Thieves will get into high places as well as low places and they should both be given economic security—in jail. But they are not a class. This is a classless country. If we hold to our unique American ideal of equal opportunity there can never be classes or masses in our country. To preach these class ideas from the White House is new in American life. There is no employing class, no working class, no farming class. You may pigeonhole a man or woman as a farmer or a worker or a professional man or an employer or even a banker. But the son of the farmer will be a doctor or a worker or even a banker, and his daughter a teacher. The son of a worker will be an employer—or maybe President. And certainly the sons of even economic royalists have a bad time holding the title of nobility.

The glory of our country has been that every mother could

look at the babe in her arms with confidence that the highest position in the world was open to it.

The transcendent issue before us today is free men and women. How do we test freedom? It is not a catalogue of political rights. It is a thing of the spirit. Men must be free to worship, to think, to hold opinions, to speak without fear. They must be free to challenge wrong and oppression with surety of justice. Freedom conceives that the mind and spirit of man can be free only if he be free to pattern his own life, to develop his own talents, free to earn, to spend, to save, to acquire property as the security of his old age and his family.

Freedom demands that these rights and ideals shall be protected from infringement by others, whether men or groups, corporations or governments.

The conviction of our fathers was that all these freedoms come from the Creator and that they can be denied by no man or no government or no New Deal. They were spiritual rights of men. The prime purpose of liberal government is to enlarge and not to destroy these freedoms. It was for that purpose that the Constitution of the United States was enacted. For that reason we demand that the safeguards of freedom shall be upheld. It is for this reason that we demand that this country should turn its direction from a system of personal centralized government to the ideals of liberty.

And again I repeat that statement of four years ago—"This campaign is more than a contest between two men. It is a contest between two philosophies of government."

Whatever the outcome of this election that issue is set. We shall battle it out until the soul of America is saved.

Packing the Supreme Court

NEW YORK CITY

[*February 5, 1937*]

STRIPPED of subsidiary matters, some of which are admirable, the President's action also amounts to this.

The Supreme Court has proved many of the New Deal proposals unconstitutional. Instead of the ample alternatives of the Constitution by which these proposals could be submitted to the people through constitutional amendment, it is now proposed to make changes by "packing" the Supreme Court. It has the implication of subordination of the court to the personal power of the Executive. Because all this reaches to the very depth of our form of government, it far transcends any questions of partisanship.

The Congress should delay action until the people have had ample time to formulate their views on it. In the long sweep of the republic, a few months are not too much in which to consider a vital change in the repeated judgment of the American people over 150 years. That judgment has always been that their liberties have depended greatly on the independence of the court, and that they themselves should determine changes in the Constitution.

Hands Off the Supreme Court

CHICAGO, ILLINOIS

[February 20, 1937]

I

I HAVE been glad to meet a long-standing invitation of this Society. The Union League Club of Chicago was originally formed in the time of a great Constitutional crisis. Its great purpose was to fight for human liberty under the banner of Abraham Lincoln. It is now and has long been a nonpartisan body. But it is no less devoted to Constitutional government. And today from President Roosevelt's proposals as to the Supreme Court we are faced with the greatest Constitutional question in these seventy years.

It is a magnificent thing for the nation that the debate upon this question has risen far above partisanship. The proposal is too grave to be dealt with on such terms. It is an inspiring thing that the leadership to maintain the integrity of the American form of government has been begun by eminent Senators belonging to the President's own party. This leadership, which we all gladly follow, places this issue on the highest plane of citizenship without regard to party, to partisan politics, to personal ambition.

Neither is the country divided upon group or class lines. Some people seem to think that all Americans can be pigeonholed into Radicals, Tories, Liberals, Conservatives, Progressives, Reactionaries, "right wing" or "left wing." These imported terms do not fit very well in America. They are used often as epithets to express our bad opinions of somebody else. But whatever they do mean, we find outstanding leaders of each of these supposed classifications carrying the banner of opposition to the President's proposals. At least our opponents who look for pigeonholes cannot place me either with the Liberty League, whose leading members so bitterly opposed my election, nor among those radicals with whose ideas of a collectivist America I have so often been in collision.

Some months ago I made an address at Cleveland in which I directed attention to the problems of human liberty. Nation-wide the press, even those who had long been my opponents, were extraordinarily eulogistic of that speech. As a method of spreading flowers over the termination of my party career the opposition press insisted on electing me to the office of elder statesman. I have not assumed that high office. But at least it marks their acceptance of the fact that the era in my life has gone by when party aspects of such an issue concern me.

I am speaking tonight not as a Republican; I am speaking as an American who has witnessed the decay and destruction of human liberty in many lands, who as President has witnessed the movement of these great floods which are testing the American levees built to protect free men.

Seldom has debate so quickly flamed up across the nation. It is not alone public men and journalists who are engaged in this discussion. It is alive today between farmers in the field, workers at the bench, women in their homes, and men in their offices. The very spread of the debate illuminates the gravity of the issue.

By this debate the issue has already been greatly clarified. That real issue is whether the President by the appointment of additional judges upon the Supreme Court shall revise the Constitution—or whether change in the Constitution shall be submitted to the people as the Constitution itself provides.

This is no lawyers' dispute over legalisms. This is the people's problem. And it is the duty of every citizen to concern himself with this question. It reaches to the very center of his liberties.

II

We may quickly dismiss the secondary parts of the President's proposals. We can accept the view that justice would be expedited if we had more Federal District Courts. There may not be enough Circuit Courts of Appeal. But there can be only one Supreme Court.

Here Mr. Roosevelt demands the power to appoint a new justice parallel with every existing justice who is over seventy years of age. This means that two-thirds of the Court, or six of them, are to be given a sort of intellectual nurse, having half of the vote of each patient. It is the implications of this proposal which have thrust us with startling suddenness into an issue greater and deeper than any in our generation.

We may also deal quickly with the reasons for this proposal to which Mr. Roosevelt has given the most emphasis.

It has been shown by the reports of the Department of Justice that the Supreme Court is not behind with its work. Moreover, more members of the Supreme Court would not speed action. The fact is each justice must in every case individually give his own opinion. Certainly each individual of fifteen justices is likely to take as long in making up his individual mind as each individual among nine justices.

One of the reasons given for the President's proposal is old age. Mr. Walter Lippmann has said, "By an act of lawless legality he would force two-thirds of the Court to choose between resignation and being publicly branded as senile." I do not for a moment believe that was the purpose of this proposal, but it might be the consequence. I wonder if those noble interpreters of human liberty, John Marshall and Oliver Wendell Holmes, would have served America as well in the last years of their lives had they possessed an intellectual nurse who also divided their vote.

III

But the President's proposal is far deeper and more far-reaching in purpose than these details. The people must probe it in the light of its background, of the incidents that have led up to it. They must probe it in the light of its real effect upon their own security. They must probe it in the light of the forces moving in the world today.

Mr. Roosevelt has sought many Acts of Congress which lead to increase in the personal power of the Executive. He has sought greatly to centralize the government. I am not for the moment debating the merits of these measures, for some of them are of good purpose. The Supreme Court has found in fourteen of these laws which profoundly affect the public welfare that Mr. Roosevelt was within the Constitution in six cases and violated the Constitution in eight cases. In many of those decisions justices supposed to be of Mr. Roosevelt's realm of thought have concurred. Of eight important decisions adverse to Mr. Roosevelt's wishes four have been decided unanimously and of the six cases where the decisions were favorable three were unanimous. There can therefore be no real charge that the Court has not decided in accord with what the Constitution means. The Court was not engaged in vetoing Mr. Roosevelt's proposals, as his Attorney-General alleges. It was finding according to the law as established by the people of the United States.

And what was the effect of these decisions which are now criticized? The unanimous decision on the NRA relieved the American people of a gigantic system of monopolies conducted by big business—a monopoly that even reached down to a jail sentence for pressing pants for less than the presidential approved price. Another of these acts was thrown out because it was based upon coercion of men to surrender their rights of freedom. And coercion is the antithesis of liberty.

IV

Mr. Roosevelt has felt it necessary repeatedly to criticize the decisions, even those which were unanimous. To complain of the umpire is real human. However, nobody in this country can believe that if these decisions had been in accord with his wishes he would have made these proposals to add six new justices. Most of the supporters of the President's proposal have ceased to defend it on the grounds of either expedition of justice or old age. Their support is now boldly that it means quick and revolutionary change in the Constitution. And that without reference to the people and we are not even told where the Constitution is at fault or what changes they would make. They are asking for a blank check upon which they can write future undisclosed purposes.

In the light of this background no one can conclude other than that the President seeks not to secure a Supreme Court that will find in accordance with the Constitution as it stands. He wants one that will revise the Constitution so it will mean what he wishes it to mean.

And this is not a loose assertion. Mr. Roosevelt himself specifically confirms this purpose. In his message to Congress he says that if these proposals be accepted then "we may be relieved of the necessity of considering any fundamental changes in the powers of the Courts or the Constitution of our government."

Thus we are plainly told that Constitutional change is sought not by open and frank amendment of the Constitution but by judicial decision.

If this is to be accomplished the new judges must necessarily be men who will ratify Mr. Roosevelt's projects. Unless they are pledged to Mr. Roosevelt's way of thinking he would not be, to use his own words, relieved of the necessity of considering fundamental changes in the Constitution. I am wondering what esteem these pledged judges would hold with the people.

V

If Mr. Roosevelt can change the Constitution to suit his purposes by adding to the members of the Court, any succeeding President can do it to suit his purposes. If a troop of "President's judges" can be sent into the halls of justice to capture political power, then his successor with the same device can also send a troop of new "President's judges" to capture some other power. That is not judicial process. That is force.

VI

The Court and the Constitution thus become the tool of the Executive and not the sword of the people. A leading newspaper which usually supports the President sums it up: "It proposes to sanction a precedent which would make any President the master of the Supreme Court by the mere process of enlarging it." Thus we are face to face with the proposition that the Supreme Court shall be made subjective to the Executive. Stripped to its bare bones that is the heart of this proposal. And that reaches to the very center of human liberty. The ultimate safeguard of liberty is the independence of the courts.

VII

In all the centuries of struggle for human freedom the independence of the judiciary from political domination has been the first battle against autocratic power.

In America we have builded over these two centuries certain sacred rights which are the very fibers of human freedom. Upon them depends freedom of speech. Upon them depends security from individual oppression. Upon the protection of these rights depends religious freedom.

Our Constitution was not alone a statement of these rights. It was a framework of government for the safeguarding of these rights. Every school boy and girl knows that the very pillars of that temple are the independence of the Supreme Court, the Legislative branch, the Executive, and the division of powers with the states.

But these securities and these rights are no stronger than their safeguards. And of these safeguards none is so final and so imperative as the independence of the courts. It is here alone where the humblest citizen and the weakest minority have their only sanctuary.

Governor Lowden has recently emphasized that the farmers of this country are less than 25 per cent of the whole people; that labor is only 25 per cent of the whole people; that the Executive and the Congress are elected by a majority. That when the day comes that the majority are displeased with farm prices or the majority displeased with wages, then protection of the rights of the minority rests upon the Constitution and the Supreme Court.

VIII

Self-government never dies from direct attack. No matter what his real intentions may be, no man will arise and say that he intends to suspend one atom of the rights guaranteed by the Constitution. Liberty dies from the encroachments and disregard of the safeguards of those rights. And unfortunately it is those whose purposes have often been good who have broken the levees of liberty to find a short-cut to their ends.

These are serious times. Liberty is crumbling over two-thirds of the world. In less than a score of years the courts in a dozen nations have been made subjective to political power, and with this subjection the people's securities in those countries have gone out of the window. And, mark you this—in every instance the persuaders have professed to be acting for the people and in the name of progress. As we watch the parade of nations down that suicide road every American has cause to be anxious for our republic.

I have said this is the people's problem. It is the Supreme Court defending the people's rights and securities guaranteed by the Constitution which time and again has protected the people from those who seek for economic power or political power or to suppress free worship and free thought. It is the people's rights that are endangered. Once political power makes use of the Court, its strength and its moral prestige are irretrievably weakened.

This meeting is the annual occasion in memory of George Washington. In his farewell address to the American people he said: "One method of assault may be to effect in the form of the Constitution alterations which may impair the energy of the system and thus undermine that which cannot be directly overthrown."

IX

It is not that our Constitution is a shackle on progress. It is a commonplace to repeat that the growth of social ideas and mechanical invention and the ingenuity of wickedness force new problems in our national life. So far as they relate to government the vast majority of them are solvable within the Constitution. When specific problems arise which do require Constitutional amendment then the people have ever been willing to grant it. Such changes are not lightly to be undertaken. But the Constitution provides an open and aboveboard method by which they may be quickly accomplished.

What is the hurry in all this? The nation is recovering from depression. There is no emergency. Surely a year or two is no waste in the life of a great nation when its liberties are the stake of haste.

If historic liberalism cannot be maintained under the present provisions of the Constitution, I shall be the first to support the President in amendment of it.

But there are certain things that must not change. These things are the fundamental safeguards of human rights. We have already gone far on the road of personal government. The American people must halt when it is proposed to lay hands on the independence of the Supreme Court. That is the ultimate security of every cottage. It is the last safeguard of free men.

Ladies and gentlemen, I offer you a watchword—Hands off the Supreme Court.

The Business of Boys

ADDRESS TO BOYS' CLUBS OF AMERICA,
NEW YORK CITY

[*May 13, 1937*]

THIS convention is dealing with the Public Relations of boys. We do not exclude their sisters—if anything, our sentiment for them is even more tender. But we are here engaged with the business of boys.

This evening I wish to examine the nature of the animal.

To explore what civilization has done to some of them.

To relate an experiment.

To lay before you a proposition which involves $15,000,000.

To give the reasons for it all.

And finally to wind up with the peroration. And to do it all in fifteen minutes.

Together with his sister, the boy is our most precious possession. But he presents not only joys and hopes, but also paradoxes. He strains our nerves, yet he is a complex of cells teeming with affection. He is a periodic nuisance, yet he is a joy forever. He is a part-time incarnation of destruction, yet he radiates sunlight to all the world. He gives evidence of being the child of iniquity, yet he makes a great nation. He is filled with curiosity as to every mortal thing, he is an illuminated interrogation point, yet he is the most entertaining animal that is.

The whole world is new to him. Therefore his should be a life of adventure, of discovery, of great undertakings. He must spend much time, if he is to expand, in the land of make-believe. One of the sad things in the world is that he must grow up into the land of realities.

He is endowed with a dynamic energy and an impelling desire to take exercise on all occasions. His primary instinct is to hunt in a pack and that multiplies his devices. He is a complete self-starter, and therefore wisdom in dealing with him consists mostly in what to do with him next.

The Constitution provides him, or at least at one time it did, with the inalienable right of liberty, and the pursuit of happiness. We are not so much concerned at the moment with his liberties as guaranteed by the Bill of Rights as we are with his processes for the pursuit of happiness. He will find the tragedies of both liberty and happiness when he becomes a taxpayer. He and his pack can go on this hunt for happiness either constructively or destructively. Our first problem is to find him constructive joy, instead of destructive glee.

To complicate this problem, this civilization has gone and built up great cities. We have increased the number of boys per acre. We have paved all this part of the land with cement and cobblestones. There are about twenty million of these human organisms in the country. Of these perhaps three million are crowded into the poorer sections and slums of our cities. They have to spend their spare time on these pavements, surrounded by brick walls. That boy has a life of stairs, light switches, alleys, fire escapes, bells and cobblestones, and a chance to get run over by a truck. Thus these boys are today separated from Mother Earth and all her works, except the weather. The outlet of curiosity in exploring the streams and the fields is closed to him. The mysteries of the birds and bees and fish are denied to him.

The normal boy is a primitive animal and takes to competition and battle. In the days before our civilization became so perfect, he matched his wits with the birds, the bees and the fish. At least he found battle with animal or plant life in zoos or parks. If he doesn't contend with nature, he is likely to take on contention with a policeman. And yet we cannot restore many of these constructive joys in a land of cement and bricks.

This is a marginal problem. It concerns only a minority of boys. And I may state generally that if the American people would only realize that our national problems are all marginal problems of eliminating evil, correcting abuse and building up the weak, rather than the legerdemain of Utopia, we would make more progress. And I dislike to refer to these boys as "under-privileged." That is only a half-truth. The government provides even the marginal city boys with better facilities for education and better protection of health than any other government in the world. And we are today doing a better job of these things than ever before in our history. Far less than his grandfather does he suffer from mumps and measles; more quickly do we heal his fractures. Far less does he have to endure stench and filth. And the electric light has banished the former curse of all boys, of cleaning lamps and everlastingly carrying them about. The light switch has driven away the goblins that lived in dark corners and under the bed. It clothes drab streets with gaiety and cheer by night. And it is the attraction of these bright lights that increases our problem.

There are other privileges that the most lowly of them have. It is a privilege to have been born in America. They live under a democracy where they have more opportunity of becoming a mayor or a policeman or an editor or even a banker than in any other country. So they have some privileges.

But we are concerned with the privileges which this civilization has taken away; and the particular ones with which we are concerned bear on his character and moral stature. Now this brick and cement foundation of life is a hard soil for these growths. Somebody will say morals are the job of parents. The better the parents are, the better the morals; the worse they are, the greater our problem. But the best of parents cannot keep him indoors all the time. And the world in the streets is a distorted and dangerous world, which the parents cannot make or unmake. So it becomes a job of public relations.

But there is more than that. The fine qualities of loyalty to the pack, competition with violent zeal yet without bitterness, the restraints that cover the rights of others—these are the spirit of sportsmanship. They are not so good on the pavements. For here the pack turns to the gang, where his superabundant vitality leads him to depredation. And here we make gangsters and feed jails.

And let no one tell you that crime is decreasing in the United States. Nor is that due to lack of vigilance on the part of public authorities. I recollect that during my administration we doubled the population of Federal jails. Crime increases despite all this repression. And with all the wave of beneficent prison reforms of the past ten years, and all the expensive attempt to make good men out of criminals, we have not decreased crime. The way to stop crime is to stop the manufacture of criminals.

And there is far more to our purpose than stopping crime at its source or to let off the boy's physical violence without getting into the police court. If there is such a thing as rights in the world, there are also rights that belong to pavement boys. There are, of course, the rights to proper homes, there are rights to education and health. But there are still other rights, and these other rights are where we come in. That is, the right to play games—the right to glimpse into the constructive joys—the right to develop an occupation fitted to his inclinations and talents—and the right to develop his personality.

There is more to this than even exercise and morals. There is the job of stretching his vision of life. The priceless treasure of boyhood is his endless enthusiasm, his high store of idealism, his affections, and his hopes. When we preserve these, we have made men. We have made citizens, and we have made Americans. But the hard pavements do not reek with these things.

Many years ago, devoted souls, apprehending these problems and difficulties, established Boys' Clubs in some of the most crowded areas of our cities. Today there are over 290 clubs embracing 255,000 boys spread in 153 cities. They represent $30,000,000 worth of property. Over these years, the clubs and the parent organization have trained a staff of skill and devotion. Some of these clubs have as many as 7000 boys causing the premises to throb with their devices. Their annual cost is near $2,000,000, to supplement the boys' own payments;

that is, about $10 per boy. And that $10 saves many hundred times as much to society.

In these clubs the pavement boy had opportunity for organization of the pack for its proper constructive joys, instead of the gang. Here they could find outlet for their superlative energy in play and the land of make-believe. These opportunities stretch all the way from checkers to sandlot baseball. There are gymnasiums and swimming pools. And here also they are given glimpses of the opportunities of a greater America. They are encouraged to music, to manufacture, to make and to construct. Their faculties and qualities are tested to find their occupational direction. They are given preliminary training in the arts and in the trades. And, above all, they are taught the spirit of sportsmanship, which is the second highest moral code in the world.

They are taught the rules of health—they are each examined and each repaired for his physical weaknesses. And the repair of boys to keep them physically fit is of the largest importance in their moral and spiritual development.

The police cases and juvenile delinquencies in the areas where these clubs work regularly show striking decreases. They have produced men of leadership in their communities. There are great editors, sculptors and actors who came from this boys' mill. And they have produced two players in major league baseball. The feet of thousands have been set on the road of American opportunity.

That is an experiment, but it is an experiment that has gone so far as to become an answer.

This movement is in no sense a competitor with the magnificent work of the Boy Scouts. There are in fact many troops in the clubs. They provide an entirely different set of influences.

I could stop at length to pay tribute to the men who have builded all this effort. They are legion. To none of them do we owe more than to Mr. W. E. Hall, for twenty-one years the President of this Association. I have but recently become officially attached, and I have had the good fortune to bring to the organization Mr. Sanford Bates, who will later address you.

Now, as to the proposition of which I warned you. There are in fact two propositions. The first is to establish buildings and equipment for two or three million more boys. That means we must expand by ten times. That takes money, that takes devotion, and that takes service. It can be done, although we cannot do it all at once. Our second proposition is to find their skilled direction and to find their annual support. That is difficult but between good folks and community chests and the energies of the managers, that is kept up pretty well by the local communities where they are started. And upon this side, I want to mention the Union League Club of Chicago. This great men's club has adopted two boys' clubs. Every great social club in the United States would be a better place if it also had such adopted children.

The most difficult job is to find land and pay for buildings and equipment. As somebody said some four hundred years ago, "There's the rub." Over a term of years we need $15,000,000 for that job. We ought to start 100 new clubs in 50 cities during the next three years.

And what do I say for a peroration? But little. You picture that pavement boy entering the door of that house of constructive joy. The light of his face—the gleam of honest devilment in his eye—the feeling of trust and security in his heart.

And here is the sense of safety and gratitude which warms his mother's heart also.

The Crisis and the Political Parties and an American Program*

[*September, 1937*]

THE time I write—mid-July—would seem appropriate for leisurely taking stock of our political parties and their relation to the great issue. Lest some suspicious person see a sea serpent in this article, let me say at once that most public men fight for re-election to office only because they are not quitters. If the voters are good enough to relieve them, there comes in time a great sense of gratitude for freedom and a determination to hold on to that blessed state. And this state develops objectivity. But objectivity in these hours does not imply neutrality.

My concern with political parties today is that they perform their prime responsibility. That is, they should align themselves with intellectual honesty and present to the people the opportunity to express their will as to the real issue of our times—possibly the greatest issue of one hundred and sixty years. The essence of the real political contest of today is personal liberty, which includes the rights of minorities. Today that issue is confused in both parties. It is obscured by indecision, by phrases, denials, contradictions, and evasion.

There is a certain obviousness in the statement that political parties are necessary to the functioning of a democracy. Also it is obvious that they must be systematically organized and constructively led. Otherwise the ballot box cannot perform its function of replacing violence or exploding feelings or advancing the welfare of the people. It is equally plain that there

*Atlantic Monthly.

cannot be more than two major parties, or the result is government by minority or by negation, which is frustration of democracy. It is likewise obvious that the party out of power has a public responsibility to oppose extreme and irrational action and to oppose it vigorously.

These are times of a new advance in humane concepts and of great social and economic restlessness. Political parties must be more than the "ins" and "outs" seeking the public jobs. They also must be more than "against." They must have affirmative purposes.

Parties can, of course, for a time avoid the real issues, or can elaborate petty issues, or carry intellectually dishonest proposals or the dodges of group apepals. But in times when the waters of the deep in human emotions are stirring, the people will sooner or later discard any such party. That is history.

The first political party in the United States in its Declaration adopted as part of its platform the demand for "life, liberty, and the pursuit of happiness." The Fathers were intellectually honest. They did not promise happiness. They only asserted that for pursuers of happiness freedom would be safeguarded.

With all our modern problems of industrial life, the miseries from war and its depression aftermath, with some who get too much and some who get too little, this method of securing happiness is being questioned in the world. That question is whether happiness is to be attained through liberty of men or whether government can take over the pursuit and deliver the happiness by coercing people into what some bureaucrat thinks should make them happy. The issue may be stated in another way. Shall coercion be limited to criminals and men of ill-will who would encroach upon the freedom of others? Or shall centralized personal government undertake to plan the lives of upright men and coerce and compel them to comply?

Despite the belief of the Fathers that they had expelled this latter concept of government, it is back again. It is not back in America with the open avowal of any political party, and of course it has new verbal clothes. It is no coincidence that the same sugar-coated phrase is used in Moscow, Berlin, Rome, and Washington—"planned economy." The American mind is confused. And there are two other problems which add to the confusion. Both bear upon the responsibilities of liberty.

The first arises mainly from our enormously increased capacity to produce. That gives rise to hopes of security to everybody. And our expanding humanitarian sense demands further action through government that those who are the most economically successful shall carry a larger burden in the promotion of the common welfare.

The second problem arises from an accumulation of hidden abuses of the capitalistic system which exploded with the depression.

The provision of greater security and comfort in life for all and the cure of abuse are objectives upon which there is no disagreement among thinking people. What we are here concerned with is the philosophy and method—for it is in these that loss of personal liberty emerges.

The question for Americans is whether or not we conceive that our system of free men is valid. If so, the current problems of social security, capitalistic abuse, or what not, are marginal problems around the preponderant honesty or preponderant security of the great free majority, and are to be cured within the framework of this American system.

The alternative has three aspects.

The first is whether individuals and a nation can make spiritual and intellectual progress unless upright men may be free to think, to speak, to worship, to assemble, and to pursue their own callings in their own way, provided they respect the rights of others.

The second is whether they can produce more goods and material happiness, and distribute them with as much justice, if they be free or if they be directed by the state.

The third is whether, if men be directed and coerced in economic life, we can at the same time maintain the spiritual and intellectual freedom of a people.

We have before our eyes in Europe the ultimates of "planned

economy" and its promises of delivered happiness. The two schools of Socialism and Fascism differ from each other mostly in execution. Russian Socialism murderd the economic middle class as a preliminary, while Fascism constituted the leaders of the middle class deputies of the state to assist in the subjugation of all the laborers, farmers, and small business people. These leaders are obviously more comfortable under Fascism.

In any event there is one common result of "planned economy" and its promises of delivered happiness. That is, it cannot continue without personal government, without suppression of spiritual and intellectual freedom and the other guarantees of life and liberty. Those are the nettles of economic coercion. These European experiments have certainly failed to produce either economic security or spiritual progress.

. . . .

The New Dealers have conceived that they can adapt a part of the European systems of coercive planned economy and at the same time preserve our spiritual and intellectual liberties and allow us the moral stature of free men. They assert that this is the only humanitarian road and the only road to cure of abuse and greater security for the less fortunate groups.

The trouble is that coercive, planned economy, with its necessary accompaniment of personal government, does not and cannot remain half and half. It spawns daily new compulsions in order to make it work. Like all drugs, it requires increasing doses.

Congress was coerced by "must" legislation and the abuse of patronage and the use of expenditures. Every session sees more and more coercive measures with further pyramiding of personal government.

The Supreme Court is now to be coerced by packing its membership.

Communities have been intimidated and beguiled by threats and promises of pork from lump-sum appropriations.

The three major guards of the Bill of Rights—the independence of the Congress, the independence of the Judiciary, and the balance of local government—are now fast being thrown into the discard in this deal.

The whole gamut of New Deal philosophy—price fixing, wage fixing, managed production in farm and shop, managed currency, managed credit, managed interest—depends on in-creasing coercion of the individual and new limitations of per-sonal liberty. Upright individuals and business are increasingly coerced not only by planned economy but by putting regulatory laws for much-needed cure of abuse in forms whereby bureauc-racy is given wide discretion in the control of men and affairs. This is the New Deal substitution for specific law which all men may read and the courts decide.

The results are not academic. Men and women in every community can bear witness to personal coercion and intimida-tion such as this country has never before seen.

And coercion is infectious. We have an outbreak of coercion when employers use spies and thugs to prevent their employees from joining unions. The very basis of liberty requires that to be stopped. But there is equal coercion in sit-down strikes and the use of "beef-squads" against thousands of workmen. And this now has tacit approval as a part of the strategy of planned economy—even the courts are flouted and disorder al-lowed to run riot. Then comes the equally terrible coercion of vigilante committees hot on the trail.

The deliberate fanning of class antagonism in a country which is more nearly classless than humanity has ever before seen is building for a Babel of coercion.

•   •   •   •   •   •   •   •   •   •

I am not here analyzing the New Deal except in one major particular. Nor is it my purpose to enter a discussion upon the inevitable economic effect of "planned economy." When the destruction of the spirit of enterprise, when the results of inflation, of restricted production, of debts, and of taxes, catch up to recovery and show in dropping standards of living and less security—then these morals will point themselves. In op-timistic or even artificially happy times every economic warning is from a Jeremiah. And Jeremiah may have been the one especially referred to as being without honor in his own country. Whether the economic consequences be for good or evil, they are of far less importance to the life of a great people than this major issue.

I am aware that the questions of personal liberty may be called academic abstractions; that it will be said they are beyond the grasp of the people. In about 1776 the people fought and many died for exactly this abstraction. And they understood what they were dying for.

There is no greater abstraction in the setup of government than the independence of the Judiciary. In the last one hundred days the people have risen to that.

II

The last national campaign was greatly confused. The public mind, and consequently the minds of both parties, were confused.

The reality of the issue was glossed over by the inevitable upward trend of the business cycle and the stimulants which had been introduced into an economic system still partly free. The people clung to growing recovery. The majority of them believed that the material benefits of the New Deal were comforting and lasting.

Both parties campaigned largely with bait to particular groups and sections. In this confused situation the Republican Party attempted to outdo some of the New Deal baits. As one cynic overstated it, "it promised every measure of the New Deal but said it would do it cheaper."

Both parties used the same phrases of Constitution, freedom, liberalism, and so forth, but to mean different things. The New Deal obscured coercion. The Republicans did not clear the issue.

. . . .

Public understanding has also been confused upon this issue

by slogans and the use of old political labels imported from Europe.

We chatter today of reactionaries, conservatives, liberals, and radicals. It is true that mental attitudes can be classified on this gamut, but in their application as political labels in the United States they have been wholly distorted.

For instance, the term "liberal" flows from the word "liberty"; it does not come from the word "coercion." Yet the New Deal has camouflaged itself with this honored term.

Of course the dictionary also gives a definition of "liberal" which connotes giving generously and spending freely. This attracts many people, but the dictionary means liberality with one's own money.

A "reactionary" in ordinary times is a gentleman who wants to re-establish the *status quo ante*. The New Deal wants to do precisely that—as a matter of fact it is *status quo George III* or *Diocletian*. This process has now attained the label of "liberal."

These and other phrases are used for eulogy, for defamation, and as refuges for intellectual dishonesty. They are set up as pigeonholes for men and groups to imply that they are righteous, stingy, malevolent, or generally sinful. They are dumdum words used to assassinate men and then to plant bitter onions on their graves.

Users of such phrases should be called upon to define precisely what they mean and what they advocate, or these words mean nothing. It would be serviceable to clarity in public thinking and intellectual honesty if the Bureau of Standards could get out a definition of each of these terms. Bureau tests of the New Deal across the genuine spectrum from reaction to radicalism would probably find its acts to be one-sixth radical, one-sixth liberal, one-third reactionary, and one-third fantastic.

.   .   .   .

Incidentally there are many blots that need to be scrubbed out if real liberty is to survive. Much of this laundry needs to be done by the cities to clean up vicious political machines. Much needs to be done nationally to stop the use of public funds to influence voters. Some of it needs to be done by the parties on methods by which private money is obtained to carry on campaigns. I have no doubt these humiliate the majority members of each party.

For instance, the Democratic Party is selling books autographed by the President at $250 each to corporations, and advising them that in merely buying books they are not violating the law against corporate funds in politics. Also in taking more than half a million dollars from one labor union the New Deal took as formidable a liability to serve special interest as if such funds had come from a group of corporation heads.

This has a counterpart in the Republican Party, which abandoned its rule of 1924 to 1932 of limited personal subscriptions and in 1936 secured nearly half a million dollars from the individual members of one large industrial firm.

Here is also illustrated the fluidity of principle in some political money. Prominent members of that industrial group were the largest subscribers to the Democratic campaign in 1928; to the Democratic smear propaganda between 1928 and 1932; to the New Deal campaign in 1932, to the Liberty League, and finally to the Republican campaign in 1936.

Another trouble in political parties is that perennial, "Predatory Interests"—that being a label which also needs definition by the Bureau of Standards.

The legitimate action of any government affects private interests of firms, groups, and communities whether they be corporations, or workers, or farmers, or local governments. It is the duty of free men to defend their rights. The spirit of the Bill of Rights does not include special privilege. Every administration is under pressure for some privilege from somewhere. The New Deal is not free from such share-croppers, as it has indeed opened new and green fields.

The list of such suspicious groups is about the same in both parties. As a matter of fact, these forces are more a spirit than specific individuals. They shift with the times and the issues. They have little if any party fealty. They certainly serve both parties for political ammunition. The spirits of special privilege and abuse will always be with us and need constantly to be exorcised. They exist even in Socialist or Fascist governments. But democracies exorcise these spirits with much more free speech, and microphones.

Be it said at once that only a small number of our business men possess such a spirit. Universal denunciation of business men is one of the most cruel and destructive tendencies in our politics. There is no more expert group of industrialists and merchants in the world than those who are piloting the production of America today. We could no more do without them for twenty-four hours than we could do without workmen or farmers.

And there are the Old Guards of both parties. They also serve as magnificent oratorical targets to prove the political purity of the orator. They again are more of a spirit than a constant group and they are not often of the predatory species. Most of them are patriotic, but slow in the uptake. They are hard political fighters and they carry their grudges, as those of us who have fought them have reason to know.

And there are the lunatic fringes in both parties who flutter with every wind of emotion. They naturally fluttered to the New Deal at the start.

As a matter of fact, when new social problems began to arise a half century or more ago the individual members of both parties divided in thought on these questions somewhat along the scale from true conservatism to true liberalism. We secured fairly progressive government over many years, because each party compromised fairly near the middle and the middles were not far apart. However, at that time both parties held to the fundamentals of the American system.

.   .   .   .

If we look over the present scene of political parties we find the New Deal throned on the prestige of an enormous victory. Its political strength rests upon the upward swing of the business cycle, upon the belief of many that the philosophy of liberty is exhausted, and upon the promise of the simple and quick delivery of happiness. Many of its proponents are imbued with a zeal and a faith that they are saving America, and with a high conviction that all who differ with their methods are wicked and selfish.

The strength of the party also rests upon the patronage which through Federal, state, and municipal offices reaches into nearly 2,000,000 families, and through Federal disbursements to unemployed and farmers reaches another 6,000,000 families—nearly one-third of the whole people. Furthermore, it controls nearly all the big city political machines.

Its political weakness lies in the fact that many members of the Democratic Party, including some of its greatest leaders, still believe in freedom, and are daily growing in their opposition to the whole philosophy of personal government, planned economy, and coercion.

It is true that the incipient revolt from its ranks by the Liberty League failed, but that revolt was based on the concept that liberty sprang from liberty for big business and not from spiritual and intellectual liberty.

The other great weakness of the Democratic Party is that sooner or later there will be the inevitable swing of dissatisfied voters away from the party in power.

.   .   .   .

If we explore the present situation in the Republican Party we find a good deal of latent strength. The sweeping defeat left it a much smaller proportion of conspicuous offices—governors and members of Congress—than any minority party since 1870. In consequence its natural broadcasting timber is limited.

Despite the fact that in 1936 it held few great public offices and no consequential patronage, its Presidential vote was about 17,000,000. Its real strength is greater than this, for the aggregate vote for the leading Republican state candidates was over 19,000,000. This constitutes numerically the strongest minority party the country has ever seen. Even on the Presidential vote the Republican minority exceeds the Democratic minority of 1924 by 9,000,000, of 1928 by 2,000,000. Carrying the brunt of world depression, the party commanded 42 per cent of the vote outside the Solid South in 1932, and, if we take the state vote mentioned above, it commanded about the same percentage in 1936.

It has other vitalities. It has an organization in more than 150,000 precincts, 3000 counties, and the 48 states, with innumerable clubs, the vast majority of which, nationally as well as locally, are led by sincere, loyal, and determined men and women. It holds elective office in many more counties than its state defeats would indicate. It thus has a moving mechanism.

The real strength of the Republican Party lies in the faith of the majority of its membership. They believe in it with a devotion second only to their religion.

It has made mistakes. It was too conservative in certain reforms during the post-war years of prosperity. Yet it was the people themselves who reflected into their government an attitude of complacency despite repeated warnings. The people were like the householder who would not allow the repair of the roof in good weather and could not repair it in a hurricane.

Republicans rightly take pride in the vast national service of their party. It was born in the defense of human liberty. The party was consecrated to that purpose in a great war. From its first day in office in 1861 to its last day in 1933 it upheld our system of personal liberty. It never deviated from the Constitution in letter or in spirit. It has at all times been a party of Americanism.

When mass production and big corporations entered national life it was the Republican Party which inaugurated the policy of regulating business to prevent monopoly and exploitation. The Sherman Anti-Trust Act, the Interstate Commerce Commission, the present Federal Power Commission, the Radio Commission, the regulation of many other interstate business activities, and the state regulatory commission were Republican concepts. It has destroyed a multitude of would-be monopolies and upheld the principle of honest competition.

It was the Republican Party which initiated the constitutional amendment authorizing income, corporation, and inheritance taxes, that the burdens of government should be distributed more justly.

Through the whole period from 1861 to 1933 it has been a party of prudent fiscal finance. Every Republican administration, except in the emergency of war,and the World War depression, has balanced the budget and reduced the national debt. Its last administration, even though dealing with the worst years of falling revenues, and against opposition, kept the debt rise down to less than 7 per cent after deducting recoverable loans.

During its whole life after the Civil War it fought for and sustained a stable, convertible gold currency right down to 1933. At every step of the party life it upheld the fidelity of the government to its obligations, and denied repudiation. All Republican administrations have contributed to and supported Federal regulation of banking. When the Federal Reserve System failed to meet expectations in the crisis of 1929, the Republican administration proposed and supported vigorous banking reform. And as sustaining agencies pending these reforms it set up the Reconstruction Finance Corporation, the Home Loan Banks, the Agricultural Credit Banks, and brought the strength of the government to protect the people from the weak banking system.

It maintained tariff protection from foreign labor and foreign farmers. It was the party that protected American workmen by first restricting and finally in 1931 abolishing immigration. It largely established and in every administration strengthened Civil Service, an essential to economical and honest government.

In devotion to public improvement it initiated Federal highways, the modernization of the waterways and harbors, the reclamation service, the construction of the Panama Canal, the Colorado Dam, the flood control of the Mississippi River.

Fortunately our foreign affairs have not been party matters. Every Republican administration has builded peace.

When the growth of humanitarianism began to press upon government it was Republican state administrations that originated the limitation of hours for women, that started the abolition of child labor, that initiated workmen's compensation acts, state old-age pensions, mothers' pensions, and a score of other social reforms. It was a Republican national administration which proposed the Federal amendment to abolish child labor. It was a Republican administration which in 1930 first announced the national obligation that no American should go hungry or cold, and first organized nation-wide relief for the unemployed. And it organized relief in a fashion which excluded politics, waste, and demoralization of community responsibility. It was a Republican administration which initiated Federal aid in support of a distressed agriculture and protection to homes.

With an honorable record and its spirit of Americanism, there is little wonder that the party has attached deep and lasting loyalties to its banner and its name. The proof is that 17,-000,000 people adhere to it even in adversity.

One weakness of the party is that it has not stood up for its substantial record of service and repelled the flood of calumny.

Another weakness in Republican organization is that it has not incorporated enough youth. Easy victories over years automatically made for much deadwood. If every one of its thousands of committees had increased its number to include a third of the men and women under thirty-five, it would have given that stir of energy and openness of view which youth alone can instill and which the youth of the party deserved.

The special weakness in the Republican Party is its failure to crystallize an affirmative and consistent body of principle in the face of this new situation.

It is in part from these weaknesses that there is some discussion over the country of new party alignment.

· · · · · · · · · · · ·

There is also some discussion among Democrats. There is certainly discontent in the Democratic Party with the New Deal. But that movement did not reach a great burning of bridges in the last election. Some prophets believe that the party must split into wings representing the older Democratic tradition and the New Dealers, and that the latter will become a class party representing labor. Those who base higher hopes on the recent cleavage from the Supreme Court controversy may underestimate the adhesiveness of party solidarity when it comes to the practical question of winning the public offices.

Who knows what may happen in 1940? Among other things it is certain that American labor will not be unanimous on the idea that a class party will serve either their own interests or the interests of America.

Nevertheless, with this incipient Democratic schism there is bound to be more discussion of a new alignment that will bring a better junction of Republicans and so-called Jeffersonian Democrats. Indeed, in the light of the fundamental issue today the differences between the two groups are not very great. Common action devoted to the cause of free men is certainly devoutly to be wished.

Such discussion is also fanned by the desire for something more effective than the futile attempts at common action in the last campaign. It is supported by a desire to shed the vicious elements of both parties.

Discussion on realignment falls into three categories. One is to create a new party. One is to change the name of the Republican Party. One is to bring about a working coalition between the two groups into a national ticket. Such political evolution in any democracy is bound to be slow, and it presents unusual difficulties in the United States.

.   .   .   .

We may explore the proposal of a new party. It may be said at once that amendment to the laws of a score of States would be required to introduce the new party to the primaries or to get its candidates upon the ballot. This would not be likely to be accomplished by 1940.

Moreover, a new party cannot be built upon a national ticket alone. To succeed and be a permanent party, it must be built upon State, municipal, county, and precinct leaders and committees, with nomination of candidates for State, county, and local offices as well as national offices.

A new party would need to reset the entire present organization of 48 State, 3000 county, and over 150,000 precinct committees so as to incorporate both old Republican and Jeffersonian Democratic personnel. It would require not only that nationally known leaders from both parties co-operate, but that State, county, and precinct leaders consolidate and many of them retire. I could dwell upon the human nature in committee reorganization at great length. Moreover, Republicans hold the offices in many counties. Jeffersonian Democrats may hold some others. Either would see little reason to "share the work." And even could all this be overcome, it would cost five or ten millions for organizers, offices, staffs, and educational expenses, and the recruiting of such money in itself would be objectionable.

But of more importance still, no such movement could wholly envelop the Republican Party. The faith in that party is too deeply implanted in the hearts of millions of people. A large part would see no reason to abandon their loyalties or banners. Such a movement for a new party, if it got under way, would no doubt develop a schism in the Republican Party and divide the front against the New Deal.

The party has withstood a number of major attempts to convert it into another party. Horace Greeley and Senator La Follette tried it. Even Theodore Roosevelt at the height of his influence, supplied with an ample sum of money, could not accomplish it. Republican leaders today, to be victorious in changing the Republican Party into a new party, would have to be far more powerful than Theodore Roosevelt's group and able to command more men and money.

Theodore Roosevelt and the Progressive Party expected to break up the Solid South with a new national party. Aside from Democratic solidarity, there is a special impediment to new organization in the South which proved fatal then and still exists. Their State and local Democratic Party organizations have the proprietorship of an unexpressed but overwhelming issue—white domination. Any new party would not be credited without assurrances on this question; nor is any new party likely to make such an assurance.

And finally, did the whole Republican Party machinery acquiesce, it must be borne in mind that many million Republicans, once their own banners were changed, would be broken from their sentimental and intellectual moorings and just as open to conviction from the enemy as by the new party.

It may be conceivable that all these difficulties could in time be overcome and a new party might be built if there were two or three national elections within which to build it. But our great issue must be determined in 1940.

.   .   .   .

The second suggestion is that the Republican Party completely change its name. The idea is that it would attract more Democrats, especially in the Solid South, where the very considerable hangover of feeling from the Civil War and the reconstruction period still remains. But the deeper emotion exists that defeated this purpose in the Progressive Party. The opposition would obviously denounce a changed name as another suit of sheep's clothing for the same bad wolf.

A change of name would encounter many of the same obstacles as the attempts at a new party—the same amendments to State laws, the assent of the national, State, and county organizations.

And again there are the Republicans who vote from faith and inheritance and loyalty, who would resist and divide the party. And there are those whose moorings would be loosened by a change of name and who would become salvage for the opposition.

Such strategies, of a new party or change of name, might bring disaster to America by dividing the major party and thereby preventing any unity of opposition. It was disunity in the opposition which aided in opening the doors to Fascism in Italy and Germany.

.   .   .   .

The third proposal is coalition. The coalition ideas take various forms, one of them being limited to coincident nomination of the same candidates for President and Vice-President by the

Republican Party and some yet undefined wing of the Democratic Party under the name "Republican" linked to some additional informal word or label. This idea has the purpose of avoiding the difficulties of a new party or a change of name and at the same time preserving the identity and organization of the two groups. Coalition, however, presupposes responsible groups and leaders to agree upon something. And this presupposes that a wing of the Democratic Party develops into a definite entity with leaders of national standing influencing large constituencies who can make agreements. What is wanted is constituencies. There is no real coalition by incorporating a few leaders. That was tried in the last campaign and failed to bring a handful of Democrats when it came to the vote. As a matter of fact, the Republican vote in the Solid South was 29 per cent in 1932 and decreased to 26 per cent in 1936.

The present influential leaders of the opposition Democrats in the Congress obviously hope to recapture their party from the New Deal or to modify its courses. It is certain that they would repudiate—and understandably so—any suggestion of leaving their party unless forced. Therefore there is no effective group with which to make agreement. No one can say that the evolution of the situation might not lead in this direction, but in any event no such proposal to Democratic leaders would get anywhere at the present time.

III

But all these discussions of new parties, changes of name, or coalition are at best merely political strategies. They place too much emphasis on politics. There is something far bigger in this situation.

The real question is, what do the parties represent? What do they stand for? The clarification of that is far more important to America.

The nation needs a party which will clearly and courageously and constructively set out the affirmative alternative to the coercive direction of the New Deal. If the word "liberalism" is derived from the word "liberty," that alternative should be the party of Historic Liberalism. If the connotation of "liberalism" is to continue to be coercion, then that alternative party may be dubbed "conservative" without disturbing my sleep.

It is important that there be given to the American people the clear opportunity to vote on this issue.

Personal liberty will live only so long as a people wants it to live. The phrases, the forms, and even the documents of liberty may continue and liberty die—if it is dead in the spirit of a people. If the people want a government of personal liberty they will declare for the party which declares it.

.   .   .   .

Our forefathers fought from Lexington to Yorktown not alone for severance from the British Empire. That was an afterthought, born of desperation. They fought for certain freedoms which they subsequently enumerated in the Bill of Rights. Those were freedoms of mind and soul. And economic freedom was to them the incident of the other and far more precious freedom. They had a new idea—unique in the history of government. They held that these freedoms were beyond the power of any government. Here is the distinction between Americanism and other conceptions of life and government.

Within the American concept there can be no real class division and therefore no substantial class conflict.

These ideals lie deep in our American heritage. The Italian collapse from a system of personal liberty was partially due to the fact that Italy's tradition of liberalism (meaning personal liberty) was not really more than half a century old, and had never overcome the Roman tradition. Liberalism in Germany in the true sense had its roots in scarcely a score of troubled years, and the tradition of German regimentation was still strong. But there has never been any other political tradition on our soil. Americanism has its roots in one hundred and sixty years—the whole of our national life—and its vitality still throbs.

.   .   .   .

The changing national scene does not change the principles of liberty. It changes the setting in which liberty is to be served. The responsibilities of liberty increase with rising standards of human relations.

No doubt others could frame a present-day creed more eloquently than I. I may, however, restate the essentials of this creed as it guides me.

I believe in the Bill of Rights—freedom of worship, of speech, of press, of assembly, that men shall not be deprived of life, liberty, or property without due process of law. These rights rest in the individual and are denied to the power of any government. These freedoms are not possible under government without the independence of the Congress, the Supreme Court, and the Executive, and without the division of Federal and State powers with their assurance of popular government and liberty.

I believe in the preservation of order under law as the first function of government. I believe that justice is inseparable from liberty. And justice requires government by specific law and not according to the whims of men.

I believe in peace as the first security of freedom, and peace cannot be had without preparation for defense in the current world.

I believe that economic freedom cannot be suppressed without suppressing also spiritual and intellectual freedom. Therefore, my creed holds for private enterprise. But freedom of men today requires that private enterprise must be regulated to prevent tyranny or exploitation. Otherwise freedom is destroyed. Government must not enter business in competition with its citizens, for that equally creates coercion and bureaucratic tyranny.

I believe in economy in government, balanced budgets, convertible gold currency, and honor in government obligations as a basic protection of the individual from government oppression.

I believe our national striving must be to open opportunity, to maintain equal opportunity. It must be to increase economic and social security to every individual. That security comes from increased standards of living for the whole people. That in turn can arise only from the maximum production within the limits of health and proper leisure, together with the stimulation to new methods, new inventions, and new enterprise which result alone from the intellectual freedom of men. These increases in production and these economies in costs, passed on to workers, consumers, and savers of capital, alone lead to higher wages, lower prices, increased consumption, full employment, and margins for old age.

I believe we should drive to put more and more of the wage group on to an annual earning basis and thus add greatly to their freedom from fear of tomorrow. I believe freedom requires that swollen fortunes must be diffused and the descent of great economic power prevented by taxes on inheritance.

I believe that if we pursue these courses we shall produce well-being for a rapidly increasing majority. Then our social problems will resolve themselves into those of marginal groups of diminishing numbers who are the victims of misfortune and of the ebb and flow of economic life.

I believe in a creed of economic fair play wherein the economically more successful must through taxes or otherwise help bear the burdens of these marginal groups in providing for old age, unemployment, better homes, and health, whether they be in the city or on the farm.

I believe our problems of abuse are also marginal problems. Child labor, the exploitation of labor, the abuses of competition, industrial conflict, and crime can be isolated and cured by law without regimenting a nation.

I believe co-operation among free men can solve many problems more effectively than government.

And finally I do not believe in any form of government or law or private action which coerces, intimidates, or regiments upright men.

This is but a part of a creed. It could be expanded. Its bare bones could be clothed with the flesh of emotion. But, however it be shaped, only the American freedoms of mind and spirit and the obligations of liberty must give it life.

IV

This is an individual creed, not a political platform, but I shall end this discussion in support of a political proposal.

The Republican Party makes a platform each four years, under the pressures of conventions called primarily for selection of candidates. In a time of confused public mind the last platform, as also the Democratic platform, was a mixture of conflicting ideas and grab-bag offerings.

It is the view of Republican leaders in more than a score of States that the Republican Party should meet officially in convention during the next year. That this meeting should be representative, that it should comprise youth as well as maturity, women as well as men. That it should not confuse its vision with candidates or attempts to solve group or sectional problems the character of which can be known only three years hence. That it meet not to form a creed, or the usual platform, but a declaration. That it should, with adequate prior preparation by able and open minds, fully debate and then declare a conviction on constructive national principles. That it should declare this with intellectual and moral integrity, with human sympathy, with idealism and emotion.

Should its declaration rise to the national need, it would infuse a renewed fighting courage in the party's own ranks; it would inspire an organization with which free men could join in coalition; it would lift the hearts of free men and women.

America needs a new and flaming declaration of the rights and responsibilities of free men.

A Program of American Ideals

BOSTON, MASSACHUSETTS

[*October 26, 1937*]

PART I

THIS club has made this evening an especial occasion for the younger Republican leaders. It is a happy participation. The same spirit should be extended over the country. The Party must have new faces and new blood. It must incorporate more youth, both men and women, in its councils. The Party needs the sincerity, the undaunted courage of youth. It is the idealism and virility of youth which bring forward motion.

The rumor has been going about for the past five years that opportunity for youth is gone in American life. We hear of a lost generation. I said once that for 150 years God-fearing people under the blessings of freedom have built up quite a plant and equipment on this continent. The nation teems with millions of farms and homes and cattle and pigs, despite the AAA. There are railroads, highways, power plants and factories, stores and banks, and economic royalists. There are towns and magnificent cities. There are newspapers, colleges, libraries, orchestras, bands, radios, and other noises. It is very sad to contemplate but it has probably occurred to you that all the people who live in these houses and all those who run this complicated machine are going to pass into the next world. Just as sure as death the job of running it is yours. And there are increasing opportunities in every inch of it. Furthermore, science and invention yearly give to us further mighty powers of progress. They create a thousand new frontiers of opportunity for youth.

But over this world have come vast problems in government

which are the challenge to youth. Unless they be rightly solved there will be less opportunity.

PART II

One phase of these solutions is political party organization. So I propose to talk to you as Republicans about the Republican Party and the service it can offer in these days of national perplexity.

I am interested in building up the Republican Party not as a partisan but as a citizen. So let us look at it as citizens and not as politicians. We are concerned now with something greater than a game or securing public office.

The Republican Party even out of office is a national necessity as a unified opposition party to check excesses and protect minorities. But it has a mission far greater than just being against. Nor can it be built solely from a collection of politicians and a mass of committees, no matter how earnest and self-sacrificing they may be.

This party must have a fighting cause; it must have an affirmative program; it must present effective methods; it must have a forward purpose; it must have idealism, and it must be responsive to the needs and crises of the people. If a party should come into power without such definite purpose it would be of little good to the nation. It would mean only that a few people have got up to the public trough.

We are concerned with service in a national crisis. Our country must have emancipation from the moral degeneration of current government methods. It must have emancipation from what Walter Lippmann so aptly calls "gradual collectivism." It must bring sanity and reform to destructive fiscal and economic policies which undermine the standards of living of the great economic middle class. It must make possible humanitarian objectives which are otherwise wrecked by wrongful and ineffective methods. Peace must be made more secure.

If that be so, all the wiles, the tricks, and the petty artfulness of politics are of minor moment.

Before I go further (not that it is of any importance but just to keep the air clean) let me repeat once again that I do not want any public office. I shall keep on fighting for those things vital to the American people. There is no form of words that will convince a suspicious politician that any man under 85 can have any other purpose for interesting himself in public affairs. The accusation of seeking office seems to be the highest intellectual level to which the opposition can rise when they are made uncomfortable by argument and new proposals.

PART III

There are five great categories of national issues today. The first are issues of moral integrity in government. The second are the vital issues of personal liberty and its safeguards. The third are those financial and economic policies which affect the standards of living of the people. The fourth are the humane issues of security and of aid for the less fortunate. The fifth are our relations to other nations.

Some of these issues are new in the last five years. Some have developed since the election. All of them are becoming increasingly vivid to the people.

The time has come when the Republican Party should be reoriented to these fundamental issues. No civilization is static. It must move forward or die. Therefore no party can be static. It must move forward with the times.

Our national question is not alone—Where are we going? But even more—Where do we want to go?

A group of important Republican leaders of all shades of thought have put forward a proposal that the party should select a Policy committee of its most distinguished men and women to draft an honest, courageous declaration of convictions, of positive principles and forward action. It is proposed that this draft should be submitted to a general conference of party leaders prior to the Congressional election. I support that suggestion. Such a Policy committee could well be continued to work out methods within those principles and convictions for solution of many national problems to be presented later on or to the 1940 convention. I am not concerned over details. I am deeply concerned that people who are losing their way shall be given a banner of moral and intellectual leadership around which they can rally as the inevitable day of disillusionment comes to them.

In the meantime no greater service can be given than discussion and debate of these fundamental questions. Governor Landon a few nights ago made a notable contribution to such discussion. Our Senators and Congressmen in their daily battles contribute to the formulation of ideas. Nothing could be more helpful than the formulation of constructive convictions and positive purposes by our State and local organizations and our Republican clubs and the press. The ideas of the Democratic Party are made by one man. We want to develop Republican ideas from the party. In the face of this crisis there is an ample area of ideas upon which to build unity.

My purpose tonight is not to forecast such a declaration. It is to urge that it be undertaken by the party and to outline something of the attitude or the point of view that could be considered in formulating it.

PART IV

ATTITUDE ON MORALS IN GOVERNMENT

Today as never before we are faced with moral questions in public life. We have had a New Deal in public honor. To indicate its significance let me ask you a few questions.

The first of these questions involves intellectual honesty in officials and in government.

Can your government broadcast half truths and expect the citizen to tell the whole truth?

Do you think you can pollute thought with framed government propaganda and maintain honest thinking in the citizen?

Do you think the government, which engages hundreds of paid publicity agents daily and hourly to eulogize its official acts, can hold the faith of the citizen in what his government says?

Is it honest or sportsmanlike to answer the argument, protest or appeal of the citizen by smearing him as the enemy of the people?

Do you believe all the official statements today?

Do you think you can let down intellectual honesty in high officials and hold up conscience in citizens?

And there are questions relating to public administration.

Does not the wholesale appointment of government officials by politics and not by merit mean a decadence in public morals? What is the morality of the recent return to the spoils system?

And there are questions involving commercial honesty.

Can your government repudiate the covenant of its bonds and expect citizens to hold to their obligations?

Can the government ruthlessly crush competition and hold the business man to fair play?

Can the Treasury deliberately manipulate the market in government bonds and expect the citizen not to do the same thing in stocks?

Is it moral for a government to collect hundreds of millions from the wages of workmen under the promise that they are kept in a fund for their security and then spend this fund on its current expenses and extragavances?

Is it moral to evade the Corrupt Practices Act by selling books to corporations for political funds?

And there are questions involving the sacredness of law.

What happens to the morals of a people when the Federal Government connives at lawlessness?

What of governors who obstruct the courts and refuse to maintain public order?

Or of workmen beaten and killed by police squads on one hand and beef squads on the other?

Do not all moral restraints disappear and the ugly spectres of vigilantes arise?

And there are questions involving the building of character in men.

When the public purse is used to subsidize, threaten, or cajole the Congressmen and the local communities, are you not corrupting the people?

When you direct the mind of the citizen to what he can abstract from the Treasury, are you building for self-reliance and stamina in the citizen?

And there are questions involving the spirit of a people.

Is it moral for high government officials to stir hate of group against group, of workman against workman?

Is not hate a moral poison to a nation more deadly than fear?

And there are questions involving the sacredness of the ballot.

What does the common expression—"you cannot beat Santa Claus" mean in public morals?

Can democracy survive with more and more of its cities in the hands of corrupt political machines?

Do not a multitude of vicious rackets, of bribery, blackmail, coercion and crime flourish under the hands of these corrupt city governments? What does this do to the moral standards of citizens and the community?

Is the Federal Government not abetting these machines when it places enormous sums of public money directly and indirectly at their disposal—too often just prior to elections?

Can we hope for self-government when these city political machines regularly manipulate the vote? Does not this influence not alone municipal but State and federal elections?

Do you think you can maintain confidence in our institutions and continually pollute the ballot box?

A nation is great not through dams in its rivers or its ships on the sea or the deposits in its banks. It is great by the moral fiber and character of its citizens. Nations die when these weaken.

Is it not the duty of the Republican Party to raise the banner of emancipation of the American people from this degradation, both national and local?

PART V

ATTITUDE ON COLLECTIVISM

The world-wide conflict today is True Liberalism against collectivism.

Huxley said the first need of debate is definitions. By "collec-tivism" we mean any system where the tendency is to make the people the servants of the government or personal power as op-posed to the government being the servant of the people. That is a complicated idea but it is the age-long fight of human liberty. We certainly do not mean collective bargaining or co-operative marketing. They begin and end among the people and are democratic processes.

I have used the term "True Liberalism." I would prefer to use the more direct term of "Americanism." The term liberal has now become the fashionable clothing of all collectivists, whether they be New Dealers, with creeping collectivism, or frank and open Socialists, or the unconscious Fascists. Its folds can apparently even be entered through the Ku Klux Klan.

Our Republicans should not use this term without distinction between true and pseudo. Gradually the public is learning that Liberal spelled with a capital L means New Deal Collectivism.

True Liberalism is liberty organized under law. It everlast-ingly reacts to one test: Does this or that act make for the free-dom of mind and spirit of men? Does it make for the dignity of all men? And let no man tell you that intellectual and spiritual liberty is not the sole anchor of American civilization.

It is the most difficult of all philosophies to realize in govern-ment, because the very freedom which fertilizes the soil of prog-ress sprouts also the weeds of selfishness and sordid ambition. It can only be realized through prohibitions and protections which prevent invasion of the freedom of others. And it rests greatly upon responsibility and self-restraint by the individual.

True liberalism does not start as an economic system. An economic system flows from it. The only economic system which will not destroy intellectual and spiritual freedom is private en-terprise, regulated to prevent special privilege, or coercion.

Every new scientific discovery, every new invention intro-duces new possibilities of privilege, as well as progress. Reform must be ever in motion. We agree with the New Deal objectives in removal of abuses. Many abuses are cured, and these objec-tives were advocated by Republicans long before the New Deal was born. But the cure is not by their method of government by men in the place of government by law. Moreover, they seek to make us believe that abuse cannot be cured without that creeping Collectivism called Planned Economy.

That "gradual collectivism" is creeping upon us should be evident by this time to any understanding American. The government manipulation of money and credit, government restriction of production, government control of hours and wages, the entry of the government into competitive business on a large scale, government coercion of upright citizens—these are but part of it. The conflict of the two systems creates at once attack on constitutional government. Undermining the independence of Congress, packing the Supreme Court, the weakening of local and State government, the new proposals to invade judicial authority under the guise of administrative reorganization are but part of the centralization of government and the increase in personal government.

Once economic life is started in this direction it creates its own demand for more and more personal power. And one of its results is a Frankenstein of hate and national disunity. There cannot be a system part collectivist and part regulated private enterprise. The very conflict of the two systems creates one economic emergency after another. We witness that at this very hour. Do you think the confidence of men, the enterprise of men, is not today chilled to the bone?

The Republican Party can declare the principles of free enterprise regulated to prevent abuse and it can set these principles against all forms of collectivism. It can do still more.

It can declare the principles for cure of abuse which will not shackle the enterprise and initiative of men. It can do still more.

It can declare the principles upon which alone a progressive economic system can produce increasing standards of living and security. It can do more.

It can declare the principles that will emancipate the American people from the collectivism which has already crept over us. It can do still more.

It can propose the principles of justice that will stamp out the fires of hate and cure the wounds of class conflict. It can do more.

It can declare its convictions on the rights and responsibilities of free men. That is the spirit of constitutional government. In those ramparts it can hold against every assault on human liberty.

And here is a paradox. The Republican Party becomes the conservative party in the sense of conserving true liberalism.

Incidentally a new form of Planned Economy has been announced from Washington. That is to be a balanced abundance. It seems to recall the trapeze.

PART VI

ATTITUDE ON SOCIAL QUESTIONS

What of the attitude toward humanitarian or social problems? After five years of New Deal remedies Mr. Roosevelt has said one-third of the people are still underclad, underfed, or underhoused. One could debate that figure as too high, but our purpose is not a statistical discussion. Whether it is one-fifth or one-fourth or one-tenth it is too high for America.

We have all of us tried to picture the kind of America we would wish to see. I pray the day will come in America when it cannot be said with truth that any one who will work shall be underclad or underfed or underhoused. We want more for our people than a minimum of food, shelter and clothing.

But America must think also of the other nine-tenths or two-thirds, or whatever it is, which are mostly the great economic middle class. I am not thinking of the drones, either rich or poor.

It is the great economic middle class who have spent years learning to do their job skilfully who must carry these burdens. The skilled workers, the farmers, the professional people, the small merchants, and manufacturers—they need to be remembered. Why should they be the forgotten men? They have worked and saved to secure the homes, farms, insurance policies and savings, which build and sustain the productivity of this country.

Government policies which tax, harry and demoralize the productivity of the great economic middle class are the greatest catastrophe which can come to the one-third of underclad, underhoused, underfed. Their redemption must come by preserving the two-thirds, not by dragging them down. In all his long years Santa Claus never increased the standard of living of a nation.

Our people want jobs. They want a just return for their labor. They want opportunity to rise in their jobs. They want security on the job. They want security from want in old age. They want collective bargaining by labor, free from coercion. They want decent returns from the farm. They want education, health and recreation. These and many others are the vital things which our civilization must produce.

They are the objectives and the hopes of every decent man and woman. They are the righteous objectives of civilization itself. The New Deal did not discover these objectives. No person or party ever had a self-righteous monopoly of them. The bright colors of wordy objectives are being used to camouflage failure. Samuel Johnson said the road to the hot place was paved with good intentions. Truly it can be said that the New Deal road to salvation is paved with objectives. That road badly needs repaving with practical methods.

The Republican Party can declare the sane principles under which we can reach our social goals and not destroy them.

PART VII

ATTITUDE ON FISCAL POLICIES

And there is the point of view of the Republican Party toward budget deficits, debts, taxes, currency inflation. When you deal with other people's money the word is conservative not Liberal, especially with a capital L.

The Republican Party can declare the principles of economy which will lift a burden from all who toil. It can declare principles of taxation that will not choke enterprise and destroy men's jobs.

PART VIII

There is discussion in the Republican Party as to whether it should undertake to declare its position upon these fundamental questions now or wait until 1940.

I realize the theory of some political leaders is that most people vote against something. It is their further theory that you only have to stand by and criticize. Give the other fellow enough rope and he will hang himself, and thereby you win elections. That is an old belief. But I insist it is inadequate for the needs of this day.

If the Republican Party has not learned the lesson that it must produce principles and program besides being against and joyriding on mistakes it has not read history.

You do not long hold the goal and devotion of men and women without definite purpose and principle. The Whig Party tried all that.

There is talk of fusion and coalition. Let me make but one remark on that. It is a result devoutly to be wished for. But the people fuse or coalesce around ideas and ideals, not around political bargains or stratagems. If the Republican Party meets the needs and aspirations of the people who are opposed to the New Deal, they will fuse and coalesce and not before. They only join in the march if they know where we are going.

Conclusion

And again I return to my opening.

There is a mighty service to be performed. This party must make the humanitarian objectives of the nation possible which are otherwise wrecked by wrongful and ineffective methods. It must reform destructive economic policies which undermine the standards of living of the economic middle class and thus all the people. It must emancipate the people from this creeping collectivism and restore true liberalism. It must emancipate them from the moral degeneration in government. The interest of the nation requires that the Republican Party shall provide the country with positive and affirmative principles and proposals that will meet these yearnings of the people today for a way out and forward. It is a gigantic task. But should we not make a beginning?

That is a task in which youth must join.

You have the blood and urge of your American forebears. You are as good stuff as they. You are better trained and equipped than they were. I have no doubt of your character and your resolution.

Free Speech and Free Press

COLBY COLLEGE, WATERVILLE, MAINE

[November 8, 1937]

ON THIS day one hundred years ago Elijah Parish Lovejoy, a graduate of this college, was killed while defending free speech and free press in the United States. A long procession of men over centuries before him had suffered and died to establish that bulwark of human liberty. His was the case of a minority fighting for a principle and of being crucified by a majority. Indignation over the murder of Lovejoy, led by the ringing eloquence of Wendel Phillips, has echoed down a whole century. Elijah Lovejoy was the last to make that supreme sacrifice on this continent. Since his martyrdom no man has openly challenged free speech and free press in America.

I shall attempt no eulogy of Lovejoy and his service. These halls have rung with those words a thousand times. It is little wonder that the precincts of Colby College are hallowed by the name of Lovejoy. To have inspired even one man to so great a sacrifice for human liberty is a service large in American education. And from it has come a spiritual endowment to this college that dollars and bricks can never make.

From the time of Lovejoy's death to a period after the Great War free speech, free press and free debate were steadily spreading over the world, for it was the very life stream of advancing liberalism.

But in the past fifteen years increasing darkness has descended upon free expression and free criticism in the world. That light has been put out in more than half the so-called civilized earth.

It is a paradox that we find every dictator who has ascended to power has climbed on the ladder of free speech and free press. Immediately on attaining power each dictator has suppressed all free speech except his own. The revolutions since the Great War were in most cases not the result of civil convulsions and the killing of many men. These revolutions were the result of implanted ideas. Magic formulas were spun which promised relief to the infinite misery of war. Propaganda confused the minds and soiled the spirits of men. The news was colored and facts were distorted. Potent catch phrases and slogans were summoned as labels for the cure of every social and economic evil. Half truths, quarter truths were amassed to prove the failure of established institutions. Just grievance was transformed into hate. Despair was fanned into destructive fear. Men were led to their own enslavement by lies and fraud from polluted speech and press. Liberty died by the waters of her own well—free speech and free press poisoned with untruth.

Untruth once triumphant could not tolerate debate and free criticism. Then free speech and free press were suppressed. Truth alone can stand the guns of criticism.

Dawn will come to these peoples again after many years. The demand for free expression of the human mind will not die. It is part of the spiritual endowment of men. It was born in human sacrifice over centuries of travail, to which those very nations made high contribution.

In the United States we do not suffer at least from any restriction in the free flow of words.

We use more billion words per capita or per minute or per decibel than any other people on earth. We start breakfast with thirty or forty thousand words in the paper. All day the tocsin rings out more and more words. Being a race fond of hair shirts we take mightily to oratory with our meals, especially after dinner. We take the radio along in our automobiles and we go to bed with it still talking.

Whatever doubt there may be as to the quality or purport of our free speech we certainly have ample volume in production.

A free press is far more than a publishers' privilege. It is a right of the people. But the publishers are its first lines of defense. They deserve the gratitude of the country for the zeal with which they have driven back every attempt at legal restrictions, but there is a problem of free speech and free press in America wider than sporadic attempts to control it.

The durability of free speech and free press rests on the simple concept that it search for the truth and tell the truth. It is only through free expression and free adventure in doubt that we explore the unknown physical world for the truth. It is only by the anvil of debate that we hammer out the flaws of untruth from social and economic ideas and mould them into shapes which are helpful to men. Progress is indeed the degree to which we discover truth—and here free press and free speech become the most powerful of human forces.

I know the philosophic view that truth is only proximate; that people differ on what constitutes truth. But despite all hair splitting there are enough standards of truth and morals at any one period to lead men and women upward. The last twenty years have amply demonstrated that free speech and free press cannot survive if they are used deliberatly to cultivate untruth or half truth. There are vast differences between mistake and deliberate planting of untruth. Free expression will not survive if it be used to stir malice in the minds of men. It will not survive if it be used to exploit hate. Nor will it survive if it be used to implant that fear which is the blood brother of hate. These emotions are the negation of all that good-will which Christianity has striven to establish during two thousand years. They can destroy civilization itself.

And this brings me to that special breed of cultivated untruth we call propaganda.

This word at one time had a reputable and even sanctified meaning. Will Irwin has pointed out that to sanctify untruth this old term was given a new occupation. Like some other ideas, it was greatly corrupted by the war.

War sanctifies murder, so it sanctifies the lesser immoralities. Lies are a legitimate weapon of war. They are a high part of war strategy. As Irwin says, propaganda became the next thing to blank lies. It is now a sinister word meaning half-truth or any other distortion of truth. It moves by tainting of news, by making synthetic news and opinions and canards. It promotes the emotions of hate, fear and dissension.

The processes were not new with the war but the war perfected greatly this device and trained many men in the artistry of its use. By it men promote subtle ambitions, opinions and a wide variety of "isms." They create bias and inflame the minds of men. With still further refinements it has been applied to politics.

The great quality of this improved poison seems to be that it must be artistically done. One of the characteristic features is the *ad hominem* argument. If you don't like an argument on currency or the budget or labor relations or what not, you put out slimy and if possible anonymous propaganda reflecting upon your opponent's grandmother or the fact that his cousin is employed in Wall Street or is a communist or a reactionary. You switch the premise and set up straw men and then attack them with fierce courage.

I am making no suggestion of law or extension of government over free speech and free press in order to suppress this improved form of corruption. Men can use brickbats for murder but that is no reason for suppressing brick houses. But we can turn some free speech on the throwers of brickbats.

So far as it reaches the press our editors maintain hourly battle against it. They have the job of discrimination between propaganda and real news, between untruth and truth. Theirs is a hard job. Considering their difficulties they do it pretty well. They would be assisted if the news services rigidly adhered to the rule that when opinion is news they refuse to quote it anonymously. That would be a hard blow to the hate makers.

And there are great problems developing from the immense expansion of speech over the radio. Possibly the maintenance of proximate truth and godly emotions is even more difficult in this area than in the press. There is less record and less opportunity for refutation.

You will ask what we are to do about it all. The first answer is reform in the morals of the users of untruth. The most important answer is more free speech. We must incessantly expose intellectual dishonesty and the purpose that lies behind it. The antidote for untruth is truth. Half truth can be defeated with the whole truth. This antidote works with discouraging slowness at times, but unless we maintain faith in our medicine civilization will despair.

It is an old saying that personal liberty will survive by vigilance. We know that vigilance can be sustained only by free speech and free press. But it is also pertinent to add that free speech and free press will survive only through honest pursuit of the truth. That is the high purpose of our schools, our churches, our colleges, and our universities. In that purpose this institution has served nobly for more than a century.

And I may conclude by quoting for your continued resolution the last words of Elijah Lovejoy, who said, "As long as I am an American citizen I shall hold myself free to speak, to write and publish whatever I please on any subject, holding myself amenable to the laws of my country for the same."

Training for Public Service

SYRACUSE UNIVERSITY, SYRACUSE, NEW YORK

[*November 12, 1937*]

THE DEDICATION of this building marks another milestone in the long march of service of American universities to the nation. This institution and some others have set out frankly to build up public service into a profession.

The major purposes of our universities outside of football are obvious. It is their purpose to train minds and to strengthen character. It is their function to transmit the accumulated learning and culture of ages on to each rising generation. Possibly the latter is in these days a good deal limited to citing references as to where it can be found.

But our American universities have gone farther than this, into the day-to-day practical problems of life. They started by giving specialized training for the professions of clergy and law. Long ago through the establishment of our medical schools they transformed medicine from a trade of quacks into the highest of professions. Later, through our engineering schools they transformed engineering from the realms of rule of thumb into a great profession. Laterally, through the establishment of schools of business administration they are endeavoring mightily to transform business into a profession.

And now this institution especially has led in endeavor to lift public administration to a profession. No doubt that is partly because we have increased the people who live on the public payroll from 1 per cent of the population to over 10 per cent, and they certainly need training.

And by profession we mean not only the addition of specialized scientific skill to general culture, but such training to be of real purpose means more than that. It means the creation of a body of ethics and honesty in professional conduct, together with pride and distinction in a calling. It is the moral standards that are built up in the great professions which have given these jobs over to the graduates of our universities.

Every citizen will welcome this new development of training for public service. We will look forward to it with the same hope and the same confidence of accomplishment that we have seen in the other great professions.

The Spoils System

Hitherto a multitude of efforts have been made to lift public service from the realm of the spoils system into the region of devotion and expertness in public interest. One of the difficulties in this advance has been the lack of men of specialized training and positive character to choose from.

But hand in hand with the development of professionally trained personnel for government we have first got to rid ourselves of the spoils system. Appointment to public office as political award is based on the notion that getting votes constitutes expertness for the job. It makes for political joy. But it produces bad administration. It undermines confidence in government by the people. It leads to corruption. It degrades politics. It is, in fact, the incarnation of immorality and subversion of the public interest.

Ours is government through political parties. But the policies of the party in power in the Federal Government can be administered with less than a hundred officials of the elected political faith. For half a century the Presidents of the United States have struggled unceasingly to uproot the spoils system from the great administrative body of the Federal Government. As a result of this long battle all but two strongholds of political appointments—the bureau heads and the postmasters—had been captured for merit selection. Upwards of 82 per cent of all federal employees were selected at the hand of a non-political

Civil Service Commission. Since then, that ratio has slipped sadly until today it is less than 65 per cent.

And let me add a word upon the plan now before Congress for reorganization of the Federal Government. It proposes to abolish the Civil Service Commission, which has for fifty years given fine service and held high standards of training and freedom from politics in public service. The new plan proposes to substitute one-man control. No matter what the words of that bill may purport to mean it is clear that the plan is to destroy the progress we have made and substitute personal political control.

Many states and municipalities have fought the battle for a non-political civil service, with varied results. It is a significant fact that where the people in local elections have the opportunity to vote directly upon this issue they have always been emphatically for a non-political civil service. Until our Federal Government, our states and our municipalities and our counties have put their two million nonpolicy-making employees on a merit service the proper field for the efforts and expert preparation of this institution will not be attained.

But again I return to the fact that until we have young men and women trained for public service no executive, no matter how willing, can adequately fill our public offices with expertness and skill.

Training for Party Organization

I have said that ours is a government of political parties. Democracy cannot function without party government. But good government is good politics—or it should be. Political parties are organizations for adult education on issues in reforms and in problems of government and the election of decent public officials—or they might be. The proper organization and conduct of political parties is a public service. One of the large services of such training as this institution proposes lies in this field. Not all your graduates will wish to enter government employment, but all of them can actively enter political organization.

On the whole, college and university graduates are playing

no such role in party affairs as the privileges of higher education demand from its beneficiaries. They are too prone to hold themselves aloof from the hurly-burly of political conflict. They content themselves with merely voting. That is often a futile affair, if the names of mediocre or incompetent candidates appear on the ballot. Mere voting is a paltry price to pay for the privilege of living under a free government. A democratic way of life is a participating way of life. Self-government exists only in name if the conduct of the parties is turned over entirely to professional politicians. These latter are performing a useful and indeed a necessary function in keeping the party organization alive. But let no one fool himself into thinking that he is enjoying self-government under the type of control which exists in many a city in this country.

If we are ever to get rid of these vile municipal political machines it must first be done by placing their employees upon Civil Service basis, and then by young men and women who are prepared to go into party organization to see that clean government is maintained. We all agree political organization is a necessity to give expression on ideas at the ballot box and to name men for public office. If this be true we cannot leave that job to people who make money out of selling rackets, crime and corruption.

And good government is not to be had by the hurricanes of reform and passing brainstorms of indignation. It can be achieved only by people who will do honest party organization. That turns the disinfectant of truth on rotten politics. We need this trained intelligence not only in the top councils of the party, but up and down the line to the very grass-roots of party organization.

The training of men and women in right understanding of politics of high purpose is not beneath our universities.

TRAINING FOR SOLUTION OF PUBLIC QUESTIONS

And there is another field for men and women trained in the arts and problems of government no less important than the others. Intelligent discussion and debate of issues, the constructive criticism of government methods, destructive criticism of government wrong, the search for truth and workable method, is the only road to progress.

This Maxwell School of Public Affairs is dedicated to youth, the standard bearers of tomorrow. Whenever we think of youth, we are moved to put on the philosopher's if not the prophet's garb. Every generation sees in its own youth the promise of a better day, the fulfillment of long-cherished hopes.

I hardly need point out that we are in a time of great, and it may be fundamental, social change. These present days are weighted heavily with potentialities. Decisions have been made and other decisions will be made in this decade that will make or break the opportunities of youth.

Many of the policies and slogans of the political parties are no longer related to the realities of the life of our country. Many of the leaders who have taken refuge and found their salvation in these policies and slogans are bewildered and at a loss in the rapidly changing currents of the time. Ours is a period for search of truth, for the creativeness, the open-mindedness, the energetic action of youth. And there is support in the wisdom and the balance of older men who have retained something of the qualities of youth—alertness, a receptive mind and the drive to be up and doing.

It is creative intelligence we need in these times. Our generation has in some measure triumphantly solved the problem of production of plenty. But there remains the difficult and unsolved problem of distributing the goods of the productive machine so that want and economic suffering may be abolished from the land.

There are those who find hopes in the gorgeous phrases of salvation by government. There are others who place their faith in unregulated competition, in the belief that human welfare will somehow automatically result. Thoughtful men have long since come to the conclusion that both of these courses lead to the destruction of the most precious possession of our race—intellectual and spiritual liberty. It is here that creative intelligence is needed.

The colleges and universities have long accepted and proclaimed their responsibility to develop young men and women for unselfish devotion and leadership in public affairs. As I conceive it, this is a time that calls for that training as has no other time in my memory.

The problems confronting us will not be solved by recourse to phrases or slogans. They will be solved by the search of new truth and the long inheritances of human experience. It is not even enough that satisfactory solutions be discovered. These must then be interpreted to broad masses of the people. And finally they fail unless there be skill in administration.

So I am moved to ask this audience, made up of educators or those interested in education: Does not the remedy lie with the educational system? Is it an insuperable task to breed a race of young people which will take seriously the privilege of living in a free country, of participating in party activities as a regular avocation—the thing to do, rather than the thing to avoid? Think of what the Russians, the Japanese, the Germans and the Italians have apparently succeeded in doing with their youth. They have developed youth to support autocracy. Can we not train our young people to everlasting faith in democracy? That means to work for and defend—not in the stress of war but in the midst of peace—their truly great inheritance of freedom.

In closing I am going to quote from the Old Guard in politics. Being authorities more than ten years old however they may be suspect as reactionaries. The first of my authorities is Aristotle who put it in his "Politics"—

"That which contributes most to the permanence of constitutions is the adaptation of education to the form of government."

My second reference is the doctrine of Old Guardsman Pericles, that the citizen is one who has united in the same person the interest in private and in public affairs, and that the man who takes no part in public affairs is to be regarded "not as one who minds his own business, but as one who is good for nothing."

Economic Security and the
Present Situation

CHICAGO ECONOMIC CLUB

[December 16, 1937]

PART I

I HAVE been led to make this address by the urgent appeal of your invitation. You said in part:

"In the main, we are a group of young men representative of the countless counterparts of the economic middle class Americans. Our future and the country's welfare are bound together. We were born without golden spoons. We cannot retire. We haven't the means. Nor does our vitality afford any inclination to do so. We have young and growing families, and these ultimate responsibilities are sacred to us.

"This group . . . have more reason to be disturbed at certain economic trends. . . . We are harassed and nervous lest the uncertainties and direction in our economic life will place an unbearable load upon our ability to plan ahead. . . . We believe you could analyze for the average younger man . . . just what is underneath this confusion, and what is wrong with it all. We need leadership in sound economic and social philosophy."

You raise the whole question of economic security and future opportunity.

Your letter echoes the anxiety of millions of Americans for the security of their jobs, their savings, the opportunity to better themselves and their children. They are thinking of the long years before they are entitled to an old age pension.

I approach that summons with great humility.

These questions range far above partisanship. The progress

of democracy requires that we present different points of view. We must pound out reason and the basis of co-operation on the anvil of debate.

By the economic middle class I take it that you mean all the people who have to support themselves. You mean the people who have sacrificed years of devotion to learn to do their jobs skilfully. They are the creative people. They are the people who want to get forward. They are the quiet, decent people who are busy keeping things going. They seldom appear in the press except when they die. Unless this great group have a chance the whole will fail. They have to carry the burdens of the unfortunate.

PART II

No Anxieties from Abroad

If we look over the national scene we will find every city, village and hamlet torn with dissension and a feeling of insecurity and even fear.

This anxiety does not come from outside our borders. America almost alone of all the countries in the world is secure from the dangers of war. There is not the remotest fear that our national independence will be challenged from abroad.

We possess the resources and the equipment to produce more than mere food, shelter, and clothing for the whole of our population.

We are still able to contend for the right to govern ourselves. Ours has been a great adventure in free men and free ideas and free enterprise. That experiment has not failed. At present it has become muddled.

PART III

The Present Recession

These anxieties, distractions and fears swell up from something far deeper in our national life than this immediate business recession.

I like this new word "recession." It is no doubt easier to bear than those old English words "slump" or "depression." It no doubt softens the pain from falling off the roof if you call it a "recession." I can be wholly objective on this depression because certainly I did not create it.

This recession need not be serious. The reason I believe this is that we are not today dragged by two of the terrible horsemen of the world-wide crisis beginning in 1929.

No major depression comes without a large element of credit collapse. There is today no inflated bubble of speculative private credit as in 1929. There is no bubble of European inflation and unliquidated war finance, the collapse of which pulled down the whole world. The world economic movement is still upward.

The grim recollections of the Great World Depression naturally contribute to fears of the present situation which reason does not confirm.

What is imperative for the moment is relief from pressures which stagnate billions of industrial and home construction and millions of jobs for men. But it is currents deeper than this recession that we are discussing tonight, although this recession is one of the indications of profound currents.

PART IV

PAST MOVEMENTS IN ECONOMIC AND SOCIAL FORCES

Perhaps we could get under the surface of these deeper distractions by a short analysis of the shift in economic and social forces in recent years.

We had for nearly a century industrial pioneers who mainly devoted themselves to building up the great industrial tools provided by scientific discovery. Those generations did a good job. They won for America the greatest economic triumph in all history. That is the unique ability to produce a plenty for a wholesome standard of living and comfort to all the people. Private initiative and enterprise proved to be the very mother of plenty.

It had social weaknesses. That generation gave too little heed to equitable diffusion among all the people of the output of their triumph in production.

Some thousands of a marginal group out of 120,000,000 got too much of the productive pie for the service they gave. Some millions of another marginal group got too little. But we had so triumphed in the long journey of mankind away from scarcity and want that we began to see the promised land of abolished poverty.

Our greatest economic weakness was the organization and shocking abuses in finance and banking. Our segment of the war depression was deepened by our credit inflations and failures. Our people were amply warned. But democracies seldom act until the shock comes. Then they get impatient.

From the miseries of the depression the whole economic system was condemned without discrimination as to its strengths or its faults.

Before recovery had been attained came a set of ideas under the euphonious title of "Planned Economy." They brought a conflict between two fundamentally opposite philosophies of government and economics in operation at the same time.

Whether Planned Economy is an infection from Europe of creeping collectivism or whether it is a native American product is less important than its actual results upon us. I shall analyze it solely from its practical aspects.

PART V

Confusion in the Present Direction of Economic and Social Forces

We must not confuse true liberal reforms with Planned Economy, which has other purposes. Constant reform is a necessity of growth. The objectives of this administration in reforms directed to cure business abuses, to remedy social ills, old age needs, housing, sweated labor, etc., are right. Nor is "Planned Economy" necessary to bring them about.

The central idea of Planned Economy which concerns me is the gigantic shift of government from the function of umpire to the function of directing, dictating and competing in our economic life. No one will deny that the government is today increasingly controlling prices, wages, volume of production and investment.

Its weapons include politically managed currency, managed credit, managed interest rates, huge expenditure in pump priming and inflation of bank deposits. Further weapons are to use relief funds to build the government into competitive business. It has stretched the taxing powers deep into the control of business conduct. Regulation to prevent abuse has been stretched into instruments of dictation. The policeman on the streets of commerce to expedite the traffic, to keep order and stop robbery, now orders our destination and tells us what to do when we get there. It will be a depressing day for America when the farmer can be put in jail for failure to obey the dictates of Washington as to what he may sow and what he may reap.

I do not agree with these New Deal objectives, for there are here fundamental conflicts with free men in which there is no compromise, no middle ground.

PART VI

Its Results

We have now had nearly five years' experience with these ideas. They were put forward as only for an emergency. And yet every session of Congress faces demands for more and more.

The very forces of Planned Economy involve constantly increasing delegation of discretionary power to officials. They involve constantly greater centralization of government. They involve conflicts with the Constitution. They involve minimizing the independence of the Congress and the Judiciary. They involve huge deficits, great increase in debt and taxes and dangers of inflation.

Somehow I do not believe these things make for either economic or social security or enlarge the opportunities of the people.

The results are obvious violations of common sense. Transient political officials cannot plan the evolution of 120,000,000 people. We cannot assume that Americans are incapable of conducting their own lives and their daily affairs for their own good. We cannot increase standards of living by restricting production. We cannot spend ourselves into prosperity. We cannot hate ourselves into it either. We cannot constantly increase costs of production without increasing prices and therefore decreasing consumption and employment. We cannot place punitive taxes on industry without stifling new enterprise and jobs.

However, the consumer is the nemesis of all Planned Economy. It may control production. It cannot control the consumer. He is on strike in residential building today because he does not like the distorted building costs.

Today in a system part free the citizen confronts a new and unpredictable factor in conducting his affairs. That is political action. The people move hourly upon their own judgments as to supply and demand, as to prices and outlook. But today every plan in life is a bet on Washington. Every investment of savings is a gamble on the currency. Every future price is another bet on Washington.

Do these things make for increase in either the economic security or enlarged opportunity of the people? Do they not lead to confusion?

When the government expands into business then in order to protect itself it is driven irresistibly toward control of men's thoughts and the press. We see it daily in propaganda. We have seen the Labor Board doing it in the last week.

Group conflicts in the country have been magnified. We have become a sadly divided America. In the words these groups use and the reprisals they undertake they have brought us fear, confusion, worry, and distraction. If every group gets all it asks for, nobody will get anything.

Do these things make for economic security or equal opportunity?

There are considerations of government far higher than money or comfort. That is its relations to moral and spiritual values. Part of these Planned Economy measures are a surrender of the spiritual for the material. Part of them proceed by unmoral steps. No government can reform the social order unless it set higher standards of morals and rectitude than those whom it governs.

I ask you: Is there economic security without moral security?

All these things affect the mind and spirit of a people. For lack of a better term we call it public psychology. And "psychology is the twin brother of economics." Politicians may be psychologists but they are a poor twin for economists.

I leave it to you to inventory the instabilities of optimism and discouragement during the past year.

In your invitation to me you asked the cause of the confusion, harassment and uncertainties of the day. Perhaps this is enough of an accounting. I could give you more.

PART VII

THE ALTERNATIVE SYSTEM

You asked for the alternative economic and social system.

What sort of an America do we want? What should be our foundations? What should be our ideals?

American young men and women should have the right to plan, to live their own lives with the limitation that they shall not injure their neighbors. What they want of government is to keep the channels of opportunity open and equal, not to block them and then send them a tax bill for doing it. They want rewards to the winners in the race. They do not want to be planed down to a pattern. To red-blooded men and women there is joy of work and there is joy in the battle of competition. There is the daily joy of doing something worth while, of proving one's own worth, of telling every evil person where he can go. There is the joy of championing justice to the weak and downtrodden. These are the battles which create the national fiber of self-reliance and self-respect. That is what made America. If you concentrate all adventure in the government it does not leave much constructive joy for the governed.

Let me shortly sketch what I conceive to be a philosophy of

government and economics which would promote this sort of living and would preserve free men and women in our modern world. It is no magic formula. It does not lend itself to oratory.

ECONOMIC PHASES

First: The main anchor of our civilization must be intellectual and spiritual liberty. Ideas, invention, initiative, enterprise and leadership spring best from free men and women. The only economic system which will not limit or destroy these forces of progress is private enterprise.

Second: In the operation of the economic system there is but one hope of increased security, of increased standards of living, and of greater opportunity. That is to drive every new invention, every machine, every improvement, every elimination of waste unceasingly for the reduction of costs and the maximum production that can be consumed. We must work our machines heartlessly, but not our men and women.

By these means we sell goods cheaper. More people can buy. And thereby we have higher wages, more jobs and more new enterprise. New industries and new articles add again to the standards of living. That is the road to more jobs; it is the cure of temporary machine displacement. That is no robbery, it is progress.

GOVERNMENTAL PHASES

Third: To preserve freedom and equal opportunity we must regulate business. But true regulation is as far from government-dictated business as the two poles.

The vast tools of technology and power can be used for oppression. They can be used to limit production and to stifle competition. There can no more be economic power without checks and balances than there can be political power without checks and balances. We must compel competition in a large area of business. It is a restless pillow for managers, but it is the motive power of progress. Where we decide as in utilities that special privilege shall be given we must directly or indirectly regulate profits. We must regulate banking and finance to prevent abuse of trust. But Democracy can be master in its own house without shackling the family.

Fourth: A system of free men implies a vast amount of competence, of self-imposed discipline, and of responsibility. It implies co-operation between groups and sections outside of government and with government. The more co-operation the less government.

Social Phases

Fifth: No system can stand on pure economics. The economic and social gears must be enmeshed. The primary objective of our system must be to eliminate poverty and the fear of it.

Men cannot be free until the minds of men are free from insecurity and want. But security and plenty can be builded only upon a release of the productive energies of men. Moreover economic security and even social security can be had in jail but it lacks some of the attractions of freedom.

Such an economic system as I have mentioned would constantly diminish the marginal group who do not get a just share of the production pie. And the pie would be far bigger.

Through income and estate taxes, we can take care of the marginal group who get too much.

The economically successful must carry the burdens of social improvement for the less fortunate by taxes or otherwise. Child labor, health, sweated labor, old age, and housing are but part of our social responsibilities. The nation must protect its people in catastrophes beyond their control.

These are indeed but highlights of a system free from so-called Planned Economy. This is no philosophy of *laissez faire* or dog eat dog. It is a philosophy of free men with the responsibilities of freedom. It requires no tampering with the Constitution or the independence of the Judiciary. It is a system of faith in the competence, the self-discipline and the moral stamina of the American people and the divine inspiration of free men. It is a system of forward movement to far greater attainment.

Our transcendent need at this moment in America is a change in direction toward this system.

A confident, alert, alive and free people, enthused with incentive and enterprise, can quickly repair losses, repay debts, and bury mistakes. It can build new opportunity and new achievement.

PART VIII

All this is but the underlying basis upon which to work. And we need to work out a host of problems. We need their reexamination within these principles that we may find new and forward solutions. Time permits me to outline but a few as illustrations.

REFORM IN REGULATORY METHODS

We need for instance an unbiased examination of the whole experience with administrative law in regulation against business abuse. As I have said, it has been stretched over into personal government and punitive action. But the border lands are not easy to determine.

Many of these measures, old and new, should be reformed into definite statutory standards of business conduct and morals. That would restore the people to government by law instead of government by whim of men.

LABOR PROBLEMS

We need fresh and unbiased consideration of many fields in employer and employee relationships.

There are areas of conflict of interest, but there are greater areas of common interest. If these groups could themselves build on these common interests they might save great tragedies to our country. Certainly the Labor Board has not been a solution.

We can well start with acceptance of the fact that collective bargaining by representatives of their own choosing makes greatly for economic security of the workers.

I have long believed that we cannot secure full economic security in the wage group until we face the question of assured annual income. The greatest insecurity in the world is fear of losing the job. I believe there are large wage groups where employers could extend this greatest of assurances of security in increasing degree to the mutual advantage of both sides. It would be a great demonstration of co-operation in industry to accomplish it.

Again I believe methods could be worked out in industry itself by which so-called technological unemployment could be cared for and thus the mistaken opposition to new improvements and individual hardships could be solved. There are a host of other constructive fields.

Sweated Labor

We need a much more exhaustive consideration of the problem of sweated labor than it has received. The present Wages and Hours Bill runs into Planned Economy fixing of wages. It will reduce productivity at a time when the productive machine because of many shocks is already hesitating. One phase of its consequences has not been ventilated. Any general minimum wage will become a sort of moral wage and will inexorably tend to reduce wages in that vast majority of unorganized labor which today supports much higher minimums.

On re-examination we should envisage this question as solely one of sweated labor. A sweated industry is an industry sick from destructive competition or devoid of effective collective bargaining. The better remedy would be to apply minimums only to those industries which have been found sick after proper diagnosis. The minimum should be applied only while they are sick. Certainly employers would be quickened to collective bargaining as a relief from the restrictions. Such a program should be administered by restraining movement of goods into states where the minimums are maintained and not by centralizing more power in Washington.

Booms and Slumps

We need a new and exhaustive examination into the causes of booms and slumps. And this involves an unbiased and searching consideration into our whole financial, credit, currency and banking regulations and their effects. Certainly the remedy of Planned Economy has not worked.

CORPORATIONS

The question of corporation life in its entirety needs study for deeper reforms than prevention of monopoly.

We need a searching inquiry by unbiased minds into our corporate structure and theory, not for purposes of destruction of this necessary engine of civilization but for simplification of the whole tangle of practice and of state and federal regulation. But more important, we need seek for a way by which we may establish, without political control, a more general institutional sense and responsibility in large public corporations. And at the same time we should search for a method in our smaller corporations by which we can restore the sense of personal relationships and the responsibility of partnerships.

TAXES

We need an exhaustive examination of our whole tax system. In old days taxes had little economic or social effect. Now when they are 20 per cent or 25 per cent of the national income they have the most profound effect. Having this effect we should devise them not to destroy initiative and enterprise. And we could devise the method of levying them to produce most substantial effects. I could imagine a taxing program that would improve our housing far more than any government loans.

CONCLUSION

My time is ending. It would require several addresses to even partly traverse our multiple problems of agriculture, of currency, of foreign trade, of child labor, of old-age pensions, and a score of others. May I say in conclusion, much of our problem of security and enlarged opportunity is more intellectual and moral than material.

Let us remember the standards of human conduct must be erected upon a far higher base than government regulations and government controls. They spring from the Sermon on the Mount.

The season from Thanksgiving to Christmas and New Years is the time that Americans give life to the highest individual qualities of good-will, and resolve to do a better job. Today as never before if we could lift these qualities into national action, it would set America on a new road of hope and happiness.

Many have rightly urged an era of co-operation. We need it. We need co-operation to place America upon the right road to progress. And we need co-operation between organized groups, outside of government.

It is difficult for timid minds to believe that free men can work out their own salvation. Arrogant minds seeking for power live upon this timidity. In the firm places of your minds you must take some new resolves.

Nations are built around important and stimulating enterprises which demand sacrifice, discipline and mutual consideration. We gave all that in war. But today the nation must have it in peace.

For we have a great enterprise. That is to build our mechanisms so as to hold the greatest possession any nation has ever had. That is human liberty.

These may be times of confusion and uncertainty. But there are lights upon the horizon, for the eternal fires of freedom still burn.

American Policies for Peace

BY RADIO TO REPUBLICAN WOMEN'S CLUBS IN
NEW YORK, CHICAGO, AND SAN FRANCISCO

[January 15, 1938]

IT IS my purpose to make some comment upon the fundamental American policies for peace. It has been my belief
that the day-to-day incidents of foreign relations should
rest upon the responsibility of the Administration. But our underlying policies which build for peace or war must at all times
be subject to debate and to searching inquiry or criticism. That
is a part of democracy itself.

The problems of peace change with the great political tides
in the world. The forces today which may affect us for good or
evil are not those which affected us in 1914, in 1919, in 1932,
nor in 1934. Despite the constant effort of men of good will to
promote peace, the world is today filled with increasing distrust
and rising disorder. There are two hideous wars in progress.
Even in the nations at peace armies have been doubled since before the Great War. International economic life is still demoralized. The world is living dangerously. It is living recklessly.

To develop sane, common-sense viewpoints on these problems
of peace is, in some ways, as difficult in the United States as in
countries of even greater danger. We are torn into confusion
by idealistic dreaming, by wishful thinking, by the illusion of
isolation where there is no isolation. We feel righteous indignation and resentment of wrong among nations. We have the in-
stant urge to fight an outrage. We have with us those weak minds
who still think that war is a cure for domestic dissension or a

source of profit. We have exponents of big armies and big navies. We have those who want America to herd the world into the paths of righteousness with the dogs of war. And there are other minds who think we can get peace and security by just deserving it. And in addition to all this we have old, diverse national origins and sympathies, with their conscious or unconscious propagandas. And there are not alone nationalist propagandas. There are the propagandas of other systems of society which seek to enlist our interest first on one side and then on the other.

Amid this emotional stew it is difficult to think straight. Yet we must have straight and sane thinking. And we must gear our thinking to the realities of a dangerous world.

Lessons from the Great War

We have, or at least should have, learned some lessons from the Great War in addition to its horrors of the maimed and the dead.

One of these lessons is that the victors suffer almost equally with the vanquished. War's aftermaths of debt inflation, unemployment, unrest and spiritual degradation halt progress and project misery for decades.

And while we are on the gloomy side of these consequences, let me add an effect of another great war on the United States. With the recent peace-time increase in our national debt, we could not finance such a war without an inflation which would confiscate the savings of all of their present holders. We do not need to worry about passing laws to conscript wealth in the next great war. That will be automatic.

Another lesson, and perhaps the most important of all these lessons, is that democratic government now, and for many years to come, probably could not stand the shock of another great war and survive as a democracy. Free economic life is not built for war. We have heard a good deal about the coming conflict between nations under autocratic governments and nations under democratic governments. We certainly learned from the last war that the area of democracy was bitterly shrunk and autocracy gained. Those who would have us again go to war to save democracy might give a little thought to the likelihood that we would come out of any such struggle a despotism ourselves.

The Policies of Peace

There are two directions from which our peace may be endangered. The first is our direct relations with other nations. These we can control ourselves, at least in part. The second is our indirect relations to other people's wars.

We do not want war with anybody. We have no purpose in war. There is no atom of craving for territory in the American people. There is no wish to exploit other peoples. There is no atom of imperialism left in us. We want to solve a thousand internal problems, we want to build a thousand edifices to progress. To do this we need peace. We want peace.

Let no one misinterpret this statement. There is one contingency where the people of the United States will and must suffer all the horrors and penalties of war. And this brings me to the first of the American policies for peace.

We must fight for our independence to the last shred of our material and physical strength. And the world should know that if we are to have peace.

I am aware that there are various events and forces which might affect our independence. One test is positive: There must be no foreign soldier on—or over—our soil. But there are other circumstances that can arise which may threaten our independence without invasion of our shores. One such is violation of the Monroe Doctrine in the sense of aggression from outside the Western Hemisphere. However, most of the difficulties beyond our shores arise from rights of trade and our citizens abroad. Interferences with them are mostly isolated incidents. Such incidents must be acted upon when they arise, but they can be solved by the processes of peace. Our citizens must live and do business abroad to carry on the foreign trade which is vital to national life. There was a time when we thought it befitted our dignity and honor to enforce their contracts with soldiers and warships. That day is gone with the other attributes of dollar diplomacy. But we must keep our nation respected and we must protect the lives of our citizens. However, where our citizens insist on acting recklessly, their faith that we will jeopardize the future of our democracy should be made more and more remote.

The present proposal to take a popular referendum before we go to war is an evidence of the public anxiety for peace. It is well to have these subjects debated. The referendum might be a good idea if all the nations of the world were democracies, and if all of them would agree to do it. But in these dangerous days, even the courtesy of advance declaration of war seems obsolete. The world seems to be reverting to the frontier practice of getting the drop on your man—and that allows little time for arbitration and conciliation.

NATIONAL DEFENSE

And this brings me to the second major policy.

The greatest assurance from aggression against us is preparedness for defense. We must be respected not only for our justice but for our strength.

The failure of our government and other governments to hold the limitations on naval arms in 1933 and the growing world dangers require some increase in our defenses. Our military expenditures were about $700,000,000 in 1932. The present programs including relief outlays call for probably $1,150,000,000 next year. And the cost of manning these extended arms will be another $100,000,000 or so. We shall be expending $200,000,000 more than any other nation on earth.

These proposals ought to have further searching examination.

That increase should not be predicated on jingo rivalry. We should really resolve that our purpose is defense, not offense. There should be a searching distinction between what constitutes weapons and preparation for defense and preparation for offense.

And at this point I wish to suggest our third policy for peace.

We should limit our arms solely to repel aggression against the Western Hemisphere.

We should not waste our substance or interest elsewhere. We have hitherto included the Philippine Islands in our lines for defense. While we should give them every friendly office, they have made their decision for themselves. There is today no moral obligation or national need upon the American people either to stand this expense or incur this danger. Our policies in naval strength should be aligned to this fact.

And let me suggest further that we should not confuse work relief with building battleships. They have to be maintained afterward at high expense.

NEUTRALITY

When war does come between other nations, at once we need a fourth policy of peace.

We must preserve our neutrality.

And let no one believe that this is a slight task. Neutrality is as dynamic in its requirements as war. It requires single direction just as does war. It has tactics and strategy. Its conduct varies with every war and it varies from day to day with that war. For that reason I have never regarded our present neutrality law with any more confidence than I would an attempt by Congress to legislate in advance the tactics and strategy to be employed in war. I believed that this law would collapse in the first contact with realities. It has already proved absurd in the first war it met. For if there is humor in such events, its only effect has been that neither Japan nor China has formally declared war, and therefore there is excuse that the law does not operate. If enforced it will sometime place us in practical economic alliance with the aggressor. If we want to be neutral in other people's wars we should not tie our hands so that we are forced to favor one side or the other. That law has some good points in it but it should be greatly amended or repealed lest if we enforce it, it will get us into some war.

PREVENTION OF WAR

Beyond all these questions of our independence and our defense lies the greatest problem of all mankind—to prevent war.

We not only desire peace for ourselves, but we want to see peace between other nations. We wish good will, justice and reason to advance throughout the world. And we realize without that advance justice and reason will lag at home. There is no such thing today as isolation in the world.

The hopes of the world lie in the prevention of war. There lie relief from poverty and the reduction of human toil.

The world has been long discussing five methods in promoting peace or preventing war among nations.

One proposal has been for every nation to build good will and preserve rectitude. That proposal goes back 1900 years. It is a sound proposal but cannot be wholly relied upon for defense so long as there are so many battleships about.

Another proposal has been that we pledge ourselves to join with others in collective action to use military force to compel peace.

Another proposal has been that we pledge ourselves to join with other nations in the use of economic weapons to compel peace.

Another proposal is that we should co-operate with other nations for economic recovery and progress of the world as a contribution to peace.

Another proposal is that we join with other nations in collective building of the moral forces to preserve peace.

We must examine these proposals in the cold light of the world today. The currents of world power may shift and we cannot say anything is final. But at this time it is certain that the proposals which imply the use of military or economic force to compel peace have been tried and found wanting. When we came out of the Great War there was real hope that with the world dominated by new and old democracies these policies would be possible. That was the concept of the League of Nations. But the picture has changed darkly.

However the proposal to force peace in other people's wars by the use of economic sanctions, embargoes or boycotts still lingers on. It is my complete conviction that the use of such measures is the stepping-stone to war and not to peace.

In this light I should like to put down what I believe should be the fifth of American peace policies:

We should not engage ourselves to use military force in endeavor to prevent or end other people's wars.

And I should at once add the sixth stone in such foundations of American peace policies:

We should not join in any economic sanctions or embargoes or boycotts in endeavor to prevent or end other people's wars.

We in America should cease raising hopes of other nations.

I have little patience with those who glibly talk of international action without boldly stating what they mean. Strong words without precise meaning are dangerous. We owe it to every other nation that there should be no misunderstanding.

Constructive World Co–operation for Peace

But there are two of these proposals of co-operation between nations which are constructive highways toward peace. They demand as much interest and devotion as the problems of defense.

I believe our seventh American peace policy should be this:

We should co-operate in every sane international effort to advance the economic and social welfare of the world.

I do not need to emphasize that prosperity of nations is the best sedative to hate. Prosperity does not come from trade wars or economic wars or combinations between some nations in economic benefits to the exclusion of others. These sow the seeds of military wars. The world has been engaged in an open or submerged trade war ever since 1932. It started using currencies as its major weapon to gain trade advantages. Mainly out of currency instability and currency manipulations there have grown unreasonable tariff walls, embargoes, quotas, subsidies on exports, discriminations between nations. They are all devilish devices which create scarcity and restrict world prosperity. The unparalleled opportunity to have brought some measure of economic peace was lost when the World Economic Conference was delayed and finally destroyed by our government in 1933.

I do not here propose to elaborate a discussion of world tariffs. Despite the campaign promises of 1932 to reduce our tariff drastically, this administration, faced with the consequences, has changed the word drastic to a minor per cent. Whether we agree with these percentages or not, we can say at once that what the world needs are moderate tariffs at levels which represent no more than the difference in cost of production between home and abroad. The world needs tariffs which treat all nations alike. But constantly higher tariffs are the inevitable destiny of "Planned Economy." The current programs of governments—including our own—to control production and to fix prices (that is, "Planned Economy") inevitably advance domestic prices. It cannot continue without building tariff walls higher and higher.

And more destructive than any tariff walls is the commodity quota. That is the child of "Planned Economy." This device in effect provides a restriction with a hole in it for favored nations. That is the implement of sheer nationalism, not of economic peace or equal treatment.

If the world is to secure economic peace, the nations should be called again to organize a searching inquiry into the methods of reducing barriers and making for currency stability.

Moral Forces for Peace

But the greatest opportunity to advance peace in the world today lies in the use of moral forces. Their implement is the public opinion of mankind. And that brings me to the eighth policy of peace:

We should by every device and on every opportunity co-operate with other nations to exert moral force and build pacific agencies to preserve peace or end conflict in the world.

We should be active in furthering disarmament. We should continue to engage ourselves in treaties of conciliation and arbitration to settle our disputes with other nations by pacific means. We should go further and support collective agreements for judicial adjudication of conflict. We should support collective agreement for submission of disputes to arbitration. We should uphold the Kellogg Pact. We should refuse to give recognition to any advantage gained by the violation of that Pact. We should join other nations in the denunciation of treaty violations that public opinion may be mobilized. We should, in fact, never hesitate to build, even by an inch, the moral foundations of the peace in the world. Our faith must be that law and moral standards can be advanced among nations.

People today scoff that there is no longer validity in treaties; that the pledged word of nations no longer has sanctity.

I know that nations have violated their agreements with us to uphold the processes of peace. Treaties building for moral foundations of the world have been weakened. Truly international lawlessness is spreading. But if we do not hold faith that the violation of international morals brings its retribution in ultimate national decay, and if we do not hold faith that keeping to obligations is the substance of progress, then this world is committed to despair. And more, this civilization is committed to destruction. We at least can keep the banner of international morals aloft.

When we survey the present state of civilization in the light of long history we can well conclude that America has three dominant and immediate missions. The first is to maintain its own independence, the second is to maintain a society of free men and women, the third is to co-operate with the rest of the world to lift the burdens of war and to build again its prosperity and its hopes. But after all it is spiritual, moral, and economic forces alone which can attain these immense objectives.

They are the stars by which the world must today return to its course. Thus our country must assume its share of leadership and responsibility.

Foreign Policies for America

PART I

OVER the years since the War I have received frequent invitations from many governments, cities and universities in Europe who urged me to be their guest. This year I felt free to accept. It has been an unique honor to a private citizen of a foreign country. I come home deeply sensible both of their hospitality and their touching memory of American aid in times of war distress.

I welcomed the opportunity to observe at first hand the political, social, and economic forces now in motion nineteen years after my last stay in Europe.

It seems unnecessary to state to an American audience that we are not isolated from the fateful forces that sweep through Europe. In 1917 we were directly enmeshed in Europe's great war. And you will not forget the fact that in 1931, after we had started to recover from our home-made slump, we were plunged into the deepest world-wide depression until then known to our history by the financial panic which swarmed out of Central Europe. While we cannot wholly protect ourselves against these intellectual, economic, or political forces, it is imperative that we understand them. Through understanding, we can avoid some mistakes. We must abate some of their violence.

First of all let me say I am not here tonight to tell governments or nations abroad what they should do. It is not the right of any American to advise foreign peoples as to their policies. But it is our duty to consider for ourselves the forces outside our borders which inevitably affect us.

In order that I may give to you my conclusions as to the American relation to these shifting European forces, I must first attempt to present to you a picture of them over the period of years which lead to today's conditions.

As you are aware, I have had other direct experience in the European scene at different critical periods during the last thirty years.

Pre–War

The first of these periods was in professional work before the Great War. That period was the Golden Age of Europe. Then Europe was progressive and virile. Through the impulses of modern invention, the standard of living and comfort was increasing. Through progressive thought, economic and social abuses were decreasing. Intellectual and spiritual freedom were on the march.

The War

The second period of my contact with Europe was the first two and a half years of the War from 1914–17, when, in the name of America, I dealt with the heart-breaking backwash of war victims while the guns still boomed on the front. I moved freely on both sides of the battle line. I saw the rise of human brutality and its sinister employment of all the equipment of modern science. I witnessed the complete eclipse of everything that made for a better humanity.

The Armistice

Then came the Armistice, and I had a third period of direct experience in Europe through government service. Again I had an unique opportunity to see another era of great human forces in motion. That time it was my duty to administer, on behalf of our country, a great effort at co-operation with the former enemy governments—to restart the wheels of life in Europe. We joined hands with some twenty nations to restore communication, transportation, and credit, to aid agriculture and industry. We sought to revive hope, to replace hate with sympathy. We fought a victorious fight against the most horrible famine and the worst sweep of pestilence since the Thirty Years' War, when a third of the people of Europe died. And we did much to nurse into promising youth the infant democracies which had sprung into being.

That intervention by America to heal the wounds of war was second only to our military intervention to end the war. Whatever the failures may have been since, we can take nothing but satisfaction at our effort to reconstruct both enemy and friend alike.

During the Armistice period the world was filled with a sense of joyous relief, of hope and confidence. The spirit of Democracy and personal liberty had sprung into being over all Europe except in Russia. Freedom and government by the people seemed to us the guarantee of both progress and peace. Men thought a new and glowing period had dawned for humanity. They believed the forces of brutality had exhausted themselves. They thought that civilization, though grievously hurt, had learned an unforgettable lesson. I confess that I myself am on record as less optimistic because of the attitudes toward Germany.

Nineteen Years After

Now for the fourth period of my direct contact with Europe— nineteen years after the Peace. While this journey has been one of glowing hospitality, it has not been a visit to review the splendors of cathedrals or castles, of art or scenery. I had no need to go to Europe to read statistics. We have plenty at home. I had no need to go to Europe to learn the history of those nineteen years. But I welcomed the opportunity of this visit to discuss the forces in motion with more than a hundred leaders whose friendship I had enjoyed in the past and probably another hundred whom I met for the first time. In all I had these opportunities in fourteen countries. It is impossible for mortal man wholly to evaluate such forces, even on the ground. It is possible, however, to learn more of the furniture in men's minds. And certainly with such contacts it is possible to form impressions of elusive yet potent movements which cannot be gained from this distance. And these forces are cumulating to affect our country greatly. They are cumulating to affect the very foundations of contemporary civilization itself.

PART II

Seven obvious forces or factors have come to the forefront in Europe over these nineteen years.

The first of these is the rise of dictatorships—totalitarian, authoritarian or centralized governments, all with so-called Planned Economies. Nationalism, militarism and imperialism have certainly not diminished in nineteen years. At one moment (if we include the Kerensky regime in Russia) over 500,000,000 people in Europe embraced the forms of Democracy.

Today, if we apply the very simple tests of free speech, free press, free worship and constitutional protections to individuals and minorities, then liberty has been eclipsed amongst about 370,000,000 of these people. But today there are 30,000,000 less people living under liberal institutions than there were before the War.

The second great movement today, partly cause and partly effect, is the race to arms. Every nation in Europe—Communist, Fascist, Democratic—is now building for war or defense more feverishly than ever before in its history. In five years their expenditures have doubled from four to eight billion dollars annually. That is probably three times as much of their national substance as before the war. Europe today is a rumbling war machine, without the men yet in the trenches.

The third process in motion is increased government debts and deficits. There is hardly a balanced budget in Europe—that is, if we strip off the disguises of words. Government debts are increasing everywhere. Another inflation in some form seems inevitable.

The fourth movement is every European nation is striving for more and more self-sufficiency in industry and food production for either military reasons or to meet the necessities of "Planned Economy." This applies not only to the Fascist and Communist areas but in some degree to even England and France. The old-fashioned barrier to imports by simple tariffs has proved inadequate to protect these policies. New and far more effective walls have been erected around each nation by quotas, exchange controls, internal price fixing, clearing agreements, and intergovernment agreements on both purchases and sales.

The fifth factor is the failure of the League of Nations as a potent force for peace, and its complete replacement by the old shifting balances of power. And they are certainly shifting.

The sixth of these forces is fear—fear by nations of one another, fear by governments of their citizens, fear by citizens of their governments and the vague fear of people everywhere that general war is upon them again. And there is the fear of the promised massacre of civil populations from the air.

The seventh force is the steady increase in some nations of brutality, of terrorism, and disregard for both life and justice. Concentration camps, persecution of Jews, political trials, bombing of civil populations are but the physical expression of an underlying failure of morals terrible to contemplate.

All in all, it is an alarming and disheartening picture. There is a brighter side. Their recovery from the depression has been better than ours. They have little unemployment. Some part of employment, especially in the authoritarian states, is due to a boom in armaments, non-productive public works and subsidized self-sufficiency programs. And I do not believe general war is in immediate prospect. War preparations are not complete. The spirit is yet one of defense, not of offense. The power of military defense has so greatly increased over the power of offense that armies hesitate to move. New balances of power emerge to neutralize each other. Some groups still recollect the frightfulness of the Great War. Other groups are constantly working for peace and appeasement of the strains of Europe. Many of their statesmen have skill and great devotion in guiding the frail craft of peace around the rocks in the rapids. But the world cannot go on forever building up for war and increasing fear and hate. Yet, so long as there is peace, there is hope. And my admiration goes out to those many leading men and women in Europe who are working so courageously and even heroically to preserve the peace.

PART III

These are the visible, apparent tides and moving storms. There are still deeper currents beneath them. I hardly need catalogue them. They comprise all the inheritances of the war and in fact of history. There were the injustices and unrealities of the Peace Treaties. There were the debts and post-war inflations that led up to the European financial collapse in 1931 with its enormous unemployment and misery, both to themselves and to us. There has been one blunder after another. Not the least of them have been the lack of co-operation by the Allies with the struggling democracy of Germany; the rejection of the American proposals of disarmament in 1932 and the destruction of the currency conference of 1933.

There is the ever-present fact of a thousand years of European history that on a score of boundaries there exist zones of mixed populations, each with its own age-old hates and aspirations. Whatever way these boundaries may be drawn, some people will be separated from their "fatherlands." Their agitations are perhaps the key to much European history and the key to one repeated war after another. Perhaps this was what George Washington had in mind in his Farewell Address.

There sounds constantly through this labyrinth the shrill note of new philosophies of government and the echoes of old orders of society disguised in new phrases. There are democracy, socialism and communism of fifty-seven varieties; there is Fascism with its variations from soft to hard; there are autocratic forms all the way from disguised democracy through authoritarianism, totalitarianism to dictatorships and unlimited monarchy.

And these movements contain as many dangers for the American people as either the military forces or trade barriers of Europe. They require examination in any inquiry as to American policies.

I need not recall to you that after the war the first rise of hope to this distraught humanity was democracy. And the steps by which this liberty was lost are as important to the American people as what actually happens under despotism when it arrives. They indeed need to sink into the American mind.

No country started with the intention to sacrifice liberty. Each started to solve economic problems. In broad terms the steps are always the same. The economic system of Europe before and after the war was relatively free. There were many deep abuses. The new democracies brought resolute reforms on a large scale. But with the handicap of the miserable inheritances of the war Utopia did not come.

Then came socialism hand in hand with its bloody brother communism crying immediate Utopia in a wilderness of suffering people. They took advantage of the tolerance and freedoms of liberal institutions to mislead the people. Their methods were the preaching of class hate, the exaggeration of every abuse, the besmirching of every leader, blame for every ill that swept over their borders. At the next step politicians arose by trying to compromise with these enemies of true liberalism. The result was governments constantly interfering with the proper functions of businessmen, labor and farmers. By these compromises they further weakened the initiative and enterprise of the men who really made the system work. They destroyed that confidence and energy by which free economic systems are moved to great production. Finally came vast unemployment, conflict and desperate people.

But socialism has not triumphed from its work. Socialism and its compromisers in Europe have invariably served only to demoralize democracies and open the door to reactionary forces.

Italy produced Fascism. Fascism promised a new Utopia through restored order, discipline and planned economy, jobs and future for the youth. It is worthy of emphasis that Fascism has always begun in the form of planned economy. And it was ushered in by the same cries and slogans that they were for the liberation of the common man.

With Economic Planning once started, each step has required another until it arrives at government dictation to business, to labor and farmers of wages, hours, production, consumption, prices, profits, finance, imports and exports. Coercion becomes a necessary instrument, and then it is but a few steps to complete dictatorship. All opposition becomes treason.

Denounce it as we may as despotism and the destroyer of liberty and abhorrent to free men, yet the Fascist form of government is today a raging power. Its acts are being rationalized into a philosophy. It has now embraced a sort of mysticism based on theories of racialism and nationalism. It is becoming a militant ideology. It does not hold within its original boundaries. Fourteen nations in Europe, with 240,000,000 people, have adopted these notions of Fascism in major part.

In Germany Fascism has had its most complete development under the iron rule of the Nazi party. In order better to understand the Nazi regime we must not overlook its apparent accomplishments. It has brought about a gigantic mobilization of a materialistic system at the hands of the government. Great industrial wastes in strikes and materials have been eliminated. Great efforts have been obtained from the people in work and sacrifice of comfort. Progress has been made toward self-sufficiency. Some sort of employment and economic security has been brought to all who comply. And concentration camps give security to the balance. New houses, jobs and more recreation have been brought to the underprivileged. The support of a gigantic growing military machine has been successfully squeezed out of an already skimpy standard of living. Germany has been restored to a first-class military power. It is today feared throughout the world. Germany today burns with a prideful sense of restored self-esteem. Youth has been fired with new hopes and high emotions.

So far as material things are concerned the average German is today better off than five years ago. Yet to a lover of human liberty there is another side to even this picture. All the remaining democracies in Europe have made sounder and greater recovery from the depression than has Germany or any of the Fascist states in the same period. And the standard of living is higher in all the Democratic states than in any of the Fascist states.

But for us there are deeper issues in all this. Under this regime the spirit of man is subordinated to the state. The individual must be developed into conformity with the national will as expressed by the leaders. Whatever is deemed by them as good for the state becomes the standard of justice, right, and morality. That has become the basis of law.

And Fascism has demonstrated a way to fool all the people all the time—by suppression of all criticism and free expression; and by drilling children and youth, stage by stage, to a governmentally prescribed mental attitude. A controlled press and organized propaganda have poured this new faith into the adults. It has stamped out, or controlled, every form of independent association from Trades Union to Universities. It has instituted a form of terrorism, for the fear of concentration camps is ever present. Its darkest picture is expressed in the heart-breaking persecution of helpless Jews. Intellectual sterility and deadened initiative and individuality are its inevitable results. It is becoming a gigantic spartanism. And let no one believe it is about to collapse.

Parallel with the rise of the Fascist philosophy, Marxian Socialism is a dying faith. They have some things in common. They are both enemies of Liberty. The gigantic experiment in socialism in Russia is now devouring its own children and shedding rivers of blood. And it is moving steadily toward a sort of Fascist regime.

Now we must distill some conclusions as to what should be the American attitude toward all this maze of forces. We may divide our relations to them into three parts. Our relations to these forces politically; our relations to them economically; and our relationship to them socially.

PART IV

INTERNATIONAL POLITICAL RELATIONSHIPS

I found most nations in Europe convinced that we would be inevitably drawn into the next great war as in the last. Some people build confident hope upon it. But every phase of this picture should harden our resolves that we keep out of other people's wars. Nations in Europe need to be convinced that this is our policy.

Yet we are interested, vitally interested, in peace among other nations. The League of Nations, except as a most useful clearing house of economic and social information, is at least in a coma. Certainly the central idea that peace could be imposed by collective action employing military or economic force is dead.

But these ideas of collective action now appear in a new form. I find in many quarters of Europe and some in America an insistence that, as Democracy is endangered by the rise of dictatorships and authoritarian governments, therefore democracies should join in some sort of mutual undertaking for protective action. These ideas were greatly stimulated and encouraged by the word quarantine from these shores. Such proposals, if sincere, involve more than mere good words. Anything honest in that direction implies the pledge of some sort of joint military or economic action by the United States with other powers. We may as well be blunt about it.

If we join with the two other powerful democracies, Great Britain and France, we are engaging ourselves in an alliance directed against Germany and Italy and all the satellites they can collect. But we are doing more than this. Great Britain has her own national and imperial problems and policies. Any commitment of ourselves will mean that we are dragged into these policies. France has her own special alliances and her own policies, including an alliance with Communist Russia. We would be supporting Stalin.

But more than all this, we would be fostering the worst thing that can happen to civilization, that is, the building up of a war beween government faiths or ideologies. Such a combination of democracies would at once result in combining the autocracies against the democracies. It could have all the hideous elements of old religious wars.

We should have none of it. If the world is to keep the peace, then we must keep peace with dictatorships as well as with popular governments. The forms of government which other peoples pass through in working out their destinies is not our business. You will recollect we were once animated by a desire to save the world for Democracy. The only result that time was to sow dragons' teeth which sprang up into dictatorships. We can never herd the world into the paths of righteousness with the dogs of war.

While we should reject the whole idea of pledging our military or economic forces to any scheme for preserving peace by making war, we have both the obligation and the interest to organize and join in the collective moral forces to prevent war. I know I will be told again that moral forces do not weigh much in a world of soldiers and battleships. But the greatest force for peace is still the public opinion of the world. That is a moral force. I will be told again that it has no weight. But I found everywhere an anxiety for the approval of world opinion. Every consequential nation supports at great expense a propaganda bureau for that purpose. The dictatorships especially devote themselves to it.

And why? Because the desire of nations for the good opinion of mankind is not dead. Secretary Hull's eloquent denunciation of international lawlessness was echoed in every newspaper in the world. Decency is still news.

I believe there are methods by which the moral forces for peace and international co-operation for progress could be better organized than they are today. At this moment of despair in the world the problems of armament and economic degeneration press dreadfully for solution.

There is a measure for very modest but long-view action by our Government that could bring great benefits to us and to other nations. It would serve to reduce greatly the area of frictions upon our war debt problem. After the Armistice we established credits for reconstruction and food to Poland, Belgium, Estonia, Latvia, Lithuania, Finland, Czecho-Slovakia, Hungary, Greece, Roumania, and Jugo-Slavia. Only Finland has staunchly maintained these payments. The others are awaiting the action of the large war debtors. There are likely to be difficulties over these matters for years to come.

I believe we should consider suggesting to these relief credit countries as distinguished from the war credit countries a readjustment of the debts and——

That each of them make these payments into a fund in their own country in their own currencies.

That this fund be used for extension of higher education, scientific research and for scholarships in their own universities; also for exchange of post-graduate students, professors, and scientific information between the United States and that country.

That these funds are to be administered jointly by Americans and their nationals.

There will thus be created a joint interest with us from which we will generate benefits far greater than we will otherwise receive. The cumulative effect over the years of building up a great body of influential men and women in those countries who would understand our country and believe in us would count greatly both in economic relations and in times of international emergency. And we shall have made a contribution to civilization which may be of no quick material value but which will later serve as a great monument to our foresight.

In summary, in the larger issues of world relations, our watchwords should be absolute independence of political action and adequate preparedness. That course will serve the world best. It will serve our interests best. It will serve free men best.

PART V

ECONOMIC RELATIONSHIPS

In the field of international business we have much to think about. The prosperity of nations is the best antidote for the poisons of fear and hate. But that prosperity will be sadly limited as long as the present barriers to trade continue. They grow worse every month, and they directly affect our American workers and farmers every week.

I must amplify what I have already said as to these barriers. In these present-day barriers the old-fashioned tariff plays but a minor part. The infinitely more potent system of quotas, exchange restrictions and internal control of the buyer erect a solid wall against imports. This wall is opened only through government-controlled gates, for specified commodities from specified countries. It matters little how low the tariff of a foreign nation may be if our American producers cannot obtain permission to move goods through the gates of the quota or to obtain payment in our own currency for the goods. Nor are these new barriers limited to the despotisms. They are increasingly in use in European democracies as well.

At this moment our exports to over 300,000,000 people in Europe meet barriers far more potent than tariffs. And to another 200,000,000 they are partly controlled outside of tariffs. These additional trade barriers now affect nearly half of the world's commerce.

When we examine these barriers we find they have developed both offensive and defensive characteristics. Their main purpose is to force self-sufficiency in internal production. That is partly a measure of military defense. It is partly a measure to solve money exchange difficulties arising from unbalanced foreign trade and unbalanced budgets with their unstable currencies. Moreover, when governments undertake Planned Economy by managed currency production, wages and prices, they must also control both imports and exports.

In other words, one of the consequences of Planned Economy is to place foreign trade more and more in the hands of the government. Thus this part of world commerce is steadily degenerating into one more implement of military and political policy.

Equal treatment of nations has been largely abandoned under these new devices. Quotas are being assigned between nations for other considerations, such as political affinity or credit advantages. For instance, the quota for automobile tire imports recently has been traded around among European nations almost to our total exclusion. I fear the reciprocity treaties in mutual lowering of tariffs will work out a one-way road under the practices of these new barriers. Some part of our workers and farmers who have been accustomed to produce goods for export are going to be out of a job so long as these practices last.

There are four alternative courses. We can, in an effort to ameliorate our situation, put penalties on the shipment to us of goods from countries whose practices in these ways discriminate against our goods. Or we could take advantage of our vast resources and by more protection establish some self-containment of our own. Or we can resume the fundamental approach to world sanity and trade peace by international co-operation as planned for the Conference of 1933. Or we can make up our minds to keep a part of our people on relief for a long time.

My own conviction is that the world muddle of unstable currencies has more to do with the maintenance of these artificial trade barriers than any other one factor. If the problem is to be corrected fundamentally on an international scale, it must be approached ultimately at this point.

It is probable that courageous discussion and action among a group of nations might be an entering wedge to the jam of barriers. Gradually the trade of the world might be re-established from such a nucleus. And these questions are not economic abstractions. They create or destroy the jobs and the happiness of millions of our people.

PART VI

The third of our attitudes which I wish further to discuss is our American relationship to the vast ferment of new and old social philosophies which boils furiously throughout the world. The wholesale eclipse of democracy must concern us. Our national mission is to keep alight the lamp of true liberalism. But it is in the United States that we must keep it alight.

Every few centuries the world gives birth to new systems of government and life. Or it resurrects old systems under new phrases. In any event they mostly revolve around two old and diametrically opposed concepts—that the development of the individual is the prime purpose of the state or the individual is the pawn of the state. On one hand the individual possesses rights and on the other he does not; in the one concept the state is the organized expression of the will of individuals within it, in the other the individual is but the transient property of the state.

True liberalism is not a mere middle ground between Fascism and Socialism. Both Fascism and Socialism hold to the other concept—that the individual is but the pawn of an all-wise, omnipotent state. Liberalism has no compromise with either of these two forms of the same concept.

Let no man believe in either of two popular misapprehensions so widespread in this country today. This philosophy of Communism is not imposed, suddenly, new born, from the bottom up. And this thing called Fascism is not imposed, suddenly, new born, from the top down. Both grew in prepared soils. Both are the aftermath of a gradual infection of Democracy, a gradual perversion of true liberalism.

And let me again repeat that Democracies are first infected by the plausible notions of "Cure the business slump" through so-called economic planning. Every step in this direction requires another. Every step further demoralizes free economy. And step by step more force and coercion must be applied until all liberty—economic and personal and political—is lost.

Let no man mistake that we in America have until now avoided the infection of these European systems. If our own so-called Planned Economy is not an infection from the original stream of Fascism it is at least a remarkable coincidence.

The leader of German Fascism in a speech last week hurled the taunt to democracies that "not a single decent nation has died for the sake of democratic formalities." To the extent that races do not actually die because they forfeit individual liberty, that may be true. But what is far more important is that when true Liberty dies, then Justice and Truth die. And intellectual progress and morality die also.

I have no doubt that Fascism will fail some time, just as Marxian Socialism has failed already. The stifling of intellectual progress, the repression of the spirit of men, the destruction of initiative and enterprise, will offset all the efficacies of planned economy. Even economic life cannot succeed where criticism has disappeared and where individual responsibility is constantly shirked for fear of the state. Even in Fascist countries liberal ideas are not dead and will not be downed. Every despotism today lives with fear of liberty at its heart—or there would be no concentration camps.

And I may add that, having listened in many countries to eulogies of Planned Economy and Fascism and of their benefits to the common man, I detected in every case the hope that some day liberty might return. The spirits of Luther, of Goethe, of Schiller, of Mazzini and Garibaldi are not dead.

Moreover there has been nothing shown me in Europe in elimination of wastes or better housing or security to workers or farmers or old age that we cannot do better under democracy if we will. Though I had little need for confirmation in my faith, I pray God that this nation may keep its anchors firmly grounded in intellectual liberty and spiritual freedom. These values can be preserved only by keeping government from the first pitfall of direction or participation in economic life—except that it shall sternly repress, by due process of law but not by edict, every abuse of liberty and honesty.

The protection of Democracy is that we live it, that we revitalize it within our own borders, that we keep it clean of infections, that we wipe out its corruptions, that we incessantly fight its abuses, that we insist upon intellectual honesty, that we build its morals, that we keep out of war.

That is the greatest service that this nation can give to the future of humanity.

Challenge to Liberty, 1938

[April 8, 1938]

PART I

I AM always glad to get back to the West. It has certain outstanding advantages. This spot is 7,200 miles from certain spots in Europe. If your imagination is lively enough to imagine California under conditions on the Continent our advantages would be even more manifest to you.

If we had 500,000 troops and 2,000 aeroplanes looking at us hatefully from over the Oregon line, another 400,000 men and 2,000 planes ready to march over the Nevada line, and another few hundred thousand being drilled in Arizona ready to pounce upon us, this would be a less comfortable place. And if we had to pay taxes for about 400,000 men in our own State to make faces at these sister States, then it would be still more uncomfortable. If each of us had by law to have a gas mask and we had by law to try them on all the kids once every little while, then it would be still more uncomfortable. And if we had to continue all sorts of shifting alliances with our neighbors to balance off their powers for evil, it would be a still more anxious place to live. And all that can happen to you even if you lived in a democratic state.

If we had an up-to-date authoritarian state, there are still other possibilities of discomfort. Then your soul belongs generally to the state. If you carry over the old idea that perhaps it belongs to you, then you go to a concentration camp to rest your nerves. If you are a farmer you plant what the agricultural policeman tells you to plant. And you raise the pigs and cows he thinks are good for the state. If you are a worker you work where you are told. And you work the hours you are told. And you get the wages you are told. Your trade union having been dissolved you can belong to a government recreation project. You will also be taught to sing cheerful songs in the recreation hours and to march all about. You have social security if you conform. If you do not conform you get security in concentration camp. You will be secure anyway. So as not to have your doubts raised and your feelings harried by critics of this more redundant life they are just put away in the same concentration camps. Your freedom of speech is a sort of a one-way street. You do gain something by saving half the public speeches in the country by doing away with all those of the opposition. Your newspaper contains what the all-powerful thinks is good for your soul. And your books are carefully chosen that your economic and romantic feelings shall not be polluted. If you kick about the way the government does it you will be placed under protective arrest to prevent harm coming to you.

There are some forces in motion in the United States which might make California an uncomfortable place. But we will at least deliver a lot of free speech before that time arrives.

There is one discomfort in California that is not a discomfort in Europe. That is where to park your automobile. Their slogan is, more guns and less automobiles.

Altogether I am glad Europe is still 7,200 miles from California.

PART II

My first purpose in visiting Europe was to accept a unique hospitality which seldom comes to men.

These hospitalities proved the occasion for great demonstrations of affection and respect for America. No American can remain unmoved when tens of thousands of school children line the streets with their cheerful yells of "Long live America," with the frantic waving of thousands of American flags. No American can remain unmoved when tens of thousands of the common people gather in city squares and remove their hats to the American National Anthem. No American can remain un-

moved to the fervent expression by men of immense responsibilities of hope and almost prayer that America shall stand fast
in liberty, that it shall not perish from the earth.

I have met some part of these demonstrations in a score of
great cities and in many countries.

PART III

I wished also to observe the forces in motion which are re-
shaping human destiny.

While outwardly the incidents of life go on much the same
everywhere, underneath Europe is seething with change which
will yet affect the whole destiny of human institutions and the
ways of human life. Europe is giving birth to a new philosophy
of government and of life.

That has happened at other periods in history. Within the
Christian Era we have seen the rise of Christianity, the rise of
Mohammedanism, the rise of Feudalism, the rise of the Ref-
ormation, the rise of Liberalism and its philosophy of free men
and the rise of Communism. And each of these great ideas has
carried a train of human conflict.

I am not going to take your time to discuss or describe this
new European philosophy or what it means today or to the future.

But let no man underestimate the dangers to free men. It
not only represents the mobilization of racial instincts and racial
yearnings for glory and power. It not alone represents ruthless
economic organization at the sacrifice of all personal liberty. It
represents the extinction of pity and mercy which Christianity
gave the world. It represents an upsurge of abhorrent brutality
from which the Jews are helpless victims. Its method is that any
end justifies the means. And that justifies every perversion of
intellectual honesty and government morals.

My great interest was to learn more of the cause of this gigantic shift in human direction. It was to learn the steps by which
fate has driven men to this defeat of intellectual and spiritual
liberty.

PART IV

And now let me return for a moment to the American scene. The real, the immediate, the pressing problem of this country is unemployment. When I went abroad we had 10 million or 11 million unemployed. I return to find they have increased by another million or two. Meantime Washington has employed most of its time debating a subject of no aid to these of our countrymen.

That 12,000,000 unemployed is obviously the indication of something terribly wrong in our own economic machine. Let me say something perhaps elementary on this American economic machine and the way it starts and stops. It moves forward and employs people only when there is confidence and hope. A large part of its movement forward depends on confidence and hope. A large part of its stoppage comes from fear. When confidence breaks down fear seizes control and unemployment becomes rampant. Prosperity and depression are greatly influenced by these two emotions. There are other factors but of later years these emotions have become immensely more potent than ever before.

One reason for this is the increasing proportion of postponable goods in our standard of living. If you will look over the country you will find that about 40 per cent of what the American people consume can be postponed. About 60 per cent are absolute necessities and cannot be postponed. A new pair of shoes can be postponed for three months; a suit of clothes six months; an automobile for a year. What we call durable goods, such as houses, can be postponed longer than shoes. If a shiver of fear comes over the country most people postpone the purchase of something. And instantly somebody somewhere has lost a job making shoes or automobiles or houses. In turn those out of a job have to postpone the purchase of even necessities. And the fellow who has a job, seeing somebody lose a job, then also postpones something out of fear of losing his job. Then we are on a downward spiral.

This danger does not arise in those Asiatic countries where

people have only the bare necessities. It existed to a much less extent in the United States fifty years ago. In other words, when we built up the American standard of living and jobs of men to include an automobile, a radio, an extra suit of clothes, and a trip to the movies, we introduced a most delicate adjustment.

In the United States today everybody has lost some confidence and everybody has some fear. It is nonsense to say that either big or little business is on a strike. It is not so. Business is yearning to sell automobiles and new suits of clothes. It is the people who are scared. Big business or little business is not scared to take on men if anybody will give them an order for goods.

With 12,000,000 people out of a job it is our business to explore the cause of these fears. I was especially interested to find if any of them were coming from abroad. One of the causes which sucked us into the whirlpool of world-wide depression in 1931 came from Europe.

There has been general recovery in Europe from that depression. There is no financial panic brewing over there to pull down our credit structure as in 1931. Their regained economic strength is even helping us now by purchasing our goods, whereas in 1931 they stopped their purchases abruptly.

In the democracies there is no unemployment at all comparable to ours. They are indeed prosperous. France is of course having trouble because she adopted the New Deal two years ago.

Even in the authoritarian states and the dictatorships there is less unemployment than we have per million of people even if we deduct those employed manufacturing arms. It is true their standard of living is less than the democracies but the people are largely employed.

Nor is there immediate danger of general war in Europe. Certainly we have no fear of war against us. There is no threat of any one pouring fire or explosives on our cities out of the sky. There is not the remotest chance that our national independence will be challenged from abroad.

Certainly this great fear among the American people does not come from outside our borders.

We ought to explore for the sources of fear at home. Today we have no inflated bubble of gambling credit or a weak banking system that we must be afraid of as there was in 1929. The banks are full of surplus credit. There is no over-expansion in industry in America. In fact we are short of equipment. There is no consequential over-stocking of goods. There is no over-expansion of buildings and homes. In fact there are not enough good homes. There is no crop failure or threatened shortage of food or clothes. Every one of the factors and forces within our borders that ordinarily produce fear and its consequence in unemployment is absent.

Yet we are stark facing the fact of 12,000,000 people out of jobs. Every one of those families is suffering some privation and worry. And there is no anxiety on earth like that of not knowing where the next week's living for your family is to come from. Some newspaper said the other day that I must get satisfaction out of this depression. I don't. I don't get satisfaction out of human misery.

I do have a recollection of a bitter slogan used against us in the 1932 campaign. They said often and harshly that it could not be worse. But some one said that was about forty billion dollars ago. And we must live in the present.

It is the first job of America to restore genuine self-respecting jobs in productive enterprises. It transcends all other questions. It transcends all party politics. It must be met without flinching, whether it be government theories, taxes, waste, corruption, unmoral acts of men in high places.

And let me say that a confident, alert, alive and free people, enthused with incentive and enterprise, can quickly repair losses, repay debts, and bury mistakes. It can build new opportunity and new achievement. That can be restored in America.

And whence do these forces of destroying fear arise?

This country should sit down and think out every force, governmental, moral, and economic, that is causing this fear, and uproot that cause. We should apply one test to the whole gamut of government action. Does this action stifle initiative and enterprise? Does it cost men their jobs? I am well aware of the importance of reforms. I am still more aware of the misery of 12,000,000 unemployed. And there are dangers to the very institutions of free men from an economic machine dislocated in this fashion.

PART V

There is one phase of all this disturbance which we got from Europe. That is the New Deal so-called Planned Economy. At least we invented both the phrase and the methods subsequent to their discovery in Europe. I have been interested to explore that idea in its European scene. I wanted to see their experience and where it led in the end.

We must not confuse true liberal reforms with Planned Economy. Constant reform is a necessity of growth. Reforms directed to cure business abuses, to remedy social ills, to provide old-age needs, housing, to end sweated labor, etc., are right. Nor is Planned Economy necessary to bring them about.

First let us examine the central ideas of New Deal Planned Economy.

No one will deny that our government is today increasingly controlling prices, wages, volume of production and investment. Its methods include politically managed currency, managed credit, huge expenditure, deficits, debts, pump priming, and inflation of bank deposits. Further weapons are relief funds to build the government into competitive business. They are used to influence the electorate. The taxing powers have been stretched deep into the control of business conduct. Regulation to prevent abuse has been stretched into instruments of dictation. The policeman on the streets of commerce to expedite the traffic, to keep order and stop robbery, now orders our destination and tells us what to do when we get there. It was a depressing day for America when the farmer could be put in jail for failure to obey the dictates of Washington.

The very forces of Planned Economy involve constantly increasing delegation of discretionary power to officials. They involve constantly greater centralization of government. They involve conflicts with the Constitution. They involve minimizing the independence of the Congress and the Judiciary.

Certainly there is a gigantic shift of government from the function of umpire to the function of directing, dictating, and competing in our economic life.

We have now had nearly five years' experience with these ideas. They were put forward as only for an emergency. And yet every session of Congress faces demands for more and more.

No more heartening news ever came to the American people than today when the House of Representatives regardless of party again halted these methods. To these men we owe a debt of gratitude.

There are here fundamental conflicts with free men in which there is no compromise, no middle ground.

PART VI

If we again return to the European scene, we find seven or eight Democracies which refused to adopt these courses of Planned Economy. They are today the most prosperous nations in the world despite the dangers under which they live. One other great Democracy, France, did adopt these ideas. They are today also in deep trouble. The other gigantic fact of European experience is that some twelve or fourteen nations belonging to Western civilization, embracing nearly three hundred millions of people, have moved from the foundations of popular government and free men to the foundations of authoritarian government where personal liberty is extinguished in the state.

And at one stage in this transformation they compromised between true liberalism and socialism or with attempts at government dictation of business, farming, and labor. That is the common denominator when democracy has fallen. They tried various breeds of Planned Economy. They tried to mix social philosophies. These attempts at mixture generated their own hates and fears.

They paralyzed with fear the delicate confidence and hope of the future with which all business moves and revives in a free system. They undermined the initiative and enterprise of men which is the sole mainspring of progress to free institutions. Out of fear they produced more and more deeper depressions and panics which finally reached chaos where men surrendered all liberty to the State to save themselves.

Western civilization does not turn to socialism or communism. They turn invariably to fascism. The only contribution of socialism and communism is disorder which leads to fascism.

PART VII

I was at the very seat of Fascism when one of our important government officials broadcasted over Europe an attack upon Fascism itself. It was received with great amusement. And I was compelled to listen to a relation of the uncanny parallel of steps taken in the United States under so-called Planned Economy with those which had bred the sort of chaos in Europe from which Fascism sprang.

I do not say that our economic system has been brought to this dangerous point where Fascism is its destination. But with all the solemnity I can command I do say that the direction that we are going in today is precisely that which in the end creates the demoralization from which Fascism invariably springs.

Whether our Planned Economy is an infection from Europe of creeping collectivism or whether it is a native American product is less important than its actual results upon us and where it leads to.

. And where have we arrived? At a discouraged and fearful people, with 12,000,000 unemployed. Is not the very system itself making the one-third ill fed and ill clothed?

The primary objective of our system must be to eliminate poverty and the fear of it.

Men cannot be free until the minds of men are free from insecurity and want. But security and plenty can be builded only upon a release of the productive energies of men from fear and handicap. That America must have.

May I say a word in conclusion? Despite the fears and gravity of our home problems I stepped on to the shores of our country with a great release of spirit. I found release from the subconscious dread that haunts all Europe. I found again that greater freedom of human mind, a wider spread of kindliness, a more general sense of individual responsibility, a stronger assertion of personal liberty than anywhere abroad.

One long-held conviction has been greatly hardened. That is that we have grown a long way from Europe in our century and a half of national life. A new race with its own soul has grown on this continent. The life-stream of this nation is the generations of millions of human particles acting under impulses of freedom and advancing ideas gathered from a thousand native springs. These springs and rills have gathered into streams which have nurtured and fertilized the spirit of this great people over centuries.

These streams are the imponderables which differentiate the races of men. Of one thing we may be sure. When a great race has been refreshed over centuries with the waters of liberty, those living waters will not be denied it.

Morals in Government

FRESNO, CALIFORNIA

[April 26, 1938]

PART I

I AM going to discuss an old old requisite of government in
a free people. That is morals in government. It has been
discussed ever since the days of Socrates in free Athens.
George Washington expounded it at his Farewell Address in free
America. But it needs emphasis now as never before in the history of this country. I raised some questions upon it some months
ago. They have never been answered. I propose to ask some
more of them.

I am impelled to this after study in Europe of why nearly
one-half of all the millions of people belonging to Western civilization in twenty years have abandoned self-government for
some form of dictatorial control. By almost bloodless revolution
they have sacrificed free press, free assembly, and all constitutional guarantees.

I may say at once that one of the decays in their freedom was
the loss of morals in their self-governments, which infected the
moral fibre in the people. On these prepared soils dictatorships
have risen through intellectual dishonesty but with high claims
to cure these moral ills. Nations can stand the pinch of economic ills, but they cannot stand the loss of moral fibre.

The greatness of nations is their moral stature, not the size of
their population or their wealth. Belgium, Sweden, Norway or

335

Finland would scarcely fill an American state, yet they are great nations. It is their moral fibre that makes them great.

Self-government by a people is based upon moral and spiritual concepts. And the government of a free people must in itself express the highest ideals of the people. If it fails in its standards it injures the morals of the whole people. It destroys its own foundations of free government.

I mean not only moral honesty but intellectual honesty. And I speak of immorality that is wider than monetary corruption. Nor am I addressing you as Republican women but as all women concerned in the preservation of self-government.

Morals in government relations with the people are positive as well as negative. Decent self-government rests upon clean public service. It rests upon honest elections. It rests upon honest enforcement of the laws by officials. It rests upon honor in all government transactions with the people. It rests upon honest debating. It rests upon the people being honestly informed.

When citizens are dishonest with each other the damage is mostly held between themselves. Also it may affect their chances in the life hereafter. But when government is dishonest it infects the morals of the whole people.

If morals cannot be sustained in self-government either one of two things ensues: civilization rots, or the people turn to dictatorial government to clean up the politicians.

And this is a subject peculiarly of interest to women. Ordinarily I have believed that the problems of a nation were common to men and women and deserved mutual presentation. But here is one problem which I believe must be eminently your own if we are to get it cleaned up.

It is not flattery but just a commonplace fact that moral instincts of women are upon average higher than men. Solomon discovered "that strength and honor are her clothing." And somebody has to do a clean-up job in this Republic. The men haven't done much of late. So as a complaining citizen, I turn to the women. Anyway, cleaning up after men has been one of the appointed jobs of women ever since civilization began.

PART II

Now let us analyze something of what is going on today as to morals in this democracy of ours. We may set down a few simple principles of government and ask a few questions as to what is going on with respect to them.

First, the principles of clean public service require that officials be selected on the merit system.

That is more than a necessity to insure efficiency. Any other course breeds corruption of a thousand kinds. The spoils seeker and the spoils giver, by their very act, are in gangster pay-off from public funds. It degrades the people who hold such jobs. It degrades public life. It withers government to "ins" and "outs" and swells the seekers at the public trough.

For example, has the present disregard of seventy years' effort to build up a national system of merit service increased confidence in free government?

Has not the patronage appointment of 300,000 officials in five years corrupted congressmen, and elections, and undermined the public faith? Does it not mean a decadence in public morals?

The Nazis, Fascists, Communists, and all authoritarian governments universally build up their grip upon the people through the use of party patronage.

Second, the principle of honest elections requires that government funds must not be spent to influence the judgment and corrupt the vote of the people.

For example does it improve national morals when the citizens see huge sums rushed to politically doubtful districts two jumps ahead of an election?

When the allocation of lump sum appropriations is used to bring pressure on members of the Congress, are you not corrupting the people?

Does not a mass of viciousness flourish under the hands of corrupt city governments? What does this do to the moral standards of citizens and the community?

Is the Federal Government not giving aid to these city political machines when it places enormous sums of public money directly and indirectly at their disposal—too often just prior to elections?

Can we have faith in self-government when these city machines regularly manipulate the vote?

What does the popular acceptance of the expression, "You cannot beat Santa Claus" mean in public morals?

What is the meaning of these Washington headlines "New Spending Program a political coup for the next election."

Third, the principle of honest accounting requires that government business be conducted with glass pockets.

Is the juggling of bureau accounts between two forms of budget, thus creating a false impression of reduced expenditures, good moral light and leading to income tax payers?

When a government claims one day that its current expenditures are less than they appear because of capital outlay on recoverable loans and later collects these loans and uses them for current expenditure, is that moral leadership in bookkeeping?

I have asked before now is it moral for a government to take hundreds of millions from the weekly wages of workmen under the promise that they are kept in a real fund for their old-age security and then spend these collections on its current expenses and extravagances?

Manipulation of budgets and obscuring the nature of government expenditures always precedes the rise of dictatorships.

Fourth, the principles of honor among men require that government be scrupulous in its financial transactions with the citizen.

The citizen is compelled to meet his taxes and debts to the government even though it deprive him of his very living. The citizen has no recourse in law against the government's robbing him. Therefore, compliance by the government with its obligations is solely a matter of the highest honor. For example:

Can a government issue bonds carrying a promise to pay in gold and welch upon it within thirty days and hold the citizen to honor in his transactions?

When the government uses public funds to manipulate its own

bond market, does it differ in morals from the corporation that uses its funds to manipulate the stock market?

Can the government ruthlessly crush competition and hold the business man to fair play?

Is it an example to Wall Street not to strip the lambs by rigging the market when the government takes the savings of the people by rigging the currency?

Manipulations of currency and government debts are the steps by which democracies move to dictatorships.

Fifth, the principle of self-reliance requires that government expenditures build up the character of the people. They must not be spent to undermine the responsibility, the self-respect, the dignity that marks free men.

Has not every community been made into a conspiracy to get its share from the Federal grab-bag?

Has not the responsibility of the local communities and States been undermined?

Does not Washington throb with greedy lobbies of all kinds?

Are not millions of chiselers rejecting all self-reliance and self-esteem in their drives to get to government funds?

Does that build for stamina and morals in the citizen?

Sixth, the principle of law enforcement and obedience to law is the first necessity of free government.

For example, what happens to the morals of a people when the Federal officials connive at lawlessness and sit-down strikes?

What of governors who refuse to carry out the decisions of the courts and to maintain public order?

Or of workmen beaten and killed by police squads on one hand and beef squads on the other?

Do not moral restraints disappear and the ugly spectres of vigilantes take control?

That is one of the hells into which European democracies have fallen and have burned with the fires of Communism and Fascism.

Seventh, the principles of national unity require that government foster good will between all groups and sections of the people.

Does it make for human brotherhood for government officials to stir up class hate in a country dedicated to no classes?

Is it moral for government officials or boards to stir up hate of group against group, such as labor unions against labor unions?

Can public money be used to favor special pressure groups among the people and not create hate and contention among them?

The first approach of all dictatorships is to divide the people by hate. They also make a popular devil out of some particular group.

Eighth, the principles of truth require both moral and intellectual honesty in statements by officials.

The pure food law should be extended to official publications. Intellectual dishonesty has become an art under the heading of propaganda.

Propaganda has degenerated to a sinister process of half-truth or any other distortion of truth. It moves by tainting of news, by emphasis of facts which give distorted slants. Its purpose is to create bias and inflame the minds of men with hate and fear.

Its special refinement lies in its application to public discussion. You appeal not to truth or fact but to prejudice and selfishness. There it relies upon the *ad hominem* argument. If you don't like an argument on currency or the budget or labor relations or what not, you put out slimy and if possible anonymous propaganda reflecting upon your opponent's looks or the fact that his cousin is employed in Wall Street or is a Communist or a reactionary. You switch the premise and set up straw men and then attack them with fierce courage.

One department in the art of propaganda is to steal righteous phrases and devote them to evil-doing. Thus we have National Planning, Planned Economy, Reform, and More Abundant Life. Another department is to attach repulsive phrases to your opponents. Thus we get Economic Royalists, Tories, Reactionaries, Witch Doctors, and Dead Cats.

Is it honest or sportsmanlike or moral to answer the argument, protest, or appeal of the citizens by smearing them as the enemies of the people?

Do you think you can pollute thought with the drugs of propaganda and maintain honest discussion in the citizen?

Can your government broadcast half-truths and expect the citizen to tell the whole truth?

Do you think the government, which has engaged a thousand paid publicity agents daily and hourly to praise and color and "sell" its official acts, can hold the faith of the citizen in what his government says?

Does anybody have 100 per cent confidence in the official statements today?

Communists, Fascists, Nazis also build themselves into power through the arts of untruth.

PART III

I do not suggest that these immoralities are new. Nor do I suggest that any political party has been free of all of them. My suggestion is that they have grown to immense size and in new and insidious forms until they endanger self-government. They must be expurgated from American life. Government in a democracy can afford some inefficiency. That is the price we pay for self-government, for intellectual and spiritual freedom. But government in a democracy cannot be immoral—that saps its very life.

There are more morals in government than the abstinence from immoral practices. There are positive moral obligations of the community expressed through the government to the people.

There is the moral obligation to war unceasingly against poverty, ignorance, disease and prejudice.

There is the moral obligation to relieve the suffering of the unemployed.

There is the moral obligation to protect the aged and the unfortunate.

There is the moral obligation to prevent abuse in business, to protect the weak against the strong.

But are these great purposes incompatible with freedom?

However, I am not trying to discuss the whole gamut of government in thirty minutes.

These are grave hours. We are in a moral recession in government. Beyond this we have for five years listened to a continuous defamation of everything that has gone before. Honest achievement of men has been belittled and attributed to improper motives. Ideals embedded in our patriotism are smeared with contempt. We are told that the frontiers of initiative and enterprise are closed. We are told that we are in ruins and we must begin anew. We are told the government must do it for us.

People speak less today of the greatness of America. Pride in her achievement is weakened. There is doubt of her destiny. We are persuaded to think of ourselves as poor and helpless. We have gigantic achievement back of us. With only 6 per cent of the population in the world, we have more youths in schools of higher learning than all the other 94 per cent. We have more laboratories dragging new secrets from nature than all the others put together. We have more developed mechanical power than all of them. We can produce more food and clothes and iron and copper and lead and coal and oil than any other country in the world. We now have nearly two-thirds of all the automobiles, radios, and bathtubs in the world. We have a larger proportion of people who own their own homes and farms than has any other nation. In a generation we raised the purchasing power of wages by 30 per cent and we knocked two hours off each working day. This has been achieved under private enterprise and free men. It has been done by a free and self-reliant people. We could do even more in another generation.

We are enmeshed in a web of fears. But are not these fears as much moral as economic? Is it not time we jerk ourselves out of this moral depression? We can fight for and we can restore the national morals of hard work, self-reliance, intellectual and working honesty and honor. Then the greatness of America will shine again.

Women have ever taken a larger view of life than men. It is now the spiritual life of America that is in question.

Will not women take this service to themselves?

The Dangerous Road
for Democracy

OKLAHOMA CITY, OKLAHOMA

[*May 5, 1938*]

PART I

I AM GOING to speak to you on the dangerous road for democracy. I wish to speak to you not as Republicans but as citizens. For these things reach to fundamentals far deeper than party labels. At my position in life, my sole concern over political parties is that they stand up and face these fundamentals with courage and intellectual honesty. I wish to see unity among all right thinking men and women in this time of national difficulty.

In a recent speech I frequently used the terms "democracy" or "democratic government." I have received many protests. No. I did not mean the Democratic Party. I meant the system of representative government where the people have personal liberty under constitutional protection.

And before I go further, let me define the economic system which is inseparable from free men.

That is private enterprise regulated to prevent monopoly and exploitation. For that the government must be a vigorous umpire and not a Simon Legree. Nor is a free system a frozen system which resists reform to meet new abuses, new inventions or responsibility for the less fortunate. And our system cannot be free unless it protects the people from exploitation and calamity and unless it strives for equal opportunity among men.

343

We Americans are travelling a road dangerous not only to such a system but to liberty itself. We are faced with 12,000,-000 of our own countrymen unemployed and in want. These things are not unrelated.

I have spent some time in Europe exploring the staggering rise of dictatorships or authoritarian governments on the ashes of democracies. By the simple test of free speech, free press, constitutional guarantees, and representative government, the light of liberty has gone out among 370,000,000 people out of the 500,000,000 in Europe alone. Among 130,000,000 in Russia the short flash of liberty in 1917 was snuffed out by Communism. And even more alarming to free men, in so short a period as nineteen years, the torch of liberty has been dashed out by some sort of Fascism in 14 more nations of over 240,-000,000 people.

In a recent address in New York, I was concerned chiefly with our foreign relations to this changing scene.

PART II

My major concern on that journey, however, was to learn more clearly what fate in these 14 nations had driven men to abandon democracy for some form of dictatorship. Nations change their way of life only under great pressures. Yet these nations made this immense change without much opposition or bloodshed.

It is cheaply superficial to say that these people became despaired, tired of unemployment, of hunger, and misery, and class-conflict. That is true, but what caused all this vast unemployment, misery, and conflict?

Ten days ago I delivered an address upon the moral degeneration in democracies which contributes to their fall.

Tonight I propose to discuss what economic causes contributed to these miseries which ended in the suicide of liberty. And I am not interested in this as an academic student of government. I am interested because it concerns the future of liberty in our country. And I am interested because the experiences of these nations point to the causes of 12,000,000 lost jobs in our country today.

Not one of those 14 nations started with the intention to surrender liberty. They started by adopting panaceas to cure slumps or overcome economic difficulties. They all undertook New Deals under some title, usually Planned Economy. In variable doses they undertook credit and currency manipulation, price fixing, pump priming, and spending with huge deficits and huge taxes. Step by step they sapped the vitality of free enterprise by government experiments in dictation and socialistic competition. They had the illusion that true liberalism was a middle road between Fascism on the right and Socialism on the left. They sacrificed free enterprise to pursue the Utopias of both of them.

Every succeeding step was egged on by politicians fanning class hate, exaggerating every abuse and besmirching every protesting voice. Every step was accompanied by greater corruption of the electorate, increasing intellectual and moral dishonesty in government. They did produce periods of artificial prosperity, only to collapse again.

These forces finally jammed the mainspring by which private enterprise is moved to production. That is confidence. Fear and unemployment paralyzed the consumption of goods.

It was at the end of this dangerous road that hunger came to their cities with violent labor conflict and final despair. Those desperate people willingly surrendered every liberty to some man or group of men who promised economic security, moral regeneration, discipline, and hope.

PART III

And just a word as to what the end of this dangerous road has been. Mark you, not one of these 14 nations turned to Socialism or to its blood brother, Communism. These never triumphed. Their only part was to aid as demoralizers of democracies. When the Socialists had carried out that mission their supporters spent their lives in Fascist concentration camps.

For in chaos the long-suffering middle class always turned to some sort of dictatorship in hope of saving itself.

The movement from experimental dictation by government to farmers, workers and business into a full Fascist system is easy. Private enterprise having been demoralized with fear, then production must be forced by more fear and coercion. The concentration camp operates for those who protest. Fascism can tolerate no objectors. It crushes labor unions, farm associations, free speech and free press. These great human laboratories in Europe have again demonstrated that economic and political freedom are organically connnected. Political liberty dies when economic liberty dies.

The end is not alone a ruthless economic organization at the sacrifice of all personal liberty. Fascism represents the extinction of pity and mercy which Christianity gave the world. It represents an upsurge of abhorrent brutality. Its method is that any end justifies every perversion of intellectual honesty and government morals.

At a terrible price Fascism has had apparent success in restoring production and employment. True, the standard of living is lower than in its neighbor democracies. But this appearance of success infects other countries who think they can play with these fires without being burned.

PART IV

In contrast with these authoritarian nations are the surviving democracies of Europe. In their economic troubles they tightened their belts, balanced their budgets, refused new deals and planned economies. Today they have had little unemployment and are the most prosperous nations in the world. That is, except France. The French, of course, are in trouble because a few years ago they copied the New Deal.

Let there be no mistake; a new way of life is rising in the world. It directly challenges all our American concepts of free men. And let me tell you that upon my recent journey over and over again men of responsibility breathed to me one prayer.

They did not seek military alliances. They did not seek loans. What they prayed was that we hold the fort of liberty in America. For that is the hope of the world.

PART V

Now what road have we been travelling in the United States? We followed a sign marked Planned Economy, the way to end all depressions. The subtitle was To Abundant Life. We at least know now where we have got to. It can be said in two sentences.

The New Deal started with a Government debt of $21,000,-000,000 and today finds itself with a debt either direct or guaranteed of $42,000,000,000. It started with 12,000,000 unemployed; it finds itself after five years with 12,000,000 unemployed.

And it is not alone the townspeople who suffer. These 12,-000,000 men and their families are compelled to skimp, save, and suffer in order to keep life together. Their reduced consumption of farm products represents more acres than Secretary Wallace's already idle fields. The farmer gets no subsidy on these.

What caused this depression? Despite all the alibis I can show you in a minute or two. Depressions arise from many causes. And the first step in diagnosis is to eliminate those which are not present. Certainly I did not create this depression, so you can eliminate that.

And seriously we can also eliminate the two major causes of the depression of 1929–32. The first of these was our crazy boom stimulated by Federal Reserve policies begun in 1927 and which cracked up in 1929. We were beginning to recover from those sins when the second and far more deadly cause intervened. That was the 1931 collapse of Europe. That European financial panic drained our credit and our gold. For months there was hardly a single new European order for a bale of our cotton or a bushel of our wheat.

I recently explored Europe to discover if they were doing anything to us again. They are not.

Europe's regained economic strength is helping us. Europe is purchasing twice as much of our goods as it did during the last depression. Omitting New Deal France and Communist Russia, their relative indexes of production and employment are running from 30 per cent to 50 per cent higher than ours. There is no financial panic brewing over there. They are not withdrawing credit or gold from us as they did in 1931 and 1932. On the contrary, they are sending vast quantities of gold over here.

Therefore our present slump does not come from Europe.

This is solely our own depression. Its causes must be searched for right here at home. And we can also eliminate the usual causes of our homemade depressions.

President Roosevelt in his message to the Congress on November 15, 1937, confirmed that fact. He said:

"The fundamental situation is not to be compared with the far different conditions of 1929. The banking system is not over-extended. Interest rates are lower. Inventories are not dangerously large. We are no longer over-extended in new construction or in capital equipment. Speculation requiring liquidation does not overhang our markets."

But if the 12,000,000 unemployed are not due to these causes, to what are they due? Why have a recession in the face of low interest rates, no over-extension of credit, no over-sized inventories, no over-extension of capital equipment, no overstock of goods, no speculation? If there are none of these sins or forces in the financial and business world, such as did exist in previous depressions, obviously the origins cannot be blamed upon finance and business.

And I may add why have a recession when we have abundant capital and are short of power equipment, railway equipment, good houses and a thousand other things that need to be done?

It is nonsense to say that either big or little business is on a strike. It is not so. We have had no such strike. We have been struck. Business is yearning to sell automobiles and new suits of clothes. It is yearning to extend power plants and build houses. Big business men or little business men are not scared to take on men if anybody will give them an order for goods. But who has the confidence to give the orders?

There is only one place left to search for the causes of this depression. Despite every alibi, this depression is the direct result of governmental actions.

PART VI

And now let us examine the dangerous road we have been travelling.

It would startle this country if our people had a detailed list of the powers over their daily life they have surrendered to the President and his bureaucracy. More and more we have submitted to authoritarian action. A large part of these powers are invisible. But they weave together and expand within a bureaucracy. And bear in mind, power is just as powerful through subsidies and favor of political jobs as it is by coercion and jail.

And the sheep's clothing of these powers is that righteous phrase, Planned Economy. The Communists first invented it. The Fascists adopted it. It still serves to fool the people. It carries the illusion that it means forward-looking. But its reality is the wolf of bureaucratic power. And it bites the flock.

Never before except in a dictatorship have such powers been given to the head of a state. And the craving of bureaucracy for more power is never satisfied. Failure does not stop their dreams; it only multiplies their alibis.

If these are not at least the infant steps along the dangerous road that European democracies took, then they are an astonishing parallel.

We also have had credit and currency manipulation, pump priming and spending with huge deficits. We have had huge increase of taxes, government restriction of production, government price fixing. We have had artificially increased prices and genuinely stifled consumption. And these manipulations are shot through with dictation and threat. They are accompanied by forays of the government into competition with private enterprise. But why recite all the creeping collectivism?

This country was definitely on the way to recovery in 1932 with all the rest of the world. These manipulations beginning in 1933 at first retarded us. Then they produced an artificial and distorted appearance of recovery claimed in 1936–37. Like all shots in the arm, a lovely time was had by all. Except for some 5,000,000 men who never got jobs. Then the President and submanagers concluded the dose of stimulants must have been too big. They gave us antidotes. They reduced bank reserves to curtail credit. They sterilized gold to reduce credit. They publicly denounced prices. They denounced and threatened business. They proposed more measures in control of wages, hours, and farmers. But if this were not sufficient to confuse and scare the people they prepared for more powers by attempting to manipulate the Supreme Court. And out of it all, we have got this depression.

PART VII

And now let us analyze this whole New Deal philosophy a little more deeply in its practical aspects. We can at least discover why attempts of government to manage a system of private enterprise must have a Nemesis—or several of them—so long as there is any freedom left in it.

The first is that free private enterprise will not mix with either the dictation or the government-competition, for one stymies the other. Germany and Italy have demonstrated that complete Fascism will work for a while. Russia has demonstrated that Socialism will not work. America has demonstrated for over 160 years that a free system will work. Just as did the 14 fallen democracies of Europe, now America is demonstrating all over again that a mixture will never work.

A drop of typhoid in a barrel of water will sicken a whole village. A few drops of Socialism or Fascism is poison to private enterprise. The Federal Government goes into less than ten per cent of the power business. At once the investor, fearful of government competition and seizure, fears to hazard his capital. And hundreds of thousands of men lose jobs. Yet the consumer and the investor can be protected by regulation.

Under these mixtures every man must conduct his business with one eye on Washington. Every plan of action is a bet on what bureaucracy may do. Every farmer must act with an eye on an agricultural agent. Every investment of savings is a gamble on what will be done to the currency. Every future price of a commodity is not a judgment on the law of supply and demand, but another bet on Washington. Every venture into new enterprise must be calculated upon what will be left after punitive taxes.

All along the line it weakens the judgment of men. It sickens initiative and enterprise. It knocks the confidence out of men. It substitutes fear. It destroys millions of jobs.

The second Nemesis is that in a partly free system the consumer has a voice. He goes on a strike as he did against building costs in 1937.

The third Nemesis is fear. Half of what people consume can be postponed at least for a time. When our Washington managers say prices are too high, buyers hold off and postpone purchases and a million men lose their jobs.

It was all with good intentions. The objectives as you have heard were magnificent. But the road to a hot spot has again been proved to be paved with good objectives.

PART VIII

But let me give you a word of comfort. It is true that we have been following that dangerous road for democracy that led to disaster in Europe. But those countries were young in freedom and weak in their fidelities to liberty. They were economically lean from the war. We are tough in our fidelities. We still have some economic fat on our national body. We still have powers of resistance. We have great powers of recovery right now.

And let me add that there should be improvement from this immediate situation no matter what the government does—but it will not be real recovery with full or permanent employment if we continue down this dangerous road. And we are not going to go down that road without a lot more fighting free speech.

PART IX

But what does the New Deal propose to do about this depression of theirs?

They propose that we travel further down this dangerous road. More bureaucratic dictation to business, more inflation, more pump-priming, more Planned Economy. We are to have more budget deficits, new inflations, more increase in national debts, more taxes for the future. We put the pea of $1,400,-000,000 of gold under the other shell. These new actions may produce another shot in the arm.

There is in these proposals a hopeless confusion of cause and effect. You do not get employment out of an economy scarcity. You do not prime the pump to any purpose by taking money out of the pockets of the taxpayer and giving it to the consumer. They are the same person. Men borrow to expand their businesses, not because money is cheap but because they have confidence in the future. The Nation gets no richer by increasing its debts. Truly you can mortgage your house and go on a spree. It does not add to your productivity and you may lose your house.

PART X

The constructive action today is to change the national direction and get off this dangerous road. That would allay fear and re-establish confidence in the future. That would release the enormous reserves of private enterprise in place of a trickle of government money. That would take men back to their jobs tomorrow and permanently.

In order that the government may give real proof that it has abandoned this road dangerous to democracy, we need to get down out of cloudy objectives. We need to take some practical steps. This cannot be done by encouraging words. It must be proved by definite acts that re-establish faith. Faith that ours is going to continue as a system of free men and private enterprise.

For a start we need to:

First, re-establish confidence that there will be no more attacks upon the safeguards of free men. That is the independence of the Congress and of the Courts.

Second, restore common morals and intellectual morals in government. In a democracy or in a Christian country the ends do not justify any means.

Third, abandon this economy of scarcity and go in for production, work, and thrift.

Fourth, stop this spending and inflation and pump-priming.

Fifth, revise the taxes so as to free the initiative and enterprise of men. The original Senate proposals were a step in that direction.

Sixth, reduce relief expenditure by one-third through decentralizing its administration. Take it out of the hands of wasters and politicians and put it back into non-political committees in each community and require the states and local communities to find 5 or 10 per cent of the cost. That will provide greater and more sympathetic care for those in distress. It will restore confidence that the Republic is not being destroyed by the purchase of elections.

Seventh, by the savings on relief, and reduction of other expenses and the end of pump-priming, drive to really balance this budget.

Eighth, stop credit inflation juggling. Make the currency convertible into bullion at the irreparable 59-cent dollar and repeal all authority for currency inflation.

Ninth, set up a court of 25 responsible non-political men representing business, labor, and agriculture to direct Federal Reserve policies and thus take that control of credit out of the hands of politicians.

Tenth, give the employer and all branches of labor the same rights before the Labor Board and appoint judicially minded men to the board.

Eleventh, stop indiscriminate defamations of business and the creation of class hate. Use the courts for purposes of prosecution.

This would at least be a start on a saner and more cheerful road. Then would begin the emancipation from this fog of ideologies. Morals in government would return again. The energies of our people would be liberated. And above all the farmer's market and the worker's job will be restored. A confident, alert and alive people free in enterprise can quickly repair losses, repay debts and bury mistakes. The pump-priming they need is confidence in the future.

And in conclusion. When I stepped on the soil of America a month ago I felt a great lift of spirit. And why? Because despite all discouragements here is a people who themselves are right. A people through whose blood run courage and honesty and faith. A people who will never surrender their intellectual and spiritual freedom. A people who will yet have a free economy free from abuse and wrong. These people will fight for it by constitutional methods as Americans have always fought for it. For it is in our blood.

Building Boys for America

[May 19, 1938]

PART I

ONE of the incessant jobs of democracies is to clean up black spots. The powerful forces of initiative under free and alert minds will constantly make new bright spots out in advance of progress. And I do not believe in looking at black spots only. It is the white spots in our civilization that keep up our courage and faith and that keep us fighting the black spots.

That concentration on black spots only is what causes the Utopia hunters and the rainbow chasers. They believe the world is all black and needs to start all over again every morning. They have no patience with cleaning up black spots, and thus bringing up the rear. They mostly ignore the bright spots. They want a new spot colored pink or red. And they would destroy all the white spots chasing after it. We ought to concentrate on a black spot long enough to clean it up.

Most of the black spots are the incidents of progress. They are in a way the proof of progress. Many of them were once bright spots. In the advance of civilization they have become black by comparison. The initiative of our people creates magnificent new houses which have more comfort and beauty than the palaces of old kings. But the old houses by comparison with newer ones become slums.

In fact, stated another way, most of our social and economic problems are marginal problems. And I may repeat that if our American people would only realize that our national problems are marginal problems of elimination and curing abuse and

355

building up the weak, we would make more progress than chasing rainbows.

And so it is with our youth problems. In all history there was never such care of youth and such opportunity for youth as 75 per cent of the children of America now enjoy. Our job is to give the same chance to the rest.

In a civilization 6,000 years old, it was only a hundred years ago that not one-third of our children had elementary schooling. Only 50 years ago only two-thirds had it. Today all but a few have it. It is not 50 years ago that less than 15 per cent of our children had secondary or vocational schooling. Today 65 per cent of that age have it. The other 35 per cent represent a black spot. Fifty years ago we had only 150,000 of our youth in institutions of higher learning; today there are 1,200,000 of them. I do not know whether that is a black spot or not. It depends on what they do with this learning.

Therefore, despite the tears of the "for Heaven's sakers" this mass of American youth is a magnificent army for carrying forward civilization. Their eyes are brighter. The satisticians tell us they are an inch taller than their forebears. In them the oncoming race is better trained and better fitted for future advance of civilization on this continent than ever before. The world has never seen anything that compared with it in the whole history of the human race. That is a white spot of American civilization.

In the large sense there are two black spots in our youth problems. They are the minority who lag behind in training, health and morals. There is a bad gap in our system in the transition of a minority of the trained army into jobs.

This last problem is one which troubles all thinking persons. To my mind it is one of the transcendent questions of our times. But it is much bound up with the problem of restoration of general employment. In periods of unemployment youth bears the brunt in the matter of getting a job, for his elders already have the jobs. In normal times it is a marginal problem, for there are almost as many vacancies by death and retirement as there are ripe youth available. But even in times of employment there still is lack of organization by which we make connection of the capacities of the individual with the openings for a job.

PART II

The work of the Boys' Clubs of America bears indirectly on this problem.

Our job in this association is cleaning up a particular black spot. Out of some 17,000,000 boys in the nation, there are some 3,000,000 who have to spend their outdoor lives upon the pavements in the congested areas of our big cities. The pavement boys do have schooling, but it is the life they lead when away from the school teacher's eye on one hand and the parents' eye on the other that troubles us. The teacher and the parents cannot keep them shut in all the time. They are a cheery lot of mischievous animals and so we do not need to weep over them. Our job is to make a place where they can let off steam in such a way as to give them constructive joy. We need to safeguard their growing pains and make them as tall and as fitted for life as the other 14,000,000 boys. We must find their occupational bent so they can start right in life. And we must supplement the moral training of the family and of the church in that other great high school of morals—that is, sport. Otherwise they wilt like wild flowers. And otherwise also they go in for destructive joy. We are doing that job for about 300,000 of them. That is the bright spot. We are not doing it for some 2,700,000 of these boys. That is the black spot. And for the future of the nation it is a very black, black spot, for many of them stay black all their lives. And some of them will trouble the police and their neighbors for fifty or sixty years.

While we do not like to dwell upon the crime argument, nor do we think it necessary to classify the boys in our poorer districts as more likely to commit delinquency, at the same time it has been repeatedly pointed out that the times when boys get into mischief are during their free time, and the places where incitement to mischief abounds are in crowded pavement districts. Whether we like it or not, we cannot for our own protection overlook these

black spots of juvenile delinquency and their inevitable consequences. If you plot the percentage of juvenile delinquency
per 1,000 boys in any city, you will find it in the congested areas,
—except where there is a Boys' Club or some other effective
agency. And there you will find it less than even in some areas
of more opportunity.

Adventure and the gang spirit are inherent in us all, whether
it be manifest in the Union League Club or the fraternal organization. The gang spirit cannot be eliminated; in fact, it is
one of humanity's precious possessions, if it be rightly utilized.
It is true that the traits in youngsters which so often unfortunately lead to delinquency are often so admirable—boldness,
independence, the pioneer spirit, the courage to take chances.
These must not be suppressed, but they must be directed to constructive joy.

I think there ought to be a special Bill of Rights for boys:

1. Like everybody else, he has a right to the pursuit of happiness.

2. He has the right to play that will stretch his imagination
and prove his prowess and skill.

3. He has a right to the constructive joy from adventure and
thrills that are the part of an opening life.

4. He has a right to affection and friendship.

5. He has a right to the sense of security in belonging to some
group.

6. He has a right to health protections that will make him an
inch taller than his dad.

7. He has the right to education and training that amplifies
his own natural bents and that will fit him into a job.

8. He has a right to a chance in getting a job.

Those are not all his rights—but these are the ones that this
association is concerned with.

PART III

The Boys' Club movement is but one of 300 or more constructive efforts to meet the challenge of youth. I am in favor of

them all. Ours is an unique appeal for it is for a particular kind of neglected boy. Its very vitality attests to this fact. Public officials, social workers and prison wardens in the 171 American cities where Boys' Clubs are located will give heartening testimony of their stimulating effect in establishing civic decency.

We can report progress during the past year. We have affiliated with the Boys' Clubs of Canada and its 21 clubs. During the year we have started 26 new clubs in the United States. We have dropped 8 clubs, some of which died and others of which did not hold up to our standards.

Today we have 330 clubs including our Canadian affiliates. Our American clubs are now established in 171 cities over 36 states. Their combined assets exceed $20,000,000. The deficit on operating the individual clubs is met by community chests, by special associations and private gift. During the past year over $1,500,000 was secured for new buildings and extensions of clubs. We need much more. And we shall beg unblushingly till we have five times as many clubs.

In our national association we balanced the budget, which is unusual in modern life. The donors to our national association increased from 647 to 2,576. We are looking for more, for next year's budget is not balanced yet.

And all this has been brought about by the zeal of a great group of devoted men and women who work unceasingly in this cause. Of our own national staff, I am not eloquent enough to express my admiration for Mr. William Edwin Hall, Mr. Sanford Bates, Mr. J. B. Kirkland, Mr. Alexander Campbell, Mr. Charles E. Hendry, and Mr. Walter Hall. During the year, they have travelled into hundreds of cities and their cajolery has been welcomed. And I wish I possessed the eloquence to pay adequate tribute to those thousands of workers on the committees of these 300 Boys' Clubs. And especially the hundreds of superintendents and leaders whose inspired souls are daily leading these 300,000 boys into the paths of health and good citizenship.

PART IV

We are here tonight to record the rapid advance of sentiment throughout the country for the establishment of more and more Boys' Clubs. And there is an outstanding service of such organizations and that is that they lend themselves so readily to the cultivation of democratic habits and attitudes.

I have lately been abroad. I was naturally interested in the organization of boys—and girls, for that matter—and their transition into jobs. The Fascist countries have devoted themselves to this organization as never before in history. The Fascist program embraces much that we try to attain in our Boys' Clubs and Boy Scouts and our multitude of institutions devoted to youth. That is, they systematically examine them physically, undertake to build up their bodies, to give recreation, to find their occupational bents, and to give them encouragement and faith in the future. It is practically compulsory. And with it all, they incessantly pound in Nazi and Fascist mode of thought in these children. They build for regimentation, for submission, and for mental and moral subjection to their masters. They build the egotism of race superiority. They deny the right of criticism and free expression. Their concept is every individual simply a molecule in a mass-directed state. It all has a military complexion of the deepest dye.

That is not what America wants. We want to build the sense of voluntary action, to build up personality, to create a sense of personal responsibility. We want to build for moral discipline, not regimentation. We want to build for the dignity and character of the individual. We want education in truth, not propaganda. These are the foundations of free men. And just as Fascists build their boys to support a Spartan state, we want to build our boys to support a democratic state.

For out of what our boys and girls absorb now will they make the America of 50 years hence. It is a solemn thought that we of our generation may be judged by what we do to solve these new problems which confront the youth.

We citizens of the largest remaining democracy have a high

duty and a high purpose in making easy the path to the democratic ideal.

Government, with its ever-expanding activities, will no doubt concern itself to a greater and greater extent with the affairs of our young people. But it will be a sign of degeneration when we as private citizens shall surrender character building to the state. That is not the place where personality and character can ever be built.

This service requires sacrifice, understanding, toleration, generosity. The methods of a dictator are too simple and too easy.

The only kind of society that self-respecting men can cherish is one which holds the common man to be worthy of its confidence, which sees in the poorest born and the least privileged boy the material of greatness, and which aims to preserve and develop their talents, their personality, their honor and their virtue wherever they may be found.

From the sum of the individual achievements of such personalities comes alone the real achievement of the nation. These ideas are being defeated in the world today. But you and I have the stern duty to carry forward.

It was the Apostle Paul who said, "Except these abide in the ship, ye cannot be saved."

On Benjamin Franklin

PHILADELPHIA, PENNSYLVANIA

[*May 21, 1938*]

THESE last few days have been given by Philadelphia to the dedication of Franklin Institute. After one hundred years of service given to the advancement of science and the arts, citizens from all parts of our country and representatives of the great educational institutions have gathered here. They come from home and abroad to mark their appreciation of great contributions to civilization.

This institution found its inspiration in the contributions to research and invention by Benjamin Franklin. It stands today marked "In honor of Benjamin Franklin." No greater honor could be given to a fellow citizen. For from here will flow the renewed stream of inspiration and progress that found its springs in his own service to our country.

This evening I have been asked to say something on Franklin and his contribution to our times.

How can I add anything new to what has been said about Benjamin Franklin? Philadelphia ought to know all about him by this time.

The rest of the country has also heard of him. With appropriate remarks his name has been fixed to thousands of counties, towns, cities, and streets. Through parents striving to implant his qualities in their offspring his name appears in five thousand telephone directories. To carry a conviction of integrity a thousand firms have labeled their goods after him.

Outside of Philadelphia even, there is one library alone of 10,000 items about him.

There have been twenty millions of orations delivered over

him. They include every man of big or little eloquence over a century and a half. Like most schoolboys of my day, I delivered a speech on him once myself. That was the same year I delivered an oration on "Rome was not built in a day." That was my last real oration.

Nevertheless I gave this support to Franklin even though the manner in which my family dinned his aphorisms into me seriously limited all my natural expansion. I even substantiated Ben's view that we could all become healthy, wealthy, and wise if we got up early in the morning. I haven't been so sure about it of late years—for I have not been able to find any one else around then except the police. I also supported Franklin in the theory that you got what we now call social security by saving pennies and producing more. That was before we discovered the theory of restricted production and spending ourselves into prosperity.

I have some misgivings about reawakening Ben's spirit just now. It might fill us with uncomfortable doubts. Moreover, since I received notice of your celebration, I have been disturbed a good deal over the shocks that staunch old emblem in his plain clothes and his radiating of thrift would meet if we waked him up and walked him around here for a few days. We might not quiet him down for the next 142 years.

On the other hand, from the stimulus to his magnificent sense of humor, he might just laugh.

I asked your committee what there was about Benjamin Franklin upon which I could address the people of Philadelphia to the profit of your minds and morals. They said, "Oh, anything. Perhaps thrift."

It is true that aside from human liberty, Ben's great plan of American life or his ideology, to use modern nomenclature, had its central idea in frugality and hard work. He conducted a propaganda on that subject for over sixty years. His slogans sunk so deep into the American mind that we practiced at it for a long time. He seemed opposed to spending. But this is not a political meeting and I do not want to give even a hint of partisanship. So I am compelled to abandon that theme.

I thought something might be said on Ben's economic and governmental ideas, however, if we did not bear down too hard on spending. Being superlatively wise he made no public speeches on the subject. But he had a fine observant mind and a command of editorial remarks generally.

He did advise on the cure of economic depressions. He asked, "What signify wishing and hoping for better times?" He asserted that "we may make these times better if we bestir ourselves" and produce. He knew none of the joys of Planned Economy.

He also had defeatist ideas about extremes in public works, and at one time observed, "It is easier to build two chimneys than to keep one in fuel." Franklin's opinion of borrowing and debts, private and public, taxed his abundant command of expression. To him they were the road of sorrow, a vice more vicious than lies, and in general the destroyers of liberty. I believe it better not to pursue those themes further.

I remembered that Franklin had made some observations on money—but I found him asserting that "The standard once fixed should ever be unvariable since any alteration would be followed by great confusion and detriment to the state." He was naturally unfamiliar with the recent theory and practice in coinage.

Ben also observed that "It is impossible for government to . . . fix the extent of paper credit," and also that "no state or potentate can settle the prices of all sorts of merchandise" . . . "plenty and scarcity must govern that." I have already commented on those themes sufficiently in other and more appropriate circles.

As to agriculture, he said: "He that kills a breeding sow destroys all her offspring to the thousandth generation." But that would not seem a happy theme to pursue.

As to the industrial front he stated firmly that "God gives all things to industry." I don't think there is agreement on that subject any more, so I will not pursue it. Some people think the government takes it away again. His further remark that "God helps those who help themselves" has been distinctly limited since his time, especially as to the public utilities.

He had many notions of government. Using the architectural metaphor, he said, "If the superstructure is too heavy for the foundation the building totters though assisted by outward props of art." That would be a sour theme for present discourse.

I then thought something might be done with the fine stimulation that Ben gave to investigation and research. The magnificent institutions which he founded have continued in that mission down to this day. Among them, he had a lot to do with creating the United States Senate. Their investigation activities would be both surprising and disappointing to him, so that theme did not seem profitable.

Ben always referred to himself as a republican but of course I cannot pursue this.

Yet on all controversial matters he was a tolerant soul. He cautioned us that "By the collision of different sentiments, sparks of truth are struck out and political light is obtained." I hope so.

He said, "It is true that in some of the states there are parties and discords; but let us look back and ask if we were ever without them. Such will exist wherever there is liberty; and perhaps they will help preserve it." That is a hopeful remark.

Ben was strong on the idea that "They who give up essential liberty to obtain a little temporary safety deserve neither liberty nor safety." Some way I feel Ben might be disappointed with us.

PART II

The building and preservation of liberty were to Benjamin Franklin the high purpose of America. Any man who helped frame and sign the Declaration of Independence, the Peace treaty acknowledging our freedom, and the Constitution of the United States was fired with the determination to secure the independence of the nation and sink deeply the very foundations of personal liberty.

Franklin had sought and associated with men keen in devotion to personal liberty long before our independence from England was even discussed. Among his friends were Burke and Tom Paine. It is sometimes overlooked that it was Franklin who paid Tom Paine's fare to the Colonies and set that firebrand of liberty on these shores. Franklin was not an emotional man. He was not an evangelist but he knew their uses. It was Tom Paine who stirred the Colonies to immediate political independence from England. It was he who stimulated the burning fires of personal liberty. It was Tom Paine, then a soldier in Washington's army, who composed that blazing document which Washington proclaimed to his dejected troops, revitalizing them to the victorious crossing of the Delaware.

Franklin was an individualist. But he was an American individualist who believed in ordered liberty and the obligations of liberty.

Franklin was the general utility man of a city and a nation. He was a laborer, a business man, a public official, an inventor, a scientist, a soldier, a diplomat, an economist, a philosopher, an author, an editor, and a patriot—all in one lifetime. He ran the gamut from abject poverty to comfortable independence. He started lowly at his trade as a printer and became the foremost publisher of his era. He was excluded by poverty from the advantages of formal education and became one of the most learned men of the world of his lifetime. He early lacked the guidance of a comforting home and became the benefactor of children and young men. He achieved independence through hard work and thrift and shared it generously. He organized institutions to help others to be thrifty, to save that they too might not become dependent upon others. He established educational institutions and libraries which have given hundreds of thousands of youth their chance in life.

Benjamin Franklin should be the patron saint of that altogether characteristic American, the self-made man. Those real men were the product from the noblest of American ideals— that each human being had the birthright of opportunity for self-advancement, that no one was by birth limited in achievement. Obviously, the ideal today has shifted from the self-made man toward the government-coddled man. The self-made man has indeed in recent years become the target for the inferiority complex of the kept and coddled. But that breed will not last, for lasting nations are not built of that sort of stuff. And ours is a lasting nation.

From Franklin's inspiration and ideals we have produced generations of hardy, thrifty, independent folk who fought their way through life in spite of adversity and reverses. The boy off the farm, or out of the small town, or from the city slums saw the same vistas, encountered the same horizons, and followed the same polar stars as those who could start life less handicapped. And in this country, in each generation, far more of those who made their own way arrived at national significance and personal satisfaction than the others. They are the men and women who builded America.

There were embodied in Franklin the traditions and wholesome morals of our ancestors on this soil, which prevent intellectual and spiritual dry-rot. He earned his own character. He accepted no crumbs of impoverished spirituality nor did he reject the glories of a hard-won battle over the handicaps which every human being meets as he goes through life.

A people cannot live on ideological dialectics or statistics about standards of living or even balanced budgets. They must have a sterner fare if they are to survive. They must possess qualities and strength of character which will give them calmness and poise in prosperity and courage and vision in adversity. They must be guided not only by patriotism of the tribe but by morality and religious faith which belong alone to the individual spirit.

Benjamin Franklin, that staunch old emblem in plain clothes radiating thrift and fine graces, offers a pattern for life which combines personal liberty and self-reliance with national order and well-being. The great characters who were associated with him in the grand adventure of founding our nation did not find liberty and independence incompatible with order and individual well-being. They would ever sacrifice well-being for the others.

That is a safer pattern for the Republic than that of those who, promising an Utopia of comfort, demand also an end to liberty. It was Joseph Choate who, addressing this city, said, "When the spirit of Franklin decays the sun of America will have begun to set."

INDEX

Index

INDEX

379

153; Federal Reserve use, 153; fiscal record, 65 ff., 254; record of freedom, 222;
financial aid by, 23; government employes,
67; highways, 254; housing, 165; humanity
in government, 38, 139, 147, 186, 202; and
NRA, 46, 154; and power regulation, 24;
recoverable loans of, 65, 205; recovery by
(*see* Recovery); relief record, 68, 188, 255;
relief, honesty, 190; tariff reform, 154; taxation record of, 193
Hoover experience, 129; Asiatic, 129; European, 129; in famine, 186; of labor, 48, 129;
in revolutions, 112; of war, 112, 129
Hoover policies: on AAA, 221; abuse, business
and financial, 17, 42; American objectives,
19, 43; on American people, 41, 61, 63, 295,
354; American system, 5, 8, 130, 293, 343;
anti-trust laws, 46; banking, 24; on Bill of
Rights, 261; boondoggling, 93; budget-balancing, 261 (*see also* Budget-balancing);
business, small, 42; against collectivism, 221;
criticism, 300; currency, 185, 261; economic
freedom, 20 ff., 261; electric power regulation, 11, 12, 24; faith in America, 15; Federal Reserve, 82; financial reform, 23; foreign, 300, 303, 309, 320; foreign trade, 322;
free speech, 280; on gold, 185; government-
in-business, 10, 11, 12, 221, 261; government
expansion, 15; government finance, 261;
housing, 165; against inflation, 221; interstate compacts, 46, 134; law, 261; merit
service, 283; monopolies, 42; Muscle Shoals,
11; natural resources, 17; opportunity, 261;
party obligations, 38; peace, 261, 300;
political creed, 261; on poverty, 18; preparedness, 261; private enterprise, 261;
production, 42, 261; Reciprocal Trade
Agreements, 108; regulation, 11, 12, 23,
24, 42, 133, 261; relief, 42, 93, 186; on Republican Policy Committee, 266; social objectives, 157; Social Security, 261; tax, income, 193, 199; profit, 196; for wages, 296;
war debts, 33, 319; for youth, 43
Hope, economy of, 52
Hopkins, 175
Hours: of labor (*see* Labor); and wages (*see*
Wages); women, Republican record, 254
House of Representatives on NRA, 45
Housing, 290, 295, 331, 348; New Deal, 165;
progress in, 355; Republican record in, 165;
taxation for, 298
Hull, Cordell (Secretary of State), 319
Human nature and social progress, 55
Humanity: American standard of, 245, 272;
government, in emergency, 38; of govern-
ment, 134, 254; problems, Republican at-
titude, 272; in Republican budget, 202
Hungary, 319
Hunger and cold: protection from, 139; pre-
vention of, 147, 186
Huxley, Thomas, on debate, 270

Hyde, Secretary of Agriculture: program of,
110; on land use, 111

Ickes, Secretary, 175
Ideals: American, 43; address on, 264; Amer-
ican system, 222 ff.; in peoples, 182
Ideologies, war between, 301, 318
Ignorance, war against, 341
"Ill-fed, ill-housed, ill-clothed," 272
Illusions, 135
Immigration, Republican record, 254
Immoralities, in government, 341 (*see also*
Morals)
Imperialism, U. S., 302
Imports: barriers, 29, 321; compared, 107; and
exports, 26; food, 41, 156; industrial, 107;
protection against, 162
Inauguration: Roosevelt, 222; and bank
panic, 90
Income, farm (*see* Farm income)
Income: national, 163; middle-class share, 70;
tax ratio, 194
Income tax (*see* Tax, income)
Incomes, real, 119
Independence (1776), 260; of Congress ,*see*
Congress); federal judiciary, 5, 246, 248,
332; personal, 158; Supreme Court record
of, 14; U. S., 302
Independence Hall, 161, 170
India, silver mines of, 80
Individual: in depression, 53; under Fascism,
323; free, progress by, 18; and government,
58; responsibility, principle of, 38; re-
straints by, 270; vs. state, 322; system of,
181
Individualism: American (*see* American indi-
vidualism); European, 3; President on, 218;
as progress, 225
Individualist, Franklin as, 366
Individualists, regulated, 101
Industrial conflicts, 54 (*see also* Strikes)
Industrial peace, 157
Industries, Franklin on, 362, 364
Industries, sweated, 297
Infant mortality, figures, 191
Inflation: credit (*see* Credit inflation); currency (*see* Currency inflation); danger of,
291; and deficits, 69, 71; and democracies,
119, 176; European, 289, 312, 314; Dr.
Kemmerer on, 167; more, 352; Napoleonic,
49; by New Deal, 88, 162; New Deal,
Budget Director on, 72; from next war, 301;
post-war, 72, 301; proposals of, 144; results of, 247; threat of, 137
Initiative and enterprise, 3, 139, 333, 342;
abuse in (*see* Abuse); achievements of, 52;
denied, 171; as objectives, 43, 55; Republican principle of, 271; system of, 131
Initiative, private: under government-in-busi-
ness, 17; principle of, 38; as productive mo-

Traditions: American (*see* American traditions; Forefathers); political, of freedom, 260

Traffic policeman, 291

Transportation, American, 21

Treasury figures, analyzed, 267; funds, and citizens, 269; raids on, 9, 10

Treaties: arbitration, 303; and conciliation, 307; violation of, 130, 308

Trojan horses, 221

Trust: accounts, government, 208; regulation of, 133; (estate), 198

Truth, 139; in government, 139; half, 267; in politics, 284

Tugwell, 175

Tugwell resettlement colony, 87

Turnpike, subsidies, 112

TVA (*see* Muscle Shoals)

Tyranny: economic, 53, 55; government, 55; out of inflation, 72; prevention of, 261

Umpire, baseball, 204; government as, 133, 164, 224, 291, 332, 343

Underprivileged, 56; and freedom, 51, 131; Roosevelt proportions, 272; source of help, 273

Unemployed: Democratic 1932 proposal to, 13; in 1932, 8, 69; comparison of, 97, 162, 178, 189; figures on, A. F. of L., 1932, 69; 1935, 149; 1936, 137; comparison of 1935, 68; and freedom, 52; obligation to, 341; and plenty, 52; Republican relief of, 179; spending for, 92; sympathy with, 92, 187

Unemployment: in all systems, 134; causes of, 185; crop reduction, 108; European, 313, 329, 344, 346; and fear, 116, 351; Hoover experience, 186; Hoover work for, 188; insurance (*see* Insurance); and managed currency, 82; and New Deal, 177, 341; and NRA, 46; post-Napoleonic, 49; post-war, 301; protection from, 42, 54, 139, 156; "recession," 328; through relief, 191; technological, 294, 297; of youth, 356; world, 27

Unemployment relief, 255 (*see also* Relief); first need, 99, 255; Hoover program for, 93; self-cure of, 146; world—relief, 33; and world trade, 28

Union League Club of Chicago, 242; and boys' clubs, 357

Unions, labor, trade (*see* Labor unions)

Universities: and character, 281; Fascist, 317; American, service of, 281; exchange proposal, 320; graduates, and public service, 284

Untruth, 277

Utilities, regulation of, 133, 294

Utopia, 201, 209; European, 315; hunters, 355; promise of, 368; and revolutions, 174

Vegetable oils, imports, 107, 111

Vested interests, 219

Veterans' bonus, 204, 205, 207, 208

Vice-President, candidate, 10

Vigilantes, 247

Vote: manipulation of, 269; presidential, analyzed, 252; Republican, 1936, 252; Republican per cent, 1936, 253; in solid South, 259

Vote getting, and appointments, 282

Voter: coercion of, 177; higher duty of, 284

Votes, power over, 220

Wages, 54; American theory of, 54; annual, 297; authoritarian, 326; and Napoleonic, 50; control, New Deal, 291, 331, 350; and devaluation, 120, 152, 184; fixing, 247, 291; increase, 7, 294; minimum, 297; power over, 220; purchasing power, 342; reduction, 297; real, 42; upheld, 147; workman's taxed, 268

Wages and hours: bill, 297; government control of, 271; sweated, 134

Wall Street, 101, 279, 339, 340; and Securities Act, 171

Wallace, Secretary, 175, 347

War: aftermaths, 53, 301; American attitude, 301, 302; American participation, 318; for democracy, 126; depression cause, 22; dogs of, 301; economic, 28, 29, 32, 33, 35; and farmers, 104; Great (*see* World); Hoover experience in, 112, 129; imminence of, 329; Japanese-Chinese, 304; justified, 53; policies building, 300; present, 300; prevention of, 35, 304, 319; prospects of, 313; referendum on, 303; religious, 321; safety, 288; threats, 313; and untruth, 278

War and Navy Departments, in Hoover budget, 210

War debt, 27; cancellation, 35; under devaluation, 206; Hoover policy for, 33; payment of, 32; debtors, 319

War service: Hoover, 310; in relief, 93

Washington, George, 11, 161, 178, 194, 225, 235, 314, 335, 366

Waste: elimination, 224, 294; mineral, 46; natural resources, 164; New Deal, 67; in relief, 42, 92, 98, 120, 186; in taxes, 199

Water resources, Democratic proposal, 13

Waterways and harbors, Republican record, 254

Weaknesses, Republican party, 255

Wealth: conscription of, 301; diffused, 19; national, President on, 91

Webster, Daniel, quoted, 123

Welfare: American, principles safeguarding, 38; general, advance in, 49; responsibility for, 245

Western hemisphere, aggression in, 303

Wheeler, Senator Burton, 3

Whig party, 182

White House, 221; class hatred from, 178, 226

White rabbits, 157

Wilson, President, 205